CROSSING BORDERS:
A Venture Capitalist's Guide to Doing Business in Latin America

Nathan Lustig

ISBN: 978-05784161-2-0

Contents

Introduction

I t all started with a question. If you could tell your 25-year-old self anything, knowing what you know today, what would it be? I'd been thinking about it from time to time since hearing Tim Ferriss ask this question to many guests on his podcast, but this time I was sitting on a beach in Colombia with real time to think. All of the sudden, the memories came flooding back.

I flashed back to November 2010, boarding a plane from New York to Santiago 11 days after my 25th birthday. I was listening to a Spanish language podcast to help me fall asleep and to get in some last minute practice before waking up in Santiago at the end of the long flight. It didn't fully hit me until I went through customs and walked out into the hot, dry Santiago summer that I was really doing it: moving to Santiago for six months while trying to build my startup as part of the pilot round of the Start-Up Chile program, an equity-free accelerator program that gives entrepreneurs $40,000 to move to Chile for six months.

I thought I was going for six months and I'd be back in the US running my business, arriving just in time for US summer. I had no idea I'd spend much of the next eight years living, working, learning and growing up in Latin America. I'd go through ups and downs, frustrations and triumphs. I'd meet amazing people, make friends for life and explore an entire continent.

I'd learn about what it's like to not be understood, for people to think I was stupid because I couldn't express myself and to not understand things happening around me. I'd experience what it was like to not feel at home in a culture and to fully realize how lucky I'd been to be born in the US, in a country where I could speak my native language, to parents who loved me, taught me, didn't pressure me to take a cubicle job, made sure I didn't have debt and allowed me to explore what I wanted.

So what advice would I give to my 25-year-old self if I could go back in time after living and working in Latin America for the past eight years? I quickly started making a list: take Spanish classes before I moved to Chile. Take intensive Spanish classes as soon as I arrived. Lose all shame at sounding stupid in front of people while I was trying to learn Spanish. Say yes to all experiences in the beginning. Take even more advantage of traveling. Play soccer more. Don't eat that street hotdog in Bahia at 4am...but that's another story.

My mind quickly jumped to lessons learned doing business in Latin America. What I'd wished I'd known at different points in my time in Latin America:

» When I first got off that plane in Santiago in 2010
» When I started working at a Chilean startup in 2012 and needed to understand how business worked in Chile, Argentina, Colombia and Brazil
» When I was teaching entrepreneurship at Chilean universities, consulting with startups and mentoring entrepreneurs
» When I was starting an e-commerce store, investing in real estate, and finally starting Magma Partners.

My mind flashed to all of the interesting people I'd met, both expats and Latin Americans, who have created the colorful world that I've been a part of as I've gotten to know the region.

I looked at the steep learning curve I'd had making investments, working with entrepreneurs and dealing with big, traditional businesses. What it was like on my first trip to Colombia to scout startups and help our startups expand. And those same trips into Peru, Argentina, Mexico, Brazil and more. I jotted down a quick list of lessons learned in my notebook, thinking that I'd write a blog post with what I'd learned. But every time I sat down to write the blog post, I realized it would need to be bigger than a blog post if I really wanted to capture what I'd learned over the past eight years in Latin America.

This book is the culmination of that initial list. It's the book about Latin America I'd wished I'd had when I first moved to Chile as a newly minted 25-year-old. I wrote Startup Chile 101 in 2012 and Expat's Guide to Chile in 2013 as actionable guides to living, working and doing business in Chile. If you're moving to Chile or another Latin American country and want to learn more about the culture and the nitty gritty of daily life, check those books out.

This book is different. It's focused on doing business, starting businesses, or getting a job in Latin America. I cover the entire region, from Mexico to Chile and Puerto Rico to Brazil, with everything in between.

This book is perfect for someone who's lived in Latin America, but maybe spent time in only one country. Or someone who's interested in working in Latin America and wants to understand how each country works, or someone who wants to start a business in Latin America, but needs a starting point. It's also perfect for an investor, family office or foundation trying to get a 1.0 version of what's going on in Latin America's burgeoning technology scene.

After reading this book, you'll have a firsthand look into each country in the region based not only on my own experiences, but also directly from the mouths of entrepreneurs, investors and government officials who have spent decades learning about their countries. It's by no means the only thing you'll want to read if you're thinking seriously about living, working or doing business in Latin America. You'll need to go deeper in your country or countries of choice. My goal is to give you first steps that will take you down the road to deeper research into whatever country piques your interest.

The book is divided into chapters with sections. We'll start with an overview of Latin America and sections about big trends that affect the entire region. We'll cover things like an overview of mobile, FinTech, blockchain and other key industries region-wide, how to find a job, some of the top startups in the region, how to raise money for your venture outside of the region and how investors and entrepreneurs view impact investing in Latin America.

After taking a look at Latin America as a region, I'll jump into a chapter focusing on each country. Each country chapter starts with an overview of what it's like doing business in each country and at least one interview with an entrepreneur or investor operating there who can help give perspective on what it's really like. These interviews are condensed lessons from episodes of my podcast, *Crossing Borders*, and the Spanish version, *Cruzando Fronteras*. They are meant to introduce you to some of the most interesting people operating in Latin America. We'll explore bigger countries like Brazil, Mexico, Argentina and Colombia in more detail, focusing on things like e-commerce, startup hubs and local support programs for entrepreneurs, while giving a more general overview of the rest of the countries in the region.

I hope my 33-year-old self can pass along some of what I have learned in my eight years in LatAm; I am certain that the entrepreneurs and investors who share their experiences in this book about doing business across borders have much more to teach anyone interested in working, living or doing business in Latin America.

Nathan Lustig
Santiago, September 2018

I

Latin America: Misconceptions and Opportunities

***

When I told people in 2010 I was going to Chile for six months, most people thought it was cool. A nice adventure. Maybe I'd learn a bit of Spanish and experience a new culture. I was only going for six months, "What's the worst that could happen?" they thought. They watched as my blog posts, news articles and travel photos rolled in during my six months in Chile, saying the requisite nice things and asking the right questions. But nearly everyone thought I'd made the right decision when I came back to the US in April 2011 and told me so.

But after selling my business, I wasn't sure what I wanted to do, and thought it was stupid that I hadn't fully learned Spanish in Chile. I'd also developed an amazing network as part of the pilot round.

So when I decided to come back to Chile in 2012, the vast majority of my friends and business contacts humored me while I finished learning Spanish and checked out any opportunities I could dig up. They assumed it was short-term and were accepting. Some were even a bit envious.

But the supportive reaction turned to puzzlement from some, and outright ridicule by others as I spent more time in Latin America and less in the US. "Come back to the US," they told me. "Move to New York or San Francisco and get serious." "You're wasting your time and money in Latin America," were the common refrains. I remember sitting in an office tower in Manhattan talking with an experienced venture capitalist in 2014 months after starting Magma Partners, our early stage venture capital firm. He told me in no uncertain terms I should come back to the US, as we were going to lose all of our money.

Most people are ignorant about Latin America. Even most Latin Americans are ignorant about Latin American countries other than their own. They've seen Netflix's *Narcos* and *El Chapo*, drug violence in Mexico, maybe some stories about corrupt politicians in Brazil, and Venezuela's self-inflicted meltdown. Many have been to touristy, all-inclusive resorts in Mexico, but they've never explored farther; and they think you're risking life and limb if you do.

Most people get basic things about Latin America completely wrong: They assume that Chilean food is burritos and hot peppers, like Mexican food. Or that Peruvian and Chilean food is the exact same. They figure that Chile is on the same time zone as California since they're both on the West Coast, when Chile is actually on a line with New York City.

Some believe that all Latin American countries are alike and that something happening in Venezuela will massively affect countries like Chile and Argentina, which are an eight-hour flight away. They're surprised to learn that most Latin American capitals have skyscrapers and good internet. And that most countries have highly talented people, including many who have studied abroad in the US and Europe. And that some even have better healthcare systems than the US.

The reality is that Latin America doesn't behave like a single entity, as many people from the US, Europe or China believe. Many people will try to divide the region into two parts, Spanish-speaking countries and Portuguese speaking Brazil, but that's not right either! In reality, each country is its own world, running the gamut from nearly developed countries like Chile, Costa Rica and Uruguay, to quick growing economies like Colombia and Mexico still trying to bring many of their citizens out of poverty. There are countries like Brazil and Argentina with massive potential, but that still huge challenges. Countries like Peru and Ecuador that are trying to find the right path, while others like Bolivia are trying build their country up from a low base. There's even Drug War-torn Central American countries, next to success stories like Costa Rica.

The ignorant narrative about Latin America is wrong, but it's not being spread by bad people, racists or even good people with bad intentions. It's being spread by people who haven't been to the region or studied its culture. Maybe they haven't taken the time to fully understand this extremely varied, fast growing region because they have amazing business and tourism opportunities at home. But they're missing the fact that Latin America is full of massive opportunities for those who are willing to look past the few sensational headlines that make it into the US or European press.

Investors and entrepreneurs in the region who believe that talent is evenly distributed but opportunity isn't, like we do at Magma Partners, are finding big opportunities. There are many talented, motivated Latin Americans who are trying to solve problems both at home and abroad. But many are blocked by poor education systems, classism, bureaucracy or having the wrong last name... but more on that later. Now that almost everyone in Latin America has access to high speed internet via mobile phones, we see a huge opportunity for people both in the region and outside of it to make money and bend the arc of an entire region, making it better for not only for people right now, but also for the next generation.

We believe that Latin America is at an inflection point and will be one of the fastest growing regions in the world going forward. Devin Baptiste, cofounder and CEO of GroupRaise, a Magma Partners portfolio company, developed an analogy for Latin America's tech scene.

When making olive oil, the first press produces the highest quantity and highest quality olive oil. We believe that we're in the first press of Latin American technology companies and are excited to share what we've learned with you.

Opportunities and Drawbacks

That's not to say that operating in Latin America is easy, or everyone should do it. If all you want to do is make money, the best market in the world is still the United States. It's the most competitive and biggest market (after China), where people are willing to pay entrepreneurs to try new things. Latin America is hard. Each country is massively different. Many people in Latin America are classist, sexist and racist, whether they mean it or not. Sometimes they're all three together! Latin American countries are unequal places and have some of the biggest gaps between the small, wealthy elite and the rest of Latin America's citizens. This inequality, along with bureaucracy, corruption and a history of foreign interference have created massive impediments to doing business for locals and foreigners alike, which is part of the reason there are so many opportunities.

Back in 2013, I was frustrated by how long it was taking me to get one of my e-commerce businesses incorporated correctly and off the ground. I did a little study that showed that you needed 6x more money to get a company off the ground in Chile than in the US. How can that be? Because you can incorporate a Wisconsin LLC online in about 10 minutes and open a bank account that same day, all for the low cost of $130. Compare that with Chile, where you need to hire an attorney, go to the notary, wait for publication in the official government newspaper and then convince a bank to accept your money. The whole process can cost up to $2000 and take weeks. While countries are making strides to allow creating an *"empresa en un día,"* or a business online in one day, these online solutions still don't solve the problem completely.

TOTAL COST OPENING A BUSINESS: USA VS. CHILE

TASK	USA	CHILE
Open LLC/ SpA	10 minutes online	4 weeks with attorney
Registration Fee	$130, paid online	$60
Notary Fees	$0	$200
Legal Fees	$0	$1000
Total Cost	$130	$1260
Tax ID Number	5 minute online	1 week
Bank Account	20 minutes	4 weeks
Requred Deposit	$55	$3000
Monthly Fee	$0	$15
Monthly Salary Required	$0	$900
Fingerprints	0	12
Trips to Bank	0	12
Total Time	35 minutes	9 weeks
Total Cost	$185	$4260

Even after getting your business incorporated, you're not out of the woods yet. In the US, you can setup a Stripe or PayPal account in minutes and charge clients immediately, who will pay you with their credit cards in your new online payment form. You can even setup recurring payments using Payform, or a similar service, on top of Stripe.

You'll have money in your account within 1-2 days. In Chile, you'll need to get official government permission to create *facturas or boletas,* government-approved invoices and receipts, and then convince your new client to pay you on time. On average, your clients will ask for net 60 day payment terms and you'll be lucky if they pay you that quickly. This means that you have to pay your Value Added Tax (*IVA* in Spanish) of 19% the next month, even before you've been paid by your client. *IVA* varies in Latin American countries, but most are similar to Chile's.

We held an informal competition in our Whatsapp group for Magma Partners Founders to see who had the most overdue unpaid invoice from a client who was happy with their service and fully intended to pay. Nearly everyone had invoices at least 30 days overdue. Most had 60 days or more. The winner? A portfolio company sold $100,000 of services to a mining company on net 75 payment terms, meaning that the mining company would pay for the service 75 days after the service was completed. They actually paid 288 days later. Another non Magma Company told me they had an overdue invoice of more than 400 days from someone who was happy with their service!

Not only do you need to have money on hand to cover your startup costs that are higher than in the US, you need to be able to finance your VAT payments for at least two months until you can take payment from your new client. Put all of these factors together, you need at least six months of operating costs to get a Chilean company off the ground, whereas you might be able to get away with 1-2 months in the US. Now remember that Chile is the easiest place to do business in Latin America and you might have nightmares about getting off the ground in places like Argentina or Brazil.

You'll need to be ready to wait in long lines to do basic things like open a bank account, pay for internet or even to buy an empanada in some cases! You think I'm joking about the empanadas, but buying an empanada in Chile, Argentina or Uruguay can be a four-step process:

» Walk into the empanada shop and select the empanada you'd like

» Walk over to the cashier and tell them the empanada you'd like to order and pay for it
» Take the ticket the cashier handed you and order the empanada from another person
» Wait for a third person to give you the empanada you ordered

Now imagine opening a bank account! You need to be ready to be infuriated by the inefficiencies and cultural differences that you'll run into each day, but then realize you have to let them roll off your back, or you won't be long for Latin America. All of these drawbacks, inefficiencies and difficulties are annoying. If you choose to look at them as problems, you're going to have a bad time. But if you look at them like opportunities, problems that need to be solved, and have someone to help you navigate them, you'll start to see why I love operating in Latin America. More people should at least evaluate the opportunity with an open mind.

Opportunity

In 2017, I was drinking whiskey in a bar in Guadalajara with Bismarck Lepe, the Mexican-American founder of Ooyala, which sold for $400M, and Wizeline, a tech services platform that raised more than $200M and is based in Mexico and San Francisco, when he said something that might be jarring to someone in the US: "Mexico is the new American Dream!" he declared. It's a variation on something I've heard from multiple entrepreneurs from Latin America, the US, Europe and China when talking about their slice of Latin America.

While each Latin American country is different and there's no way anyone would say Venezuela is the new American Dream, some variation of Bismarck's theme rings true for entrepreneurs solving real problems that affect Latin Americans in their day to day lives. Entrepreneurs are solving problems from financial inclusion to insurance, to healthcare to transport, e-commerce and more.

Entrepreneurs are also starting to change the narrative in countries where a small upper class of generational wealth controls most of the economy and the "work hard and you'll be successful" themes haven't historically resonated. Unlike the US, where the culture celebrates creating a business and earning money, many Latin American countries have negative views of successful people and the "have nots" don't believe they can move up in society or get a fair shake. And they've been right to be cynical for most of history. But the internet, mobile devices and entrepreneurship are changing things.

The rewards for those who solve Latin American problems are outsized for three reasons: First, the problems are so big. 80% of Latin Americans don't even have access to a bank account to deposit their money, much less access to mortgages or consumer credit. We're talking big problems that have big rewards if you can solve them. Second, there's not much competition in Latin America. If you can solve a problem, it's not likely that others will compete with you successfully. Third, if you are successful, you have the opportunity to help millions of people better their lives, send their children to schools for a better education and potentially help people join the middle class, or even building generational wealth themselves.

Unlike the US, where a majority of people now think that their children will live worse lives than they did, Latin America is a region on the upswing, where people are generally excited to see growth and new ideas taking root.

Next, I'll dive deeper and cover the four megatrends that are impacting Latin America and creating opportunities for entrepreneurs, investors and the general population in Latin America.

The Four Megatrends Creating Opportunities in Latin America

I n 2010, a few weeks after getting to Chile, I met a guy at a friend's *asado*, a Chilean barbecue. We talked about taking a trip to his beach house with some of his friends that next weekend and exchanged numbers. I texted him the next day…Radio silence. I sent another message a few days later. Nothing. I assumed he'd made the offer just to be nice. But when I ran into him two weeks later, he was happy to see me and was puzzled that I hadn't called. I asked why he hadn't texted back. Two reasons: I must not have been interested if I couldn't be bothered to call rather than send a text. And text messages cost $0.40 and it would run down his prepaid credits on his dumb phone too quickly. I clearly wasn't worth the $0.40 since we'd just met!

Flash forward to ~2014. Everyone has WhatsApp. Nobody sends text messages except spammers, scammers and old school companies like banks and big retailers. A younger friend from the US who moved to Chile in 2016 said he's never called a woman he's been interested in; always WhatsApp. Why? Because WhatsApp is free, representing a huge cultural change from 2010 when everything was done by phone,. This little story is fun, but it illustrates a larger point: these same changes, influenced by technology, are happening across industries and cultures where change moved at a glacial pace for hundreds of years until smartphones and broadband internet started to impact the region.

Starting in the late 2000s, a few years before I moved to Chile, Latin America's economy, mores and culture, like much of the rest of the world, started to change, mostly influenced by technology. This wave was late to hit Latin America, but is starting to gain steam in ~2014. You can see it by mobile broadband penetration, more young people moving out of their parents houses to live on their own instead of staying until they got married, Uber's domination of the Latin American taxi market (for now) and Whatsapp's ubiquity.

Change is in the air. Governments have been increasing investment in technology and innovation to shift their economies away from their reliance on natural resources that some day will run out and to diversify their monocultures. At the same time, investors, entrepreneurs and tech companies from the US and China have started paying attention to Latin America and investing in the local ecosystem; investment in Latin American technology startups has nearly doubled in each year from 2014-2018, according to the Latin America Venture Capital Association (LAVCA). And in an eight-week period spanning the last two weeks of August 2018 to the first two weeks of October 2018, there was more venture capital and acquisition activity ($600M) than in all of 2016 ($500M)!

I see four megatrends playing out in Latin America that are creating opportunity which will shape a region for the next generation:

1. The rising middle class powered by increased technology penetration rates
2. The maturing regional technology ecosystem
3. China's recent involvement in Latin American tech
4. US investors making investments in Latin American startups.

These megatrends are creating a perfect storm that will allow Latin America's ecosystem to jump forward, potentially leapfrogging legacy technology and business models, jumping directly to new, technology-enabled models. The businesses that win now will likely be the winners that will lead a continent for the next few generations, replacing many of today's incumbents.

1. LATIN AMERICA'S RISING MIDDLE CLASS, POWERED BY INCREASED TECHNOLOGY PENETRATION RATES

Latin America is massively unequal, but it's moving in the right direction. While the US middle class has struggled since the 70s, Latin America's middle class has grown by 50% since 2008 and now represents 30% of the region's population[1]. Better education, improved safety nets, better government (in most countries), and higher workplace participation for women have all played a role in bringing a large portion of Latin America's population out of poverty.

Increased access to the internet, especially through mobile phones, is helping spur development. More than two-thirds of the population in Latin America, over 415 million people, are mobile users. Of those users, more than half are connecting via smartphones. Just as Africa leapfrogged over landline phones straight to mobile, Latin America has quickly adopted smartphone technology, while still lacking many basic services like access to a checking account, online bill pay and more that US consumers take for granted. Newly connected Latin Americans face different challenges than US and European consumers do.

90% of the population in many Latin American countries have mobile broadband connections, but more than 50% of Latin America remains unbanked and up to 85% don't have access to financial services that people in the US assume everyone has access to.[2] While smartphone penetration has grown at 12% per year, the banked population has only increased by 2% yearly.[3] Because of increased mobile broadband penetration and the legacy finance system's inability or unwillingness to innovate, Latin America is a massive opportunity for FinTech startups, especially for companies that are looking to connect the young, technological middle class to financial services and insurance.

2. The maturing Latin American tech ecosystem

Most early Latin American startups were "copycats," companies that tweaked or outright copied proven business models from the US to build successful startups in Latin America.[4] While some of the region's largest tech startups like MercadoLibre, Despegar, and OLX were founded during the early 2000s, initiatives like Start-Up Chile and Brazil's growing startup scene in the 2010s marked an inflection point in the development of the region's entrepreneurial ecosystem. Latin America's tech ecosystem has matured significantly since the launch of Start-Up Chile in 2010.

A second wave of copycats led by Clandescuento and Peixe Urbano, the Groupons of Latin America, Restorando, the OpenTable of Latin America; Viajala, the Kayak of Latin America, Dafiti, the Zappos of Latin America; Linio, a big e-commerce in Latin America; and PedidosYa, the GrubHub of Latin America, VivaReal, the Zillow of Brazil, found success. These companies were initially more attractive to US and European investors because they understood the business models from investing in the US or European versions of the business. Additionally, some new models started to emerge, but many failed to take off.

Latin America's startup ecosystem is now in its second wave as battle-scarred founders from the early 2010s are building their second or third companies and disrupting the tech market. For example, Maria Paz Gillet, founder of Jooycar, an Internet of Things (IoT) connected-car platform, originally built HappyShop, a rewards platform, in 2006 and raised US$6M. HappyShop eventually failed, despite its viral beginnings, and Maria Paz is now applying what she learned to Jooycar. Federico Vega, founder of CargoX, the Uber for trucking in Brazil, had to close down the company twice and even live in his car, before it reached its 2018 US$200M run rate. Latin American unicorns like Fabricio Bloisi's

Movile, Latin America's mobile business leader, are pushing the ecosystem forward by investing and acquiring startups.

As the ecosystem has matured, bringing hundreds of new entrepreneurship programs to the region, investment continues to grow. According to LAVCA's 2017 State of the Industry Report, Latin American startups received US$1.1B in venture capital funding in 2017, doubling invested dollars in 2016.[5] Investment should reach at least $2.5B by the end of 2018, and may reach $3B.[6]

This new wave of Latin American startups, investors and government institutions is pushing the ecosystem forward, improving the quality of startups, access to capital and most importantly access to lessons learned from starting previous businesses.

3. CHINA'S INVOLVEMENT IN LATIN AMERICAN INNOVATION

In 2017, I traveled to China with Jie Hao, a Partner at Magma Partners based in Beijing, to raise money for our second fund. It was the culmination of five years of hard work to educate Chinese investors, entrepreneurs and government officials about what was happening in Latin America. We'd first tried to raise money in early 2017, but we got flat "No's." We decided to help educate the market and wrote articles and created a training seminar with 36Kr, the TechCrunch of China. It was a success, tapping into China's appetite for new, interesting deals.

Unlike many US investors, Chinese investors are generally less afraid of Latin America's past. Right after the US elections in 2016, China pledged to increase trade with Latin America by $500 billion and foreign investment by $250 billion. To show they mean it, both of China's development banks now provide more financing for development to Latin America than the World Bank, the IDB, and the Andean Development Corporation (CAF), combined.

While Jie, Magma and I were early movers, big Chinese tech companies like Alibaba, Huawei, Qihoo, Xiaomi and more had already started investing and operating in Latin America. China's growing interest in Latin America became evident in January 2018 when Didi

Chuxing, China's Uber clone, acquired Brazil's Uber clone, 99, for a rumored US$1B.[7] Didi had already invested heavily in 99 at the time of the acquisition, hinting at the importance of this megatrend over the next few years.

Other examples of increased Chinese interest in Latin America include Alibaba's expansion of Aliexpress services throughout the region, Mobike's debut in Chile, and Tang Xin's development of news app, Noticias Aguila, for the Mexican market.[8] Chinese online security service Qihoo previously invested US$25M in Brazilian antivirus company PSafe.

While Latin America has traditionally partnered with the United States for investment and support, the political climate in the US since 2016 has pushed Latin American governments to seek connections elsewhere. China has stepped in to fill the void. Chinese investment in Latin American mining and infrastructure projects is expanding into tech businesses, investment and acquisitions from China. In 2018, in a meeting in Santiago, Chile, China officially added Latin America and the Caribbean into the Belt and Road initiative, a world-wide, multi-trillion dollar infrastructure program funded by the Chinese government. China will likely invest hundreds of billions into Latin American infrastructure and mining projects by 2028.

Adding Latin America to the Belt and Road initiative is significant. The Belt and Road initiative kicked off in 2013 by China's President Xi Jinping and pledged $900B to infrastructure projects to connect China with Europe via overland routes and China with the Middle East, Africa and Europe via shipping infrastructure. The Belt and Road Initiative has since expanded to $3T in investments into projects designed to project Chinese influence, make peoples' lives better and add new markets for Chinese exports. According to a CNBC article titled China invites Latin America to take part in One Belt, One Road from January 2018:

The so-called Santiago declaration, signed by China and CELAC [Community of Latin America and Caribbean States] delegates, also calls for bolstering trade and taking action on climate change. Chile

Foreign Minister Heraldo Munoz, who has criticized [President] Trump in the past, said the agreement marked an 'historic' new era of dialogue between the region and China. 'China said something that is very important, that it wants to be our must trustworthy partner in Latin America and the Caribbean and we greatly value that,' said Munoz. 'This meeting represents a categoric repudiation of protectionism and unilateralism.'

China has sought a bigger role overseas since Trump was elected, presenting its Regional Comprehensive Economic Partnership trade agreement as an alternative to the Trans-Pacific Partnership, which the United States has abandoned. The country is already testing U.S. dominance in Latin America, offering the region $250 billion in investment over the next decade. It is the top trading partner of many countries in the region, including Brazil, Chile and Argentina.[9]

Latin America's digital economy of 2018 looks like China's digital economy 10-15 years ago. China jumped directly from an unbanked, underdeveloped ecosystem to serving their highly-connected, youthful middle class through the internet. China now has the most advanced FinTech tools in the world and has shown Latin America a path to follow.

Unlike the United States, China and Latin America did not have to manage legacy technology and industries that resist innovation. For example, only ~7% of people in the US are unbanked, whereas up to 80% are in Latin America.[10] These 80% are not being served by the traditional financial system and are more likely to use mobile-based neobanks or loan options based on your behavior on your mobile phone. China's growth from a lower base might be a better example for Latin America than looking for solutions from the US, where the financial system was more developed previously. In October 2018, Brazilian Challenger bank Nubank had 5M Brazilian customers and received an $180M investment at a $4B valuation from Chinese internet giant Tencent.

Latin American entrepreneurs like Fabricio Bloisi, founder of Movile, wants his company to improve the lives of 1 billion people over the next ten years and is setting his sights on becoming the Tencent of Latin America. Tencent's WeChat platform is ubiquitous for everything from messaging to payments to loans to entertainment to ordering transportation and more.

Jack Ma, Alibaba's founder once said, "eBay may be a shark in the ocean, but I am a crocodile in the Yangtze River. If we fight in the ocean, we lose—but if we fight in the river, we win." Federico Vega, founder of CargoX, the Uber for trucks in Brazil, decided to dominate the Brazilian market, rather than compete globally from the beginning. He was inspired Jack Ma's strategy of dominating China first and then expanding internationally. Vega believes Latin America is similar because of market complexity, which requires entrepreneurs to have local knowledge and market understanding in order to win.

Chinese venture capitalists and entrepreneurs increasingly see Latin America as a huge market opportunity with a population of 600 million people that still requires solutions for significant development problems including energy, water, agriculture, and economic inequality. After years of investing in Latin American infrastructure, Chinese companies are starting to support (and profit from) Latin American tech growth, which could prove to be a crucial exit strategy for many Latin American startups over the next decade.

In the first 11 months of 2016, China's VC and Private Equity firms made 265 investments worth 31.7 billion yuan (~US$5 billion), according to Zero2Ipo Research, a Beijing-based researcher of financial institutions.[10]Although Zero2Ipo Research data shows only reportable investment deals and the number of unrecorded deals is likely much greater than this, it shows that the number of investments and the amount of money invested increased 105% and 189% respectively year-on-year from 2009 to 2015.[11]China also set up US$35 billion in multilateral finance platforms for Latin America, the US$20 billion China-LAC Industrial Cooperation Investment Fund and the US$10 billion China-Latin America Infrastructure Fund which were established in 2015. China also pumped another US$5 billion into the China-Latin America Cooperation fund that was set up in 2014.[12]

While trade between the US and Latin America has doubled since 2000, China's trade with Latin America has multiplied 22 times, according to OECD economist Angel Melguizo. As of 2018, China is the top trading partner for the major economies of Brazil, Chile and Peru. Furthermore, Argentina, El Salvador and Guatemala are well-placed to profit from China's booming demand for global food products. In Mexico, China's JAC Motors invested over US$200 million into a factory with Giant Motors, a company backed by billionaire investor Carlos Slim.[13]Latin American countries ties with China are poised to continue their rapid growth.

Tech giants like Alibaba are making their move

In addition to trade deals, Latin America's burgeoning tech scene is also capturing the attention of China's biggest technology companies and venture capital firms.

Alibaba, the largest Internet retailer in China and the world, has been steadily examining the Latin American market over the past few years. So far, the e-commerce giant has signed three memorandums of understanding with governments in Latin America. The first one established a partnership with Brazil's national postal service, Correios in 2014. In 2017, Jack Ma flew to Argentina to work out an agreement that would help bring food and wine from Argentina to China. In September 2017, Alibaba also created a special program specifically for Mexico, in which it agreed to share best logistics and payment practices with Mexican companies so they can bolster their cross-border business activities.

So why does Alibaba have such a strong interest in educating and helping online merchants in Latin America? The main reason is that the e-commerce space in Latin America is incredibly under-developed compared to other regions of the world and Latin America consumers are already buying direct from China on AliExpress. Over the next five years, the region's e-commerce market is forecast to grow 18% annually, however, currently represents just 2% of the world retail market despite being 9% of the population.

After almost 40 years of development, China's middle class is one of the largest and most powerful in the world. There is an increasing demand from Chinese consumers for the best products from all around the world, for example Chilean and Argentine wine, and bringing those products to Chinese consumers is just one more part of Alibaba's strategy.

MercadoLibre, the largest e-commerce marketplace in Latin America with 174.2 million users in 15 countries, will try to make it very challenging for Alibaba to grow its presence in the region without a fight. Because Amazon doesn't have a widespread local presence in Latin America, it seems that Alibaba may ramp up its Latin American presence, or even try to acquire MercadoLibre, as some in Latin America have speculated.

Growing VC interest in Latin American startups

Founded in 2012 by Brazilian entrepreneurs, 99 (formerly 99Taxis) is an app-based, on-demand ride service much like Uber. 99 took off quickly in Brazil, reaching more than 10 million user downloads in the world's second-fastest-growing Internet market. 99 is available in 550 cities in Brazil and is the leader in both São Paulo and Rio de Janeiro, two of the largest consumer markets in all of Latin America.

In 2016, Didi Chuxing, China's largest ride-sharing companies, announced a sizeable investment in 99 to help the company expand its services into other countries in South America. Though undisclosed, a 99 spokesperson claimed the investment was in excess of USD$100 million.

"We welcome Didi to Latin America. Didi's financing, state-of-the-art technology, and operations knowledge will play a key supporting role as 99 actively expands our network and services in

Brazil and reshapes the competitive landscape in Latin America," said Peter Fernandez, CEO of 99.[14]Cheng Wei, the founder and CEO of Didi, highlighted their cooperation with more global partners: "China and Brazil are the world's foremost emerging markets with enormous opportunities for our rideshare industry." In 2018, Didi acquired 99 for a reported US$1B and also launched services in Mexico City and Guadalajara.

The potential of a tech partnership

The biggest names in China are already making their mark outside of China. While the Chinese government has invested heavily in other regions, it has recently started programs to build strong relationships with Latin America's young and innovative leaders. For instance, the Future Bridge Training Program aims to invite 1,000 young Latin American leaders to China over the next ten years. Magma Partners' Jie Hao was invited invited to speak at the 2017 China-CELAC Forum, and hosted the Future Bridge Training Program in Beijing in 2017.

This type of talent exchange is not only happening at the Chinese government level. Over the last two years, Magma Partners has seen an increasing number of talented entrepreneurs with businesses in Latin America interested in learning about opportunities in China.

As a result, Magma Partners, which offices in Chile, Colombia, Mexico and the US opened a new office Beijing, and is working with organizations like 36Kr, one of China's largest technology media companies, to provide Chinese investors and partners with a full review of Latin America's technology environment and opportunities.

Led by our partner Jie Hao, we published 40 educational articles with 36Kr in 2017 and now have a weekly column where we write about what's happening in Latin American technology and startups. Magma Partners will work with the Chinese technology media, our established connections in the Chinese venture capital ecosystem, and with our connections to the 40+ Chinese incubators, to keep the educational exchanges going. We are also educating young entrepreneurs and startup teams in Latin America on the many ways they can find opportunities in China and how the regions can work together to build a better future for Latin America.

For more information about how China is impacting Latin America or how you can leverage China for your startup, contact us at china@magmapartners.com.

4. US INVESTORS TAKING NOTICE OF THE LATIN AMERICAN ECOSYSTEM

As China has begun investing in Latin American startups, the US venture capital industry has also made inroads into supporting the LatAm tech ecosystem. Some funds made investments in the 2000s, but by 2016 investments started to become more common.

In 2014, many top Silicon Valley firms asked entrepreneurs and venture capitalists uninformed questions about Latin America when evaluating opportunities. They asked whether Latin American capitals had internet and were surprised to see skyscrapers in big Latin American cities when we showed them drone videos during meetings. It's no wonder that many didn't show much curiosity about seriously evaluating Latin American startups.

That's starting to change. In 2016, 2017 and 2018 Andreessen Horowitz and Sequoia Capital invested $380M in Rappi, Colombia's last-mile delivery service founded by Felipe Villamarin, Sebastian Mejia and Simon Borrero, after Rappi became one of the first LatAm startups to go through Y Combinator. Sequoia Capital also invested in Brazil's NuBank, founded by Colombian David Velez and Brazilian Cristina Junqueira, as did Tiger Global, Founders Fund, and Redpoint eVentures and Chinese giant Tencent. Accel Partners made their first Mexican/Chilean investment in CornerShop, a Chilean grocery delivery app founded by Daniel Undurraga and Oskar Hjertonsson, in 2016, which was acquired by Walmart for $225M in 2018. The Mexican version of Square, Clip, founded by Adolfo Babatz, received one of Mexico's largest Series A investments from American Express in 2015. Goldman Sachs also made investments, leading a US$20M Series C round for CargoX in Brazil.

While Brazil has historically received most of the international investment sent to Latin America, Argentina and Mexico are beginning to gain attention from the US, as well. Venture capitalist Tim Draper has made investments in Argentina through Draper Cygnus, and George Soros deepened his commitment to the Argentine ecosystem in early 2018 with an investment in neobank Ualá. Goldman Sachs, Ribbit Capital and more invested into Ualá's late 2018 Series B. Apax Partners made a US$43M investment in Wizeline, an outsourcing platform founded by Bismarck Lepe based in Guadalajara, Mexico and Silicon Valley. Naspers continued to support Movile, highlighted by their $500M investment into Brazil's iFood.

Finally, during 2013-2018, YCombinator accepted Latin American startups, including Authy, Rappi, Platzi, Runa HR, Hogaru, Ropeo, Brainhi, Podcast App and more. The US will likely continue to play an increasingly large role in supporting Latin America's tech ecosystem over the next decade as some of the first US invested companies show that they are successful and highlight Latin American opportunities.

These four megatrends are key to understanding doing business in Latin America. They showcase a dynamic region bursting with opportunities, on the cusp of real change. It will be interesting to watch these trends over the next decade as China and the US begin to have a larger involvement in Latin America's tech ecosystem, while new technologies help Latin Americans continue to join the middle class. In the next chapter, we'll look more in depth at Latin America as a region, including my advice to foreigners looking to do business in the region, deeper dives into how to get a job, how to work remotely and some of the opportunities in Latin America.

Endnotes

1   *World Bank.* http://www.worldbank.org/en/news/feature/2012/11/13/crecimiento-clase-media-america-latina

2   *eMarketer.* https://www.emarketer.com/Article/State-of-Mexicos-Mobile-Market/1014148

3   *AMI Perspectiva.* http://amiperspectiva.americasmi.com/tapping-the-un-banked-smartphone-user-market-in-latin-america/

4   *TechCrunch.* https://techcrunch.com/2017/09/08/copycats-vs-disruptors-in-latin-america/

5   *LAVCA.* https://lavca.org/industry-data/inside-latin-americas-break-out-year-tech/

6   Ibid.

7   *TechCrunch.* https://techcrunch.com/2018/01/03/didi-confirms-it-has-ac-quired-99-in-brazil-to-expand-in-latin-america/

8   *Bloomberg.* https://www.bloomberg.com/news/articles/2018-03-04/chinese-startups-export-playbook-to-latin-america-for-new-riches

9   *CNBC.* https://www.cnbc.com/2018/01/22/china-invites-latin-america-to-take-part-in-one-belt-one-road.html

10   *Zero2IPO* Research. http://www.zero2ipo.com.cn/EN/service/28/

11   Ibid.

12   *TechCrunch.* https://techcrunch.com/2018/01/03/didi-confirms-it-has-acquired-99-in-brazil-to-expand-in-latin-america/

13   https://www.forbes.com/sites/doliaestevez/2017/03/28/billionaire-carlos-slim-and-chinas-jac-motors-to-manufacture-cars-for-latin-american-mar-ket/#5600e86a6ac8

14   https://venturebeat.com/2017/12/17/chinese-investors-target-latin-ameri-can-startups-as-u-s-vcs-shy-away/

II

Advice for Doing Business in Latin America

I always say "Don't treat Latin America as a monolithic region," but I'm going to do just that and make some generalizations in this chapter. This chapter is all about laying your Latin America foundation for the region as a whole. From my quick advice guide (up next), to later sections that cover specific region-wide topics like e-commerce, FinTech, Blockchain, Venture Capital and getting a job in greater detail, my goal is to build the foundation for the rest of the book.

So before we go any farther, want to know the basics about Latin America? Or you don't want to read the rest of the book? This is the quick and dirty overview for Latin America, which lays the foundation for the rest of the book. If you can't read anything else, read this.

In 2010, I made friend at an *asado* (BBQ) after a talk that Start-Up Chile had invited me to give at Universidad Católica, Chile's highest-rated university. We'd met up for beers and he invited me to go with his friends to the Chilean coast the next weekend. We talked about leaving on Friday and returning on Sunday. As Friday rolled around, I assumed he's shoot me a message about where to meet up, when we were leaving and what I needed to bring. But I got crickets. I figured I'd been disinvited or that my friend's invitation was a courtesy invite. Later, my friend told me that they'd had an *asado* in Santiago and wondered why I wasn't there!

Things like this happened multiple times and for the first month or so. My business partner Jesse and I figured thought that maybe our "new friends" were just being nice to us, but really didn't want to be friends. But when I finally asked a Chilean I'd met at Wisconsin while at university what was going on, he told me it was just the local culture. Plans aren't set until they're set. Most people don't commit strongly. It wasn't just us, it was everyone! What a relief. We learned we had to reconfirm the day of, and then again in the evening or we'd risk missing things.

When I first got to Chile in 2010, I knew there were cultural differences, but I thought that if I worked hard in the same way I did in the US, I'd be successful, as I had been in the US. Working hard helped, but there were many cultural misunderstandings that hampered my progress.

It may sound obvious, but each country has different cultural norms that you need to learn if you want to be successful, rather than being the proverbial bull in a china shop. Hopefully this guide will jump start your learning curve so you can be culturally proficient more quickly than I was.

1. LEARN SPANISH (OR PORTUGUESE)

Don't give your potential client or business partner another excuse to not do business with you. Most people in high level business positions across Latin America speak decent English, but many don't. And if you end up in meetings with multiple people, there's a good chance at least one person won't understand what's going on because you're speaking in English. Business meetings are hard enough when language isn't an issue. It becomes nearly impossible when one party isn't understanding what the other is saying. It may sound obvious, but if you want to be successful in Latin America, learn Spanish. Same goes for Brazil, but in Portuguese.

2. If Cloning, Adapt to the Local Market

Many entrepreneurs think that they can bring an already existing product to Latin America. Some have had success (Groupon, food delivery etc.), but others have struggled or failed entirely. The successful startups adapted quickly to the local market and tweaked the model so that locals would be comfortable. Cloning isn't copy paste in Latin America.

3. Latin America is Not Monolithic

Many people who don't know much about Latin America see it as a monolithic place south of the border. Others think a bit harder and imagine a place with two cultures: Spanish speaking Latin America and Brazil. Both are wrong. The reality is that each Latin American country has its own traditions, cultural norms, history and business practices. Doing business in Chile is very different than doing business in Argentina even though they share a massive border! Colombia and Venezuela are worlds apart business-wise, but connected on the map. Many countries even use different words for the same thing, others use words differently, and others use different grammar entirely (I'm looking at you Argentina!), meaning that you likely need to create country-specific websites with translations for each country.

4. Latin America Isn't Silicon Valley, It's not Madison, WI Either

Silicon Valley is a special place where venture capital flows freely, people share ideas and work on world-changing projects. The United States is a special place, where business is competitive, generally straightforward and people are willing to take chances. Latin America is a conservative place and can't be compared with Silicon Valley, much less the business climate in a smaller city in the middle of the United States.

5. Don't Expect Silicon Valley Valuations

Exits are hard to come by in Latin America and when they happen they're for small multiples. Venture capitalists must invest at lower valuations to have any hope of making money under these conditions. There may be more exits for high multiples in the future, but investors won't bet on them.

6. Hiring Employees: Conservatism

Most Latin American workers are generally conservative. It's prestigious to work for a large, well-known company. One of the first questions people ask you in Latin America is "Where do you work?" I remember people looking at me with pity when I said I worked at a startup. I could see the gears turning in their heads "Oh man, he's unemployed, poor Nathan."

Many Latin Americans would prefer to earn less money at a prestigious company with a safe long-term contract than to work at an uncertain startup where they might earn more money and get to work on more interesting problems.

7. Most Employees Don't Understand or Value Stock Options

Equity and stock options still aren't popular forms of compensation in Latin America and many employees either don't understand their value or prefer to make more money in cash rather than taking a risk with stock. In some countries like Chile where trust between employees and employers is very low, some employees even think that they're getting screwed if the employer offers them something out of the ordinary and just reject a stock options offer out of hand.

8. It's Hard to Raise Money

There aren't many private VC firms in Latin America and very few seasoned angel investors. Most family offices don't invest in startups or new businesses and when they do, they invest old school, valuing early stage businesses based on cashflow and trying to get as much equity as they possibly can.

There's government money floating around in countries like Chile, Peru, Colombia, Brazil and Mexico, but it usually comes with strings attached, sometimes with terrible terms and may not come from sources that will actually help you. The venture capital market is improving, but it's hard to raise money.

Most US VCs have so much deal flow from the United States that they ignore Latin America startups and pass on investing in them unless they have a physical presence in the US with US clients.

9. Sales: People are Terrified of Getting Fired

Sales requires a different strategy than in the US. If you walk into a potential client's office in the US with a new technology, offering to make (or save) the client $1000 per month if they buy your $500 a month product, many potential clients might take the risk for a month or two to try it out. They understand and value the monetary benefit immediately. And they know if they miss out on a new product or services that ends up being used by the competition, it could lead to them getting a stern talking to from their boss or potentially even fired.

In Latin America, leading with a monetary benefit isn't usually going to work. Businesses are generally conservative and many rule by fear. Many employees only want to keep their head down, earn a steady paycheck and make sure they continue to earn it next month and next year. They take a massive risk if they buy your product and it doesn't deliver the promised results or worse, causes a problem.

In Latin America, it's almost always best to lead with the fact that your product is low risk and how the employee isn't going to risk their job by trying it. Show a path toward getting buy-in from other employees to spread the risk and then talk about the benefit once the potential customer is more relaxed.

10. Exits are hard(er)

Large Latin American companies haven't acquired many startups. Foreign startups sometimes do, but spend less on Latin American startups than they would on similar startups in other parts of the world. Big businesses aren't scared of startups yet, so they don't feel much urgency to buy up startups to kill off the competition. Many large businesses are owned by families that have to take the cash out of their own pockets if they want to acquire a startup, whereas in the US, most companies acquire startups using VC money or public market money. And we all know that spending your own money is much harder than spending someone else's!

11. Income Inequality is Massive and Incomes are Low

It's really hard to build a Business to Consumer (B2C) startup in LatAm because most people don't have much money. In Chile, Latin America's richest country on a per capita basis, 85% of households earn less than $1250 per month and 70% earn less than $750. 50% of workers earn $450 per month, minimum wage. These households don't have much money in absolute terms to spend on B2C startup products, so it's challenging to build a business. Other countries have similar distributions, but the income tranches are even lower.

12. Software hasn't eaten Latin America yet

If software is eating the world, Latin America might be dessert. I've seen companies with hundreds of millions of dollars in sales using pen and paper to track inventory, Excel to keep track of work orders and even typewriters to do some business! Many US technology products aren't in Spanish or don't fit local needs, which presents a massive opportunity for tech entrepreneurs.

13. B2B is Where the Money Is

Most Latin American countries are not poor countries, but Latin America is incredibly unequal. Large companies and their owners have massive amounts of money and Chile has one of highest number of billionaires per capita in the world. Many of these businesses still have large inefficiencies that need to be sorted out and provide large, potentially lucrative opportunities for entrepreneurs to solve. If you have tens of hundreds of millions of dollars from US investors, you can afford to take on a B2C opportunity in the long term.

14. Think About Operating with Latin American Costs, but with US Income

Latin America is home to some great tech talent, especially in Mexico, Colombia, Chile, Argentina, Venezuela and Brazil. Many can't move to a startup hub in the US because of visa issues and others don't want to for quality of life reasons. These talented engineers earn up to 90% less than top engineers in the US.

Latin America also has thousands of native English-speaking expats who might not speak Spanish (or Portuguese) fluently yet. Their only options are to work teaching English for low pay or fight for the few English only jobs in the market. If you create a sales or customer support team of native English speakers, you can create a massive competitive advantage.

15. Don't Follow Cultural Hiring Biases

If you're willing to hire the best person for the job, you have a big advantage over many traditional companies and can get great talent as many Latin American countries have biases based on class, race and gender that don't always lead to hiring the best talent.

16. Yes Can Mean Yes, No or Maybe. No Can Mean Yes, No or Maybe

It can be really hard to get a straight answer out of many people in Latin America. People don't like to say no, but many times they'll say no when the answer is yes to avoid doing work, taking a risk or trying something new. Check out my blog post on Weonomics for more information at: http://www.nathanlustig.com/2013/06/05/weonomics/

17. Being Early is the Same as Being Wrong

It's true in any market, but many services in the US aren't ready for the Latin American market or the market isn't ready for them.

18. Press Means Nothing

The Latin American tech press is starved for a good story. And there aren't many startups. So many mediocre-to-bad startups get covered extensively in the press. Remind yourself that just getting covered doesn't mean anything and the "superstar startups" that keep showing up may be hemorrhaging money.

19. Bureaucracy

Be ready. You'll need to get proficient at the notary, dealing with government regulations and checking the boxes at the bank. Most banks won't give you a personal or business bank account without jumping through hoops and there are many arcane and illogical governmental rules.

20. Connections Matter

If you do succeed in getting a meeting, your clients may believe they deserve the lion's share of the benefits. For example, if your service creates $100 of value for your client and you're not in the elite circles, the client might demand $97 of value and let you keep $3. When you have a partner in the elite circles, with the right last name, who went to the right high schools or church etc., your business might get $50 and the company might take other $50. And in extreme cases, you might even get more than 50% of the $100.

21. AVOID THE GRINGO PRICE

Make friends with at least one local or a foreigner who's been in the country for long enough to understand the market. Verify pricing and other issues with them to make sure you're not getting Gringo-gouged.

22. TAKE MY MONEY...PLEASE!

It took me 2.5 months to get internet in my new office. It took one year to open a business bank account to deposit my money. It took five trips to the tax office to be able to sell legally. It took three trips to the tax office to verify my company's business address with the government. I wanted to spend money with companies, but in many cases the companies make it extremely difficult. So frustrating! Be ready for it and learn to laugh it off, there's not much you can do about it.

23. IF CUSTOMER SERVICE DOESN'T GIVE YOU SATISFACTION, HANG UP AND CALL AGAIN

Hang up and call back until you find someone who can really help you. It might take 10 calls, but it'll likely work eventually. I was shocked to find that this works, but it does nearly every time.

24. PROPOSE SOLUTIONS TO PROBLEMS

Most customer service reps, whether on the phone or in person, have a script. They don't go off script. They don't want to. They get paid to churn through people. If you let them follow the script, you'll be in customer service hell. Many times, you can propose a solution and walk the rep through your solution and it will work. If you try this multiple times and get the same result, the reps are probably telling the truth. Do it nicely and you'll have more success. I always say "Y que pasa si..." which means "Well what if..." and go from there.

25. Don't take no for an answer right away

The 25th and final piece of advice is related to points 16, 22, 23 and 24. If someone tells you that it can't be done, make sure it really can't be done before giving up. Most of the time, it can be done, but with much more work for the business. If you accept the first story, you'll never get anything done.

Conclusion

The more business you do in Latin America, the more you'll be able to add to my list. Read on for more in depth explanations of each country, additional cultural lessons and ideas for living, working and doing business in Latin America.

Getting a Job in
Latin America Tech

As the tech ecosystem has grown rapidly from 2010 to 2018, I've been flooded by people from the US and Europe who want to get a job in tech in Latin America. Programs like Start-Up Chile, Ruta N, Seedstars, Hackers/Founders, 500 Startups are seeding Latin America's tech ecosystem and providing incredible resources for local entrepreneurs. I've seen a surge in not only Latin American companies launching in local markets but also in US startups opening offices here, along with local entrepreneurs attacking the US market. This growth has generated a new wave of highly-skilled, international tech companies operating in Latin America.

Because I operated a tech company in Latin America and worked with countless startups with a Latin American presence, I always try to give advice to US-based tech workers who are curious to know what the technolgoy job market looks like and how they can get into it.

The short answer is, as of 2018, the most in-demand professionals are Ruby on Rails, Blockchain and Python developers, UI/UX designers, and online marketers. But there is also a significant demand for native English speakers to fill sales and customer service roles. As the Latin American startup ecosystem gains traction and more tech companies around the world are granting their tech workers the flexibility and/or option to work remotely, the number of emails asking me for advice on how to land a tech job in Latin America has picked up.

Here are the four options for expat tech workers who are looking for job opportunities in Latin America:

1. Working remotely for a US company
2. Working for an established Latin American company
3. Working with a Latin American startup targeting Latin America
4. Working with a Latin American startup targeting the US market

If you're interested in landing a job at a startup in Latin America or just learning more about how you can work remotely from Latin America, here's a breakdown of each of these options as well as a list of the top tech hubs in Latin America to help you get started.

1. WORKING REMOTELY FOR A US COMPANY

If you have the opportunity to work remotely for a US company and still make a US salary or hourly rate, you can live exceptionally well in most Latin American cities.

Of course, the downside of working 100% remote is you won't really be exposed to the local tech ecosystem, and it will be harder to make friends with locals. If you're a freelancer with established US clients, a good way to tap into the local tech ecosystem is to work from one of the numerous, affordable coworking spaces across Latin America.

Keep in mind, if you're working remotely for a US company, you will have a harder time getting a work visa because the US company does not have local infrastructure to offer you a job. For example, you may be required to leave the country or change countries every 90 days so that you can stay on a tourist visa.

2. Working for an established Latin American company

If you would like to try working for an established Latin American company, remember that tech salaries in the region are much lower than in the US. Fortunately, so is the cost of living in most countries. If you choose to go this route in countries like Chile, getting a work visa can be easy. More established companies favor fluent Spanish speakers and professionals with degrees from top Latin American or US universities.

Similar to working for larger companies in the US, you probably won't be working on the most cutting-edge technologies. You might also have a manager who doesn't know all that much about technology, and you might find the working conditions unorganized and chaotic compared to a well-organized big company in the US. However, the advantages of a stable income, decent salary (even if it's less than what you'd make in the US), and a work visa can offset some of these challenges.

3. Working with a Latin American startup targeting Latin America

From 2008-2018, the number of work visas being granted by Chile alone has risen by an average of 25 percent per year, as the demand for more foreign professionals has spiked.[1] According to Cisco, Latin America will have nearly half a million IT professional shortfall by 2019, with the largest skills gap in emerging technologies such as video, cloud, mobility, big data, cybersecurity, IoT, and software development.[2] Most of the Latin American companies hiring tech workers in these fields will pay $2,000 – $3,500 per month. Good places to search for positions like these at Latin American startups is Workana or Chiletrabajos (a Magma Partners portfolio company).

Although the founders of most Latin American startups and some of the tech team will speak English, be prepared for most, if not all, of the product and marketing to be in Spanish. On the plus side, working for a Latin American startup can make it easier to get a work visa, and your team can help you quickly integrate with the local tech scene. You'll also have a chance to polish your Spanish – it's how I learned!

If you don't currently have any tech skills, or you are looking for an entry-level position, consider coming to Latin America to work as an intern where the costs of living are lower, and learn some new skills. This will help you get connected with the local startup scene and then you can try to stay to work full-time afterward. Latin American boot camp programs, such as World Tech Makers, Coderhouse, Desafío LatAm, and Digital House, will teach you the tech skills startups are looking for and even help connect you with companies during and after the program.

4. Work with a Latin American startup targeting the US market

The last and perhaps best option for English-only speakers is to work with a Latin American startup, or a foreign startup with offices in Latin America, that is targeting the US market. There are countless startups with a product or service for US consumers that have back offices for their tech and sales teams in Latin America. For example, did you know there is an agile team building core parts of Eventbrite's global platform in an office in Mendoza, Argentina?

Working for a Latin American startup targeting the US will bring a monthly salary similar to working for a traditional company in Latin America; however, if you have a lot of experience or a specific skillset that is in high demand, you could bring in upwards of $6,000 per month, which is 2-3x higher than an average technology salary in Latin America.

Even though it's difficult to find a job with a salary that matches US salaries for the same position, your day-to-day expenses will be significantly lower in most Latin American countries, allowing you to live as if you were earning 2x-10x as much in the US. Companies that target the US market will likely allow you to work in English and obtain a work visa while working on interesting tech problems, while still having the opportunity to learn Spanish.

Tapping into this tech scene can be challenging as job offers and businesses information is often outdated or dispersed across various networks. Just as in other parts of the world, the best opportunities often come through word-of-mouth. There are many ways to get connected to the Latin American tech scene, such as attending networking events, workshops at local universities, and meetups. A good place to start is Hackers and Founders, Founderlist.la (a Magma portfolio company), or Meetup.com, which offers dozens of groups related to tech and startups in Argentina, Colombia, Chile, and more. To find job postings, be sure to frequently check Craigslist, LinkedIn, and expat groups on Facebook, which are widely used to share opportunities in English.

Where to start your search: Latin America's booming tech cities

So where are the tech hotspots in Latin America with the most potential? Here are some of the best cities to start your search. We'll go into greater detail about the pros and cons of these cities and more in later chapters, so treat this as a short preview.

» **SANTIAGO, CHILE:** This capital city is home to Start-Up Chile, one of the most successful startup programs in the world. The program has placed the country on the global map and turned the city into Latin America's "Chilecon Valley." In 2017, the Chilean government introduced a new tech visa allowing tech workers, investors, and entrepreneurs to obtain a work visa in just 15 days.

» **MEDELLIN, COLOMBIA:** The tech scene in Medellin is growing fast with support from talented entrepreneurs, smart venture capitalists, and programs like Ruta N that offer grants to help entrepreneurs and local tech talent succeed. A short plane ride away from major US cities, Medellin is uniquely positioned to continue expanding its position as a key tech hub in Latin America. Don't sleep on Bogota, Colombia's capital city, either!

» **MEXICO CITY, MEXICO:** With a population over 25 million, Mexico City is home to many tech companies that have found success solely by servicing the local market. However, proximity to the US still attracts entrepreneurs with a global vision, and many US companies also have offices of their development teams in the city.

» **GUADALAJARA, MÉXICO:** Though a smaller city, Guadalajara is another booming tech hub in Mexico to keep on your radar. Some of the best engineers in Mexico are located here, which has also attracted US companies to set up their development teams in the city.

» **BUENOS AIRES, ARGENTINA:** Home to one of Latin America's most vibrant venture capital ecosystems, Buenos Aires has a wealth of IT talent and tech companies in a range of sectors. In 2017, the government introduced a new Entrepreneurs' Law that promises to help companies launch their businesses in 24 hours and give more incentive to local VCs to fund new ventures. As a result, local companies are going to find it much easier to scale their teams.

» **SAN JUAN, PUERTO RICO:** With a highly-trained workforce and attractive tax structure, Puerto Rico is turning to technology and entrepreneurship to revitalize its economy. Programs like Parallel 18 have helped the island quickly make a name for itself as an emerging tech hub in the region, and it shows no signs of slowing down, even after the devastating 2017 hurricane.

Latin America's tech scene is thriving, and there's never been a better time to be a part of it. If there is one thing startups struggle with, no matter where they're located, it is finding top tech talent. So if you're amazing at what you do and eager to immerse yourself in the local startup ecosystem, Latin America could be a good move for you. Feel free to reach out at **jobs@magmapartners.com** and we'd be happy to answer any questions you might have or direct your resumé to startups in the region looking for employees.

Endnotes

1   *Reuters.* https://www.reuters.com/article/us-chile-immigration-idUSB-RE90O17G20130125

2   *Cisco.* https://blogs.cisco.com/news/filling-the-it-skills-gap-in-latin-america-with-qualified-it-talent

How to Recruit Talent In Latin America

O ne of a founder's most important duties is identifying and recruiting top talent. Finding and convincing the best people to work for your startup can be the difference between success and failure. There are hundreds of great resources on how to find top talent in the US, but Latin America is very different. US strategies don't usually work in Latin America. This section is worth reading even if you're not a founder, but are on the other side of the table, looking for a job. It'll give you an idea of the labor market in Latin America.

Recruiting for startups in the US is difficult because the market is extremely competitive and well developed. But it can be easier because many people want to work at a startup because "startups are cool." Sometimes they even pay well.

Many US workers choose a mission-driven company that aims to change the world, or a company that offers workers the opportunity to work on interesting problems, rather than the company that pays the most or has the highest brand recognition. Additionally, structural advantages like recruiters and well developed stock option plans showcase startup opportunities and push more people to take a risk with a startup.

In Latin America, it's different. It can be difficult to recruit for startups, but not necessarily because of competition from other startups.

Difficulties of Identifying Talent and Recruiting Employees in Latin America

1. STARTUPS AREN'T COOL YET
In the US, working for a startup is cool. In Latin America, it's cool to work for an old, conservative business. Your parents, your significant other and your friends will likely be more impressed that you have a middle management job at a stodgy retailer than if you earn the same money at a startup nobody's heard of.

2. LATIN AMERICANS ARE GENERALLY CONSERVATIVE
In addition to wanting to work for conservative companies, most people would rather work for a big company because they perceive it as more secure than working for a startup. Since the Latin American slowdown started in 2016, Latin America is going through the job losses that the US experienced in the 2008 financial crisis. Most Latin Americans don't realize that those jobs are never coming back, so people don't view traditional jobs as risky yet.

3. EMPLOYEES DON'T VALUE STOCK OPTIONS
Stock options are a new idea for most Latin American workers and, in many cases, an alien concept. Most people generally think employers are trying to screw them by offering less money, while offering stock options. They can't understand why a founder would want to give away equity to a lowly worker!

In addition, there haven't been many examples of successful employees making tons of money from working at a startup because there haven't been many successful startups in Latin America yet. The perceived value is low, so founders lose another tool from their tool kit.

4. TOP UNIVERSITY GRADUATES EXPECT HIGH SALARIES (FOR THEIR COUNTRIES)

If a Latin American went to one of the top 2-3 universities in their country, they expect a top salary that's likely out of reach for a local startup and may even be expensive for a US startup for non-engineers.

5. UNWILLINGNESS TO MOVE

In the US, if you're a young single person and you get recruited to a top startup in California and you live in Wisconsin, chances are you'll think about going. The US has a much stronger culture of moving for jobs. In Latin America, family usually comes first, second and third, so it can be hard to get top candidates to move.

6. RISK TAKING IS VIEWED AS DANGEROUS

Finding risk takers can be difficult. Most Latin Americans are generally conservative because they've been trained to optimize for keeping their heads down and not getting fired. That's antithetical to a startup, where founders push their team to take risks, fail fast and small, so they can avoid a big failure and be successful faster.

7. INTENSE WORK ETHIC IS HARDER TO FIND

Many people like their 15+ public holidays and 3 weeks of vacation and have a 9-6 mentality. If something needs doing outside those hours, they're not working. Those are valid choices, but a startup needs people who are willing to be a bit more flexible and are generally optimizing for other things.

8. UNIVERSITIES TRAIN FOR BIG BUSINESSES

This is true in the US too, but it's even more true in Latin America. Most workers were trained to work in a big business and lack the skill set for startups.

9. PEOPLE ARE SKEPTICAL OF COMPANIES THAT TREAT THEM WELL

Many large companies rule by fear and require constant face time to succeed. It can be strange for a worker to find a company that treats them well and doesn't require them to put in facetime for their bosses, but focuses on getting things done and efficiency.

10. WORKERS VALUE FULL-TIME EMPLOYMENT CONTRACTS

In the US, you can hire a new worker as a contractor and most people will be happy. In many Latin American countries, people need and want government social benefits that only come with full time employment on a standard contract, so doing the contractor route can be more difficult. Many people would rather work for an established company as an employee rather than make 3-4x as a contractor.

11. CLASSISM AND RACISM CAN MAKE FINDING TOP CANDIDATES DIFFICULT

Many local companies and recruiters reject top talent based on classism and racism, which makes some good candidates self-select out of applying. Sometimes these biases are overt. Job descriptions can say things like "I'm looking for a young woman" or "I'm looking for a man" that don't leave the door open for talented people don't fit the description. Others have code words like *buena presencia* which has historically meant light skinned and upper class. Still others don't say it publicly, but HR will automatically throw out resumes that don't come from specific high schools or universities.

Strategies to attract Latin American talent for your startup

Make no mistake, there are incredibly talented people in Latin America who would love to work for a startup and would be great cultural fits. Here are the strategies I've seen successful funds and startups use to recruit the best people in Latin America.

1. SHOW ME THE MONEY!

If you're a funded startup or a US-based startup...show them the money! Hire at or above market salary, legally incorporate a local entity, use local employment contracts and you can likely buy yourself a good team. Chile has the highest average wages in Latin America but you need to earn only $1400 to be in the top 5% of wage earners. Other countries are even lower. If you pay an employee US$3000/month, or even US$5000/month, you'll be able to pick top talent. But this top talent that's clearly motivated by money isn't ideal, as they'll be likely to jump ship at the first higher offer. It can be hard to find top performers, so think about acqui-hiring a small startup team and letting them do the hiring for you.

If you're interested in learning how you can build a tech team in Latin America, please feel free to reach out to us at **aquihire@ magmapartners.com.**

2. LOWER AN EMPLOYEE'S (PERCEIVED OR REAL) RISK

At least four top funds in Latin America, including Magma Partners, guarantee people jobs in other portfolio companies if the startup they work for goes bust. We give top workers peace of mind so that they can "take a risk" by working at a startup, knowing they won't miss a paycheck.

3. HIRE THE BEST PEOPLE

Latin American countries have varying degrees of classism, racism and sexism which excludes some of the best people from top jobs in traditional companies. Or precludes them from advancement above lower level jobs. The biggest upside is hiring smart, talented women who might have been passed over by bigger companies.

Second, most large Latin American companies won't even look at a person's resume if they didn't complete university. Or just as bad, didn't go to one of the top 2-3 universities in their country. No degree/lower tier university=low wage work for the rest of their life. Hiring from non-university graduates represents an untapped talent pool.

Some of our best employees didn't finish university, either because they ran out of money, had to start working to help their families, or weren't prepared to succeed in university when they were 18-20 years old. But they're brilliant and hard-working. Give them an opportunity and you'll likely have a loyal, hard-working employee who is just as qualified, if not more so, than someone who did finish university.

50% of Chileans earn minimum wage. 90% earn less than $1400/month. And Chile is the wealthiest country on average in Latin America. Hire the best people, give them paths to advancement and you'll find an enormous untapped pool of great employees. If you treat them well, they're more likely to be loyal since you gave them an opportunity.

4. Support Individuality

Most Latin American companies value copious in office face time, rigid rules, punish failure harshly, require employees to punch the clock… literally. Many rule by fear and don't offer opportunities for advancement.

Show that you value productivity, allow flexibility, allow space for small failures and you'll attract great employees.

In Latin America, as in the US, "Would I want to have a beer with that person?" is one of the bigger, yet unspoken, hiring criteria. In Latin America, so many smart, dedicated, people get passed over if they don't fit the prevailing culture. I think this sentiment is even stronger than it is in the US.

5. GIVE TALENTED PEOPLE SOMETHING FUN TO WORK ON

As in the US, many big companies in Latin America are extremely conservative. A programmer can work on maintaining old code from the early 2000s, or they can come work on the cutting edge, learning something new every day. Show you offer these opportunities.

6. TRAIN AND TEACH YOUR EMPLOYEES

Many Latin American large companies don't push personal growth and employees can stagnate, doing the same thing over and over. Emphasize that you train your employees and teach them the newest tricks of the trade.

7. CULTURE OF PROMOTING FROM WITHIN

Most large Latin American companies don't promote from within. Employees who start in an entry level position may get a promotion or two, but aren't going to be able to advance very far. Show that you're different and promote from within.

8. INTERVIEW FOR CULTURE AND TEST

More people in Latin America prefer a more laid-back lifestyle than people in 2018 USA. And that's fine. But it's better to be sure that the person will fit a startup culture ahead of time, rather than just being really smart. I always do a 1-3 month test with all new startup employees to make sure that they can do the job and that they actually want to work for a startup rather than just thinking they want to work for a startup. If at the end of the trial period the company doesn't offer them a full time job or the person doesn't accept an offer, the project ends, no hard feelings.

9. LOCAL JOB BOARDS + REFERRALS

The best places to find locals are on local job boards. International boards don't work well and you have lots of competition with big international companies. Find the two biggest local job portals in your country and post there. Join expat groups on Facebook and post there, too. Overqualified expats who don't speak the language well enough, don't have a university degree that local companies recognize, or don't have the required paperwork can make amazing employees.

10. INVOLVE C LEVEL OR FOUNDERS IN THE RECRUITING PROCESS

This tip was recommended by Welcu's Nicolas Orellana, a Chilean entrepreneur, and it's spot on. He says "People love to work with passionate teams that love what they're doing. In Latin America, most companies push hiring onto HR managers. You can be different by involving top level people in your startups."

If you'd like to work for a Latin American startup, shoot us a note at **jobs@magmapartners.com**. If looking to build a Latin American tech team, reach out at **acquihire@magmapartners.com**.

Venture Capital Overview

R aising venture capital is hard. Raising in Latin America is even harder. There are very few venture capital firms in Latin America compared to the US and China. Many of the firms that do exist don't have a strong track record, don't have operational experience in startups or are subsidized by government programs, misaligning incentives. Additionally, there are very few regional venture capital firms, which means that most entrepreneurs have few options when seeking capital. Most firms offer terms that would no longer fly in the US, very long decision processes and slow feedback loops.

Government backed accelerators, incubators and funds do their best to help the ecosystem, but many create perverse incentives and set unreasonable expectations for startups, while pushing early stage valuations higher. More firms have joined the ecosystem over the past few years, including established firms from the US and China, along with new Latin American funds, but there is still room for many more.

Our firm, Magma Partners, has tried to take the best of both worlds: the US venture capital ecosystem's founder-friendly deals and Latin America's focus on building real businesses. We're part of a group of investors who are doing things the right way, helping support Latin America's best entrepreneurs. Magma focuses on entrepreneurs who want to launch and scale in the US, or continue to build out their startups in Latin America.

We invest early stage and like to be first investors into companies. Our initial investments are in the US$25-$75K range and we can follow on with up to US$500K per company at seed stage and up to $1M to help lead Series A rounds. Since 2014, we've invested in

38 companies with founders from 11 different countries and now have offices in Chile, Colombia, Mexico, US and China.

Since 2014, the industry has started to mature at an accelerating rate. According to LAVCA's State of the Industry Report, Latin American startups received a total of USD$500M in all of 2016. In just the first 6 months of 2017, they received USD$477M, closing 2017 at $1.1B.[1]

Latin America is experiencing a substantial uptick in venture capital activity. Series C rounds in Latin America totaled USD$314M for the first half of 2017, compared to USD$208M raised in all of 2016.[2] Didi, China's largest ridesharing company, investments in 99, Brazil's largest rideshare service, represented two of the top three largest investment rounds of all time in Latin America at the time.

The report also showed that 93% of the VC funding that Latin American startups received in 2017 went to the IT sector, almost triple the amount that was invested in 2016 through the same number of deals.

Big-ticket investments are more popular in Latin America and there's still room for early stage investors to help startups reach their potential. VC attitudes are also changing for the positive, with most VCs planning to maintain their investments in the region over the next three years or more. In August 2018, Colombian last mile delivery startup Rappi raised a $200M round at a $1B valuation, furthering the trend of big-ticket follow-on investments from international VCs. In October 2018, Nubank raised $180M from Tencent at a $4B valuation.

Just two years ago, most VCs from the U.S. and China avoided Latin American startups, except for a few select deals in Brazil. 2017 marked an inflection point with US-based Andreessen Horowitz, Sequoia, Redpoint, Accel and other top-tier VCs making significant investments in Latin America.

Below is an overview of some of the organizations driving the venture capital growth in Latin America as of 2018. For an up to date list of investors in the region, check out my blog, http://www.nathanlustig.com, LatAmList.com, or LAVCA, the Latin America Venture Capital Association.

Argentina

» Kaszek Ventures – This Latin American venture capital firm focuses on high-impact technology companies in Brazil, Argentina and the region that want to operate in Latin American markets. The fund managers have connections to MercadoLibre, one of Latin America's startup unicorns that was founded in Argentina. Kaszek provides not only capital but also hands-on mentorship, networking, product development, team-building, and plenty of resources to help entrepreneurs develop viable businesses. So far in its three funding rounds, Kaszek has supported the growth of 43 companies in the Southern Cone region of Argentina, Chile and Uruguay. In 2017, it raised its third and largest fund of $200M.

» Patagonia Ventures – This Buenos Aires-based private investment fund focuses on high potential Latin American Internet businesses. The firm has already had eight successful exits out of 21 investments. The team is focused on active and global investments that bring investors and entrepreneurs together to nurture innovative ideas.

» NXTP Labs – NXTP Labs is one of the most active funds in Latin America, with operations in Argentina, Chile, Colombia, Mexico, and Uruguay. The firm has backed many of the region's top startups and acquisitions, including Fundacity, Aventones, Sparkflow, Cookapp, ComentaTV, WeHostels, and more. NXTP Labs also offers programs for Agtech and Fintech companies in Latin America.

» IncuBAte – Started in 2018, IncuBAte is a Buenos Aires based incubator program open to Argentine and international entrepreneurs. Offering a network of mentors and elite connections, startups that are chosen to participate will also receive a US$30K equity-free grant and office space.

» DRAPER CYGNUS – Draper Cygnus is an Argentina/Silicon Valley VC fund for Argentina that focuses on supporting entrepreneurs whose tech or business models have the potential for massive social change. They focus on Fintech, Agtech, Cleantech, and Nanotech and have thus far invested US$105M into 28 Argentine companies.

Other notable venture capital firms in Argentina include CAP Ventures, Quasar Ventures, Pymar Fund, Cygnus Ventures, Enzyme Venture Capital, South Ventures, Alaya Partners, Victoria Capital Partners, Jaguar Ventures, Wayra, and Incutex.

Brazil

» MONASHEES+ – A global venture capital firm based in São Paulo, Monashees+ invests in innovative entrepreneurs at the early stages of their ventures. Its portfolio includes companies focused on improving lives through technology, such as 99, Rappi, VivaReal, and Petlove.

» VALOR CAPITAL GROUP – Valor focuses on US/Brazil cross-border opportunities and is based in New York, Menlo Park, and Rio de Janeiro. They look for early- to late-stage US or international technology companies seeking to expand to Brazil, as well as Brazilian technology companies. Valor Capital Group's companies solve the problems that face the middle class, especially in fields of education, financial services, and health.

» REDPOINT EVENTURES – Redpoint eVentures is an early-stage venture capital firm located in São Paulo, Brazil. The firm is partners with Redpoint Ventures and e.ventures in Silicon Valley and boasts an impressive portfolio of 15+ companies, including big names like Rappi and Gympass.

» ACE – ACE is a major player among accelerators in Brazil, investing over $500 thousand reais in promising startups each year. Previously known as Aceleratech, ACE is considered among the top funds in Latin America, nurturing over 130 startups during its operations. ACE was voted three times as the best accelerator in Latin America.

In Brazil, other notable venture capital firms include Criatec Fund, SP Ventures, Instituto Inovacao, Ideiasnet, Confrapar, Astella Investimentos, Warehouse Investimentos, W7 Venture Capital, and DGF Investimentos.

Chile

» MAGMA PARTNERS – Magma Partners is the only fully-private investment fund in Chile. With offices in Chile, Colombia, Mexico, USA and China, Magma has invested in 42 companies at a pre-seed and seed stage across the region as of October 2018. Magma backed companies have gone on to raise $34M of follow on capital, generate $25M in annual sales and employ more than 500 people around the world. Magma will invest in 10+ early stage companies per year through 2020 from its Fund II.
» MOUNTAIN NAZCA – In 2015, Nazca was acquired by Mountain Partners, a successful German/Swiss VC and company builder. The firm invests USD$200-$500K in companies that can scale regionally and potentially expand to other Mountain offices in Europe, Asia, and Africa. Nazca has offices in Argentina, Chile, Brazil, Colombia, and Mexico in Latin America.
» START-UP CHILE – Start-Up Chile is the flagship program by Chile's public/private economic development entity CORFO and the Chilean government. The program has financed more than 1,400 Chilean and foreign startups since 2010 with its Seed program that provides CLP$20M pesos (USD$30K) equity-free grants. In 2015, Start-Up Chile added the Scale program, a CLP$60M pesos (USD$90K) equity-

free follow-on fund, as well as the S-Factory, a CLP$10M (USD$15K) pre-accelerator program for female entrepreneurs.

Other firms investing in Chile include Dev Labs, NXTP Labs, Chile Ventures, FEN Ventures, Endurance Ventures, Manutara Ventures, Scale Capital, and Aurus.

Colombia

» FIRSTROCK CAPITAL – Firstrock Capital (previously Social Atom Ventures) is an investment fund with offices in Medellin and Bogota. The firm specializes in connecting Latin America's tech talent with US startups that need technical support. It mostly invests in early-stage companies that have technology teams in Latin America, but whose target market is the US.

» FCP INNOVACIÓN – FCP Innovación is a USD$40M capital fund that is 100% backed by Empresas Publicas de Medellín, Medellin's utility company. Its investments are mostly focused on natural resource management, such as oil, water, natural gas, and waste management innovations. Currently, they have seven active investments across five Latin American countries.

Other venture capital options in Colombia include Torrenegra Labs, Axon, and more.

Mexico

» 500 STARTUPS – 500 Startups is a Mexico City-based accelerator and the most active fund in Mexico. It's invested in 300+ Latin American companies since its inception and have some very successful companies in its portfolio. 500 Startups is part of a trend of US funds and accelerators investing in the Mexican market. Successful graduates of 500 Startups in Latin America include Konfio, Clip, and CinePapaya.

» HACKERS/FOUNDERS – Hackers/Founders is a US-based company that helps accelerate startups and helps them raise money in the US. It has an office in Guadalajara and have helped at least 20 companies in Mexico so far. Hackers/Founders charges equity for its services and creates a stock pool so that all 20 companies in a round receive equity in each other. So far, they have over 200,000 entrepreneurs as members in 47 countries worldwide and a portfolio worth USD$400M.

» JAGUAR VENTURES - Jaguar Ventures is a Mexican/Argentine early stage venture capital firm that has invested in 10+ companies and closed its second fund in 2018.

» ALLVP - ALLVP is a Mexico based venture capital fund that has invested in 40+ early stage, Series A and Series B companies in Latin America. It has had 4 exits as of 2018, including Cornershop's $225M exit to Walmart.

» MITA VENTURES - Mita Ventures is a US/Mexican venture capital firm focused on early stage Mexican startups and later stage Silicon Valley startups that want to open offices in Mexico.

» ANGEL VENTURES - Angel Ventures is a Mexico based Latin American venture capital firm that closed a $120M fund to invest regionally.

Mexico is home to many other venture capital firms, including Mountain/Nazca, Variv Capital, Alta Ventures, Arkfund and more.

Peru

» ENDEAVOR – Endeavor is a global organization that promotes high-impact entrepreneurs in over 25 countries worldwide. The organization arrived in Peru in 2014 and became a leader developing the ecosystem, supporting over two dozen entrepreneurs who represent 14 companies.

» ANGEL VENTURES, a Mexico-based VC, has a local presence in Peru through its Angel Ventures Peru branch office. Angel Ventures Peru has sourced deals from Latin America for the regional fund and raised a $2M early stage Peru only fund in 2018.

» STARTUP PERU – Startup Peru is a Ministry of Production government program based on the Start-Up Chile model. It has financed more than 150 startups with its equity-free grants, and finances up to 24 projects at a time, depending on the stage of the startup.

In Peru, other notable venture capital firms include UTEC Ventures, Wayra, EmprendeUP, and Fledge.

US Firms investing in Latin America

» LATINSF – LatinSF is a new economic development initiative that promotes business and trade between San Francisco and the Latin American region. This initiative comes from a public-private partnership between the Mayor's Office of Economic and Workforce Development (OEWD) and the San Francisco Center for Economic Development (SFCED), with the goal of creating a welcoming environment for established Latin American companies to expand and for startups to relocate to San Francisco.

» LEAP GLOBAL PARTNERS – LEAP Global Partners is a US-based VC firm focused on training and empowering Latin American entrepreneurs that are making an impact in finance, health, education, the shared economy, or in media. They have ~US$15M in funding available and have invested in three tech companies in Latin America.

» BABEL VENTURES – Babel Ventures is a Silicon Valley-based venture capital firm raising $30 million to help accelerate Latino-owned businesses in the U.S. and Mexico. The founders, Bárbara Kunde Minuzzi and Daniela Arruda, are both from Brazil and previously raised funds for other real estate and tech funds.

Other notable funds include: Quona Capital, Elevar Equity, Plug and Play, Alpha4Ventures and more.

Regional Firms investing in Latin America

The following firms, many of which are mentioned above, also invest regionally:

Magma Partners, Mountain Nazca, NXTP Labs, Angel Ventures, ALLVP, Kaszek Ventures, Monashees+, Valor Capital, Wayra, and 500 Startups.

If you're looking to raise money and would like advice, please reach out via our application form at **http://www.magmapartners.com/apply.** Don't take more than 5 minutes to fill it out with some bullets points and don't worry if you're not raising money or don't fit our investment thesis. We're happy to give advice on launching and scaling in either Latin America or the US.

Endnotes

1 *LAVCA.* **https://lavca.org/2017/10/31/state-of-venture-capital-industry-2017-deal-activity-highlights/**
2 Ibid.

Raising VC Money in the US

I t was around 1am on a Friday night when I got the call. One of our portfolio companies that has offices in the US and Latin America had been offered a Series A investment from one of the best investment funds in the world and the founder couldn't believe it. He had great numbers, was at break even, had an amazing team and was growing 25% each month. The offer was for $5M at a great valuation.

But the founder told me he wasn't going to take it. Why? Because one the requirements was that he move his entire team to Silicon Valley and fire anyone who couldn't or didn't want to move. The founder knew he couldn't take the risk of firing the team that got him to where he was today. He also knew he'd be beholden to future VC funding if he replaced his Latin American team with Silicon Valley talent that would raise his burn rate 4-5x.

Unfortunately this story isn't an isolated incident. It's happened to multiple Latin American entrepreneurs, even those who have a base in Silicon Valley, but keep a second office in Latin America. One of our best portfolio companies went through one of the top two accelerators in the world and has been offered multiple term sheets from top VC firms that require them to fire everyone on their team and open up shop in the valley or NYC.

So how can you fund your startup's growth if you're not able to bootstrap your business and you're located in Latin America? It's much harder to raise a Series A in Latin America that it is in the US. And Latin American startups still struggle to raise money when they make the jump to the US in hopes of raising money in Silicon Valley or New York. Many times, a US incorporated startup targeting the US market that happens to have a Latin American team would go up in value 5-10x if you changed the founder's last name from Spanish to English and moved them to San Francisco.

As of December 2018, Magma Partners has supported 45+ companies with bases across Latin America to build their businesses. Many of these companies are really US companies that just happen to have a tech and sales team in Latin America and want to raise capital in the US. Others are Latin America B2B companies that would love to raise money in the US, but have found hard sledding.

When I first got started, I didn't realize how hard it would be to find investors to follow on in our companies and our strategies were all wrong. My hope is that this section will help you avoid the mistakes that we made when we first came to the US, and that US investors now have a more open mind when looking at Latin American tech companies.

In 2015, I got on a plane to California with Adrian Fisher, the founder of PropertySimple, to take his company to the US market. He'd built an amazing product, similar to Zillow, but in Chile. He had 1000+ real estate agents using his product and millions of people using his product to find properties.

He'd created a US version of his product, called it PropertySimple and moved to the US to focus 100% on the US market. We started in Los Angeles and over the next two months met with investors, entrepreneurs and friends in the Bay Area, Chicago, Wisconsin, New York and other areas in between. We figured that we'd be able to raise a small seed round in the US, as we'd seen our friends raising money with less developed products in the States. We figured that we'd already de-risked the business by having proven we could build a great product in Latin America. We only needed a cash infusion to jumpstart the US market.

We were wrong. Most investors seemed to think that Adrian's Latin American traction was a negative, not a positive. Others had never seen a company with a Latin American tech team and weren't sure it would work. Others loved the initial traction, but wanted to see it working in the US with US clients before investing.

After our trip, we realized it was going to be much harder than we expected to raise a round in the US and the team and Adrian began to build out the product and generate sales. After 12 months in the US, we'd built a business that was not only cash flow positive, but was in a position to choose investors, not the other way around as when we first arrived.

During that same time, three other Magma portfolio companies were in the process of raising US capital and had similar experiences. A few of our companies finally broke through, including PropertySimple, which raised $3M from US investors. As of December 2018, the portfolio companies we support have raised $37M+ in follow-on-funding, most of it from the US. I pooled everything we learned from successfully raising funds from US investors to create our playbook for raising money from US funds even if you're based outside of the US. Here's what we learned.

What to do before your investor meetings

1. **Build a great product and team.** This sounds obvious, but having a great product and team is table stakes. We like to see balanced teams with complimentary skillsets solving real problems, with solutions people will pay for.
2. **Follow standard procedures.** US investors want to invest in businesses they understand. They have such great deal flow where they are that it doesn't make sense to try to understand foreign investments, laws and teams. If you're doing business in the US, Incorporate in the U.S., ideally with a Delaware C corporation. If you're doing business in Latin America, look at a Delaware LLC and/or potentially incorporating in Cayman Islands, United Kingdom or Puerto Rico. Use a standard share structure and include founder vesting. It's what most U.S.-based VCs are used to and is quick and easy to set up.

3. **Open a US office.** Get a membership in a US coworking space in the startup hub where you plan to raise money to show you have a US office. You can then use the space every three-to-four months. We have portfolio companies that have been in WeWork, The Port and similar coworking locations. Some of our startups have used extra space in other startup offices, which works well too.

4. **Get US clients.** Investors like to see US dogs eating US dogfood. There are so many great US startups and deals that come across a VC's desk. When doing due diligence, they want to be able to call clients in the States. We suggest first getting US clients while you are still based in Latin America so that you don't spend on higher US costs while you're prospecting if you can avoid it.

   If you can sell product over the phone or internet, do it. If you can't because you're in an industry like larger B2B SaaS sales, set up two weeks' worth of sales meetings over the phone and then plan a US sales trip, ideally in a secondary city with less competition and lower costs. Austin, Denver/Boulder, Madison, Chicago, Los Angeles, Miami, Houston, Dallas, Phoenix are all good options. Make sure investors can call your U.S. clients in due diligence.

5. **Make inroads into the ecosystem.** Interact with locals from the ecosystem where you'd like to raise money, either online or in person. The best way to get on their radar is to get direct introductions.

6. **Get introductions from people who have a good track record or a connection to Latin America, but are based where you'd like to raise money.** There are likely top startup founders with a US track record from your country. Connect with them and show them you're serious. A good place to find these entrepreneurs is on the *Crossing Borders* podcast, where I interview entrepreneurs doing business across borders, with a

focus on those with a connection to Latin America. http://www.nathanlustig.com/category/crossing-borders-podcast/

7.   **Research U.S.-based VCs who have invested in non-US teams.** Some VCs invest only in a specific geographic area. Others are more open. Try to get meetings with these funds.

What to do during investor meetings

1.   **Take Mark Suster's advice and offer to hold board meetings in the investor's home city.** Many investors will not invest outside of their geographic location because of travel time. Take this objection off the table up front.

2.   **Don't focus on your foreign track record; emphasize your US product.** Our company's foreign track record was seen as neutral or even negative. Go straight to gaining traction in the States. While counterintuitive, we found that investors were scared that you'd take the money for the US product and invest in the Latin American product, or get distracted by the Latin American market and neglect the more lucrative US market.

3.   **Don't assume investors know anything about your home country.** Some investors might even have misconceptions. Answer questions and address misconceptions directly, but respectfully.

4.   **"Be so good they can't ignore you."** Steve Martin's classic quote is our mantra with foreign entrepreneurs when they come to the U.S. to raise money. You have a barrier to raising money in the U.S. if you don't fit the pattern of what a U.S. venture capitalist sees each day. Make this quote your mantra and you'll be more likely to succeed, with or without venture cash.

If you're looking to raise money and would like advice, please reach out via our application form at **http://www.magmapartners.com/ apply.** Don't take more than 5 minutes to fill it out with some bullets points. Don't worry if you're not raising money or don't fit our investment thesis. We're happy to give advice on launching and scaling in either Latin America or the US.

An Overview of Fintech Startups

In 2013, the German founder of a Chilean startup wrote me a cold email. He had a dilemma. He'd gotten $250k in funding from a German investor and wanted to deposit this investment into a Chilean bank account. Sounds straight forward, right? But he'd gone to multiple banks, but they'd all told him he needed to show at least US$2000 of monthly income in Chile for a period of 2 years, plus have a cosigner on his account. $2000 would have put him in the top 10% of family income in Chile, the wealthiest country in Latin America.

Unfortunately, I couldn't help him and it took him months to find a local connection who could convince a bank to open him an account to deposit the $250k. I wish this were an isolated incident, but I had to deposit $5000 that I couldn't touch for two years in order to open a personal bank account. We're not talking about credit cards or lines of credit, only a simple bank account to deposit money. At the same time a majority of Latin Americans lack access to financial services, Latin American banks are among the most profitable in the world.

Latin America isn't a poor region. It's massively unequal and lack of financial services is one of the reasons for this inequality. Only 11% of Latin Americans have access to credit from formal institutions.[1] In Chile, Colombia, Peru and Mexico ~40% of adults have no accounts with a formal financial provider, even though Chile has one of the highest levels of financial inclusion in the region.[2] In other Latin American countries, lack of access to financial products can be 90%!

In one of the most chronically underbanked parts of the world, improvements in financial technology have started to open the doors for widespread financial inclusion throughout the Latin America. That's why Fintech startups are a core part of the Magma Partners investment thesis.

People are accessing mobile payments, credit systems, and Peer to Peer (P2P) lending opportunities through recent advances in local Fintech, and investors are catching wind of the enormous opportunity.

While there have been advances in financial technology in Latin America in the past five years, many solutions are still available only in the countries where they were founded.[3] Few have made the leap to offer financial services more regionally. It's hard to navigate Fintech regulations across the region, which may create a fragmented group of successful companies, or the biggest success stories from the biggest economies may move into neighboring countries and dominate the region.

Whether we get regional players or increased consolidation, financial technology in Latin America is filling a persistent gap in the access to financial services across the region.

Why is Fintech so Important in Latin America?

By 2016, less than half the population of Latin America had access to a bank account or debit card. Even fewer people had access to credit. In a region where micro, small, and medium enterprises (MSMEs) make up 99% of the private sector in terms of raw number or businesses and people impacted, financial inclusion for individuals and small businesses continues to be a significant challenge for economic development.[4] Latin America's banking sector is relatively strong and profitable compared to the rest of the world, despite (or more cynically, because) most Latin Americans lack access to the system. During the 2008 recession, Latin American economies were surprisingly resilient, growing around 3.8% in 2010, after a mere 2% contraction in 2009.[5]

This growth was fueled by commodities exports and a strong, conservative banking system, avoiding the toxic investments that were crippling banks in the U.S. In comparison, exports in the US and Europe shrank by 10% in 2009 and did not bounce back for several years.[6] A 2016 study found that Latin American MSMEs are less competitive than their counterparts worldwide, in part because of a US$210 – $240B deficit in financing options.[7] Across the region, small businesses struggle to grow because access to credit continues to be a highly formalized and bureaucratic process that excludes many business owners. Since these enterprises employ at least 67% of the population regionally, the need for widespread financial inclusion is pressing.[8] In the past decade access to technology and the internet has changed how Latin America does business. There are opportunities to provide financial services to MSMEs and people who fall outside of the traditional banking systems.

In 2018, almost 50% of Latin Americans have access to a smartphone.[9] While mobile banking has long been accessible in places like China and Kenya, Latin America has also become a front for new technologies that increase access to financial services for all.

Opportunities in Latin American Fintech

A 2017 report by Finnovista and the Inter-American Development Bank (IADB) found a total of 703 Fintech startups in Latin America, over 50% of which were launched between 2014 and 2016.[10] This sector received over US$186M in venture capital funding in 2017, and one-third of that went to startups.[11]

It is clear that Latin America is at the beginning of a Fintech revolution, with recent improvements in access to internet and technology driving this boom.

Diego Caicedo, CEO of OmniBnk, a Magma Partners portfolio company, published an article in 2017 identifying the current trends in the Latin American Fintech industry and what Fintech companies plan to do to change the region.[12] Electronic invoicing and factoring, digital banking, smart contracts, blockchain technology, and digital authentication processes are all driving efforts toward financial institutions that accept more Latin American clients. These technologies are helping lower the risk of providing credit to or signing contracts with individuals.

Here are a few of the most exciting Latin American Fintech startups using these technologies:

Mexico

» KUESKI: A Mexican startup focused on providing small loans to middle-class individuals, received US$35M in funding in 2016 in a round led by Variv Capital, Richmond Global Ventures, Rise Capital, and CrunchFund.

» CLIP: Latin America's answer to Square, Clip simplifies cashless payments for small businesses. In 2016, General Atlantic made an undisclosed investment in Clip after the startup had raised a US$8M Series A round led by Alta Ventures in 2015.

» KONFIO: An online lending platform for micro-business loans that has raised $100M+ in debt and equity, Konfio is focused on extending lines of credit to MSMEs in Latin America by using an algorithm to measure creditworthiness for financially underserved people.

» ALBO: A Mexican Neobank that allows anyone to open a bank account and transfer to and from any account in Mexico for free. Albo is a Magma Partners portfolio company.

Other notable fintech startups in Mexico include: Bitso, Conekta, ComproPago, and Kiwi.

Colombia

» EPAYCO: Founded in Medellin, Epayco provides e-commerce solutions to individuals and small businesses in Colombia. Think Venmo meets Square. Wayra invested US$50K in Epayco in 2016.

» OMNIBNK: OmniBnk helps SMEs find the most business-friendly terms from factoring companies. OmniBnk evaluates electronic invoices from companies and provides information to investors, which allows investors to make financing offers quickly and transparently.

OmniBnk is a Magma Partners portfolio company and has raised more than $250M in debt and equity investments as of 2018.

Other notable fintech startups in Colombia include: La Vaquinha, Prestamela, and Banlinea.

Chile

» CUMPLO: A Chilean crowdlending platform that connects companies applying for loans with networks of investors. Founded in 2012, Cumplo is certified as a B Corp and has helped generate US$180M in loans.
» FOUNDERLIST: Latin America's answer to AngelList. A crowdfunding platform that creates syndicates of private investors to finance startups across Latin America. FounderList is a Magma Partners portfolio company.
» QVO: An online payments system aimed to simplify transactions for small businesses. QVO is a Magma Partners portfolio company.

Other notable Chilean fintech startups include: ComparaOnline, Flow, Buda, CryptoMKT, Destacame, and PuntoPagos.

Brazil

» NUBANK: A São Paulo-based Neobank that provides mobile banking and credit card options for Brazil's unbanked population. Since its founding in 2013, Nubank has raised over US$377M with several rounds led by Goldman Sachs and became a Latin American unicorn in early 2018. Nubank raised $180M at a $4B valuation from Tencent in late 2018.
» CREDITAS: Creditas is an online secured lending platform that is working to lower borrowing costs for Brazilians by increasing the efficiency of lending systems.

» GUIABOLSO: Brazil's only personal finance platform that allows users to fully integrate their bank accounts. GuiaBolso currently has over 3.3 million users and has raised over US$67.2M in funding.

Other notable Brazilian Fintech startups include: Triunfei, Verios, and Iugu.

Argentina

» AFLUENTA: Currently, this Buenos Aires-based startup is the only marketplace lending company for individuals and SMEs with operations in more than one country in Latin America. It operates in Argentina, Mexico, and Peru, with plans to expand to Colombia and Brazil in 2018.
» RIPIO: One of Latin America's foremost blockchain payments companies, Ripio is helping make the Latin American financial system more accessible through blockchain technology.
» UALÁ: Founded in 2016, Ualá is Argentina's answer to Nubank in Brazil. Ualá has raised more than $40M in VC from Goldman Sachs, George Soros, Ribbit Capital and more.
» Other notable fintech startups in Argentina include: Wayniloans, SeSocio, Increase, and ComparaenCasa.

Ecuador

» KUSHKI: Kushki is an Ecuadorian Stripe that has operations in Ecuador and Colombia.

This list of startups only scratches the surface of the movement that is growing in Latin America. While Mexico, Argentina, Colombia, Brazil, and Chile are leading the Fintech revolution, these technologies are also popping up in Peru, Ecuador, and Paraguay, where the population is still highly underbanked.

Investments in Latin American Fintech

A rush of investments has followed this wave of growth. Eighty-one percent of venture capital deals in Latin America in 2016 involved Fintech companies.[13] LAVCA pointed out that Fintech companies received over US$186M in venture capital in 2016 and a majority of these rounds were led by syndicates of local investors, including VARIV Capital, Jaguar Ventures, FEMSA Comercio, Kaszek Ventures, Redpoint e.Ventures, Magma Partners and Valor Capital.[14]

2016 marked an inflection point in Fintech investments, with more international firms paying attention to Latin American startups, with 26% of investments made by co-investments between local and international venture capital firms[15]. QED Investors partnered with Scotiabank in 2017 to create a platform that "will identify, invest, and promote the growth of innovative startups across the Fintech spectrum that look to improve customer products and experiences in Latin America," and Visa Brazil recently founded its own LatAm Fintech accelerator to empower Latin American companies and help them grow.

Latin America's Fintech ecosystem used to be dominated by cross-border payments and processing solutions that helped bring US$74B of remittances into the region.[16] But in the past five years, the Fintech industry has finally moved forward. Smart contracts, electronic payments, and online-lending companies are dramatically improving financial inclusion in Latin America. This movement is just getting started.

Startups are providing individuals and MSMEs the resources they need to grow, which in turn has increased regional competitiveness and generated economic growth. If you're interested in learning more about what's happening in Latin America Fintech, check out my blog posts on nathanlustig.com by searching the tag Fintech, or looking at LatamList.com's Fintech news articles.

Endnotes

1   *Brookings.* https://www.brookings.edu/blog/techtank/2015/10/29/financial-inclusion-in-latin-america-regulatory-trends-and-market-opportunities

2   Ibid

3   *Oliver Wyman.* http://www.oliverwyman.com/content/dam/oliver-wyman/v2/publications/2016/dec/HARNESSING-THE-FINTECH-REVOLUTION-ENGLISH.pdf

4   Ibid.

5   *Seeking Alpha.* https://seekingalpha.com/article/182166-latin-american-banks-attractive-to-investors-as-loans-and-profitability-grow

6   *World Trade Organization.* https://www.wto.org/english/news_e/pres09_e/pr554_e.htm

7   http://www.oliverwyman.com/content/dam/oliver-wyman/v2/publications/2016/dec/HARNESSING-THE-FINTECH-REVOLUTION-ENGLISH.pdf

8   Ibid.

9   *Statista.* https://www.statista.com/statistics/203719/smartphone-penetration-per-capita-in-latin-america-since-2006/

10   *LAVCA.* https://lavca.org/industry-data/2017-industry-data-analysis/

11   Ibid.

12   *Tech Bullion.* https://www.techbullion.com/the-latest-fintech-trends-transforming-latin-america/

13   *LAVCA.* https://lavca.org/2017/04/25/fintech-dominates-latam-vc-investments-2016/

14   Ibid

15   Ibid

16   *AMI Perspectiva.* http://amiperspectiva.americasmi.com/traditional-remittances-are-under-attack-by-online-competitors/

Blockchain in Latin America

M ost people have heard about cryptocurrencies and ICOs, but most only know about the ability to gamble on token prices and the 2018 price crash. But blockchain may have important use cases that could be especially interesting in Latin America.

In March 2018, Venezuela launched the "Petro," the first-ever cryptocurrency created by a national government in Latin America.[1] The currency is supposedly backed by Venezuelan oil production and is supposedly worth a barrel of crude oil from the country's Orinoco Region. The government's stated reason in connecting the Petro to a natural resource is to create a stable currency that could provide an alternative to the Bolivar, which is experiencing crippling inflation.

While correctly panned by the vast majority of crypto experts and many human rights activists as a money grab by a corrupt regime, the launch showed how cryptocurrency, and the blockchain technology that supports it, could revolutionize the financial infrastructure of countries in Latin America if executed correctly and by a non-corrupt institution.

In a region where 70% of the population still has no access to formal banking institutions, blockchain represents a route to financial inclusion.[2] Latin America has been one of the fastest adopters of the blockchain, primarily because of the urgency of financial inclusion in the region. However, blockchain still faces many local challenges from powerful government regulators and the financial sector, which is one of the most profitable in the world and is reticent to allow potential competition into the market. Here's an overview of the state of blockchain technology in some of Latin America's biggest markets.

Blockchain in Argentina

Argentines have been some of Latin America's earliest adopters of cryptocurrency. With 6.1 businesses that accept bitcoin per million people in Buenos Aires, Argentina's capital has adopted cryptocurrency faster than almost any other city in the world.[3] The use of blockchain-backed currencies is not necessarily sanctioned by the Argentine government. Instead, citizens have adopted the technology as a safety net against the extremely unstable Argentine peso, the restrictions on foreign currency exchange within the country, and the 2018 reported ~32% yearly inflation rate. Argentina experienced an 80% devaluation of the Peso against the dollar in 2018, which may lead to even more crypto adoption.

The Argentine Parliament recognizes cryptocurrency as property, not as currency, so for now, the exchange of coins is legal. Argentinian entrepreneurs had installed 200 Bitcoin ATMs as of late 2017.[4]

As one of Latin America's top destinations for software development, Argentina has also become a hotbed for blockchain startups that are using new technologies to revolutionize contracts, financial exchanges, and fundraising. One notable example is CoinFabrik, which provides several blockchain technology development resources as a service to other companies. RSK Labs is also active in Argentina's blockchain development ecosystem, creating Rootstock, a smart-contract platform connected to the Bitcoin blockchain. RSK recently partnered with the Universidad de Buenos Aires (UBA) to provide courses in blockchain technology as part of the Information Engineering program.[5] RSK has been active in the blockchain network since 2013 and raised a US$3.5M Series A round in 2017.

One of Latin America's most prominent blockchain startups, Ripio, is also based in Argentina. Ripio provides electronic payments solutions for businesses in Latin America, allowing merchants to process payments from international credit cards and Bitcoin using the blockchain. Ripio raised a US$400K Series A round in 2017, and their coin, the Ripio Credit Network, had a US$40.44M market cap in 2018.

The founder of the Xapo, a cryptocurrency wallet that is the largest custodian of bitcoin in the world, is also from Argentina. Wences Casares is now building Xapo in Silicon Valley and has raised over US$40M to support the venture. After building the first internet provider in Argentina in 1994, Casares has founded countless technology companies that revolutionized Argentina's tech ecosystem even in the early 2000s. As of 2018, he sits on the board of PayPal, Endeavor, and Kiva.

Blockchain in Brazil

Latin America's largest economy has adopted blockchain technology to reduce corruption, legitimize legal decisions, and even track votes.[6] In a country of 215 million people, dealing with land titles, citizen petitions, and voter registration can be overwhelming, and the government is looking to the blockchain to eliminate discrepancies and corruption.

In January 2018, Brazil's state-run technology company Serpro launched a blockchain platform to regulate land titles in the world's fifth largest country.[7] The platform is meant to reduce corruption by recording every action taken in the system so officials cannot delete files without other stakeholders knowing about it. Serpro is joined by U.S. blockchain startup Ubitquity, which helps prevent deforestation by fighting the corruption that allows land titles in the Amazon to be bought and sold illegally.

In 2017, Brazil's Central Bank began exploring blockchain options to back the country's financial infrastructure.[8] It is testing four platforms: Ethereum, Quorum, HyperLedger Fabric, and Corda. It plans is to back-up the central bank's current real-time gross settlement system (RTGS) to keep up with other central banks that are beginning to innovate using blockchain technology.

Some of the other notable blockchain startups operating in Brazil include Bitcoin to You, which sets up bitcoin exchange centers across the country, and CoinBR, which offers services for mining and exchanging cryptocurrencies. Chilean-founded and Magma Partners portfolio company CryptoMKT expanded their operations to Brazil in March 2018, allowing for exchange of Ethereum, Bitcoin and Stellar Lumens.

Blockchain in Chile

In 2015, Chile's government invested money in SurBTC via a grant, and supported the creation of Chile's first bitcoin exchange, now called Buda.com. This decision made people think that Chile might accept and regulate blockchain technology for financial transactions, as SurBTC and CryptoMKT, a competitor, are currently governed by Chile's Financial Intelligence Unit which monitors money-laundering, which makes Chile was one of the first countries in the region to open its doors to blockchain technology and cryptocurrency exchanges.

Further, in 2017, Chile's largest stock exchange, the Santiago Exchange, partnered with IBM to implement blockchain into the country's financial services sector to increase the accuracy and security of transactions.[9]

Chile took a step back in 2018 as Chile's banks closed all cryptocurrency companies' accounts simultaneously in March, 2018.[10] As of September 2018, Buda.com and CryptoMKT are in court fighting the banks' collusion to shut down the cryptocurrency market and were granted an injunction forcing banks to reopen accounts while waiting for a court's decision, which may come in 2019.

Paradoxically, in early March 2018, Chile's National Energy Commission announced they would begin using blockchain technology to authenticate information from the national energy grid. The plan is to add regulatory strength and security of the data collected by the agency, building trust with consumers and key stakeholders.

Chile's government has been open and welcoming to blockchain technologies as a way to revolutionize payments and contracting across the country. The question remains whether banks will follow the same pattern.

Blockchain in Colombia

While Colombia has not adopted blockchain technology as readily as its counterparts, the Colombian government has been exploring opportunities to use blockchain to improve security and prevent fraud. The Colombian Central Bank was one of the first to meet with blockchain development firm R3 in 2017 to discuss opportunities for partnership.[11] Citizens have also begun to ask when Colombia will implement blockchain to help authenticate electronic voting, following in the footsteps of Sierra Leone.[12] However, the government has yet to recognize cryptocurrencies officially, meaning bitcoin exchange platforms like LocalBitcoin and Colbitex are on shaky ground, although some local merchants already accept bitcoin as payment.

Colombia is one of the world's top adopters of electronic invoicing, with the government enforcing mandatory e-invoicing for all businesses starting in January 2019.[13] Colombian startups like OmniBnk are using blockchain to create tools that help businesses understand and leverage the data produced by electronic invoicing and make more informed business decisions. Colombia has frequently struggled to become integrated with international currency exchange platforms, like PayPal, so blockchain technology and cryptocurrencies may help streamline cross-border payments in Colombia as well.

Blockchain in Mexico

Mexico became one of the first countries in Latin America to regulate financial technology by passing the Fintech Law in early 2018.[14] The Mexican Congress officially recognized cryptocurrencies as digital assets – but not as currency – and set up rules to control exchanges to prevent corruption and money laundering. The law puts the Mexican Central Bank in charge of monitoring startups working with cryptocurrencies.

Blockchain could be a massive opportunity for Mexico, where more than 80 million people do not have access to formal banking services.[15] Companies like Bankcoin.global, a project by the Universidad Autónoma de Baja California Sur, are piloting smart contracts and cryptocurrency e-commerce in Mexico. Mexico also has two cryptocurrency exchange startups, Bitso and Volabit, which are helping coordinate remittances through simple-to-use apps that lower the cryptocurrency learning curve. Magma portfolio company CryptoMKT opened its Mexican exchange in August 2018.

Other industries have caught on to the potential usefulness of blockchain technology, including the Mexican car insurance industry, which is notoriously poorly-regulated. The Mexican Association of Insurers is exploring blockchain solutions to transparently validate insurance policies, save the government time, and improve compliance. In the banking sector, Santander has reportedly invested ~US$800M in Mexico to develop blockchain technologies that will strengthen security and integrate cryptocurrency exchange into the financial system.[16]

In a region where more people have smartphones than bank accounts, blockchain technology and cryptocurrencies represent an opportunity to improve regional financial inclusion. However, not all governments are thrilled about the arrival of a technology that allows for decentralized currency circulation. Bolivia, Ecuador, and Mexico have all banned or restricted cryptocurrency transfers because of concerns about illegal activity and money laundering.

Nonetheless, startups across the region are exploring blockchain technology to improve transactions across almost any industry, from car insurance to land sales. Some of the region's wealthy are even seeing cryptocurrencies as an alternative to unstable fiat currencies, and some family offices are buying up Bitcoin and other cryptocurrencies rapidly.[17]

Latin America has proved itself as an early adopter of blockchain technologies, with both the private and public sectors seeing the potential to use the network for economic development, financial inclusion, and transparency. Still, as we've seen in Chile, Ecuador, Bolivia, and other regions, entrenched interests, including banks, government agencies, big businesses, and financial industries are beginning to push back. It will be exciting to see how this battle evolves as the Latin American blockchain industry matures.

Endnotes

1   *Washington Post.* https://www.washingtonpost.com/news/worldviews/wp/2018/02/20/venezuela-launches-the-petro-its-cryptocurrency/?noredirect=on&utm_term=.78bbdb0ee093

2   *AMI Perspectiva.* http://amiperspectiva.americasmi.com/tapping-the-unbanked-smartphone-user-market-in-latin-america/

3   *Coindesk.* https://www.coindesk.com/bitcoin-thriving-argentinas-black-market-economy/

4   *Coin Telegraph.* https://cointelegraph.com/news/argentina-jumps-on-bitcoin-atm-bandwagon-with-200-expected-in-october

5   *PulsoSocial.* https://pulsosocial.com/2018/04/03/universidad-buenos-aires-incorpora-blockchain-programa-educativo-rsk/

6   *News BTC.* https://www.newsbtc.com/2018/01/08/brazilian-electoral-system-to-use-ethereum-network/

7   *Reuters.* https://www.reuters.com/article/us-brazil-property-blockchain/can-blockchain-save-the-amazon-in-corruption-mired-brazil-idUSKBN1FE113

8   *Coindesk.* https://www.coindesk.com/immature-no-longer-brazils-central-bank-is-ramping-up-its-blockchain-work/

9   *BTC Manager.* https://btcmanager.com/chiles-santiago-stock-exchange-leads-blockchain-implementation-in-latin-america/

10   *LatAm List.* https://latamlist.com/2018/03/30/chilean-cryptocurrency-industry-asks-banks-to-clarify-regulations/

11   *R3.* https://www.r3.com/blog/2017/08/29/banco-de-la-republica-colombia-se-vincula-con-r3-para-fomentar-innovacion-financiera/

12   *El Espectador.* https://www.elespectador.com/noticias/politica/cuando-se-podra-implementar-el-voto-electronico-con-blockchain-en-colombia-articulo-744568

13   *Observatorio E-commerce.* https://www.observatorioecommerce.com.co/la-facturacion-electronica-sera-obligatoria/

14   *Brave New Coin.* https://bravenewcoin.com/news/bitcoin-adoption-accelerating-in-mexico/

15   *El Financiero.* http://www.elfinanciero.com.mx/economia/santander-listo-para-utilizar-blockchain-en-mexico.html

16   *Bloomberg.* https://www.bloomberg.com/news/articles/2017-12-08/latin-america-s-wealthy-families-are-buying-up-bitcoin

Impact Investing in Latin America

M any entrepreneurs and investors want to build business that generate an impact. They want to make people's lives better. According to Wikipedia, impact investing is defined as investments "made into companies, organizations, and funds with the intention to generate a measurable, beneficial social or environmental impact alongside a financial return." These types of funds and companies are popular in Latin America and many solve real problems and help people live better lives.

But I think we should be expanding the definition. I believe that supporting almost any forward-thinking, technology-based venture in Latin America is a form of impact investing.

Investing in companies that are using technology to close the region's inequality gaps or to simply stop the brain-drain to other countries, is not just good for business. It is also an act of support for a knowledge-based economy and job growth in the region.

Many Latin American countries still face extreme levels of social and economic inequality. In 2014, the richest 10% of people in the region held 71% of Latin America's wealth.[1] Latin America is not poor region, it's unequal.

Latin American entrepreneurs are showing us that they have the power to solve some of region's biggest challenges, while benefitting more than just the top 10% of Latin Americans. Funds like Mexico's IGNIA Fund and Adobe Capital, Brazil's Vox Capital, and global funds like Elevar Equity, Accion and Village Capital have invested in a wide range of companies focused on financial inclusion, education, cleantech and more.

Magma Partners has invested in 42+ companies with sales and development teams based in both Latin America and the US. The investments we've made in these companies have introduced a new generation of Latin American entrepreneurs to startup best practices—such as stock options, good paying job opportunities, an open business culture, and flexible work schedules. The startups we've supported have helped break down barriers caused by racism, classism, and sexism.

So is my definition really impact?

When I got pushback about my broader definition of impact investing, I clarified my position in an interview with ImpactAlpha, an impact investing website. I've included a short excerpt:

Most investments in Latin America should be considered impact investments if they're creating jobs, training employees, and seeding the next generation of entrepreneurs, while not creating an extractive business model.

We believe that the founders we support will be able to build real, sustainable businesses with teams in Latin America, not only helping stop the brain drain, but also taking the best parts of global entrepreneurial culture like stock options, flexible schedules and working on cutting edge technologies, and helping make them more common in Latin America.

We'll be investing into 60 companies across Latin America with Magma Fund II and our goal is for all of them to build teams in countries across Latin America, while targeting clients from around the world.

Technology has the ability to help bend the arc of the entire region for the good. We believe that the founders we support will be able to build real, sustainable businesses with teams in Latin America, not only helping stop the brain drain, but also taking the best parts of global entrepreneurial culture like stock options, flexible schedules and working on cutting edge technologies, and helping make them more common in Latin America.

Our companies will have impact by building teams, creating good, high-paying jobs, and most importantly, transferring tech industry knowledge from global markets into Latin America by allowing entrepreneurs and team members to work on cutting-edge technology. We also believe that many of the companies we've invested in are solving real problems for both the region and the world, even if they wouldn't be considered an impact investment by all traditional standards. If we're talking about dumping toxic waste into rivers or neighborhoods, then no, it wouldn't be an impact investment, or even a morally justifiable investment.

We wouldn't invest into a payday loan company that had extremely high interest rates, even if it employed hundreds of people and was extremely lucrative, as the overall impact would be negative. There are plenty of Fintech companies that aren't abusive and provide investor returns for us to support.

We've helped create jobs in Latin America since our companies generally have most of their teams in Latin America, supporting a small office in the US. Companies like GroupRaise, PropertySimple and Keteka have their high tech and sales jobs in Latin America, generally headed by a co-founder, and then a smaller office headed by a cofounder in the US. They're helping create jobs, polish talent and transfer knowledge between Latin America and the US, which stops the brain drain and trains the next generation of Latin American founders and tech talent.

Local impact investors

Until recently, most impact investments in Latin America have come from foreign investors. Local impact investments have been held back by challenges in big businesses and by a lack of support for early-stage companies, according to the World Economic Forum.[2] That has created a so-called "pioneer gap," in which many enterprises are too large for microfinancing but too small for banks and investment funds.[3] The impact investing ecosystem in Latin America is fragmented at both regional and national levels.

Local impact investment funds are bridging the gap between the social entrepreneurs and the resources they need to grow. Firms enter the impact investing space in Latin America at the rate of approximately 15 firms every two years, according to a recent study by the Aspen Network of Development Entrepreneurs, Latin American Private Equity & Venture Capital Association, and LGT Impact Ventures.[4,5]

Mexico's emerging impact investment ecosystem

According to The Impact Investing Landscape in Latin America report in 2017, there are 42 impact investing firms in Mexico, 15 of which are exclusively investing in Mexico.[6] The attention of these firms, like Village Capital, is primarily on companies making an impact via financial inclusion, health, and agricultural innovations.

Backed by Adobe Capital, SalaUno is a healthcare social enterprise that launched in 2011 based on the successful Aravind Eye Hospital model in India. More than two million people have cataracts in Mexico, 700,000 of whom are blind. SalaUno has treated over 70,000 patients and performed over 10,000 surgical procedures—65% of which were cataract surgeries.[7]

In Mexico, local financial institutions extend credit to the private sector at a low rate, below 35% of GDP, compared to 68% of GDP in Brazil. Afluenta, backed by the IFC and Elevar Equity, is another startup that is revolutionizing the market with its approach to credit and investment. As a technology-enabled marketplace that connects lenders and borrowers, Afluenta is increasing the access and affordability of financial services in Mexico and beyond. IGNIA also recently invested in Afluenta to allow the company to continue its consolidation in the local and regional market.

Each year, Miami Dade College and the Inter-American Development Bank bring together creative minds from Latin America to tackle development challenges at its Demand Solutions event. In 2017, companies selected from Mexico included Xintiba, an educational startup that develops therapeutic video games that accelerate the acquisition of cognitive skills in children with special needs.

Brazil's Impact Ecosystem

The number of both domestic and international impact investors is on the rise in Brazil, despite the political and economic issues plaguing the country. According to The Impact Investing Landscape in Latin America report, the number of active impact investors in Brazil increased from 22 to 29 between 2014 and 2016, with key impact investment sectors including health, agriculture, education, and finance.[8]

Vox Capital, the first certified impact investing fund in Brazil, has invested in multiple companies offering innovative and scalable solutions to enhance the lives of low-income Brazilians. For example, ProRadis is a software company that helps offer low-cost medical care to the Brazilian population that lacks health insurance.

Avante is another Vox Capital portfolio company that provides financial solutions for micro entrepreneurs in low-income regions, mainly in the Northeast of Brazil. The company's goal is to become the most transparent and reliable channel for the Brazilian micro entrepreneur.

The Ford Fund Lab was also recently established in Brazil to provide training and guidance to startups that develop mobility programs geared to the needs of the country's low-income population. The Ford Fund Lab plans to provide acceleration for up to 20 entrepreneurs in the early stages of business development with a focus on promising social impact projects and innovative solutions that address the basic needs of communities that lack transportation.[9]

Colombia's Impact Ecosystem

According to the same report, international funds dominate the impact investing ecosystem in Colombia, with only three local firms focused solely on the Colombian market.[10] Unlike Mexico and Brazil, Colombia's private equity industry is still in its early stages. Impact investments have helped develop the industry quickly and turn the country into a stable place for investing activities.

As a result, new impact funds are being created in Colombia. Elevar Equity and Odiseo are funds focused on Colombian entrepreneurs and building profitable, scalable and impact driven companies.[11] Over the next five years, Odiseo plans to impact at least one million lives through products and services accelerated through the program and generate at least 4,000 new jobs in the country.

According to Harold Calderon Meza, Managing Director of Odiseo, [Colombian fund managers and family offices confuse] impact investing with philanthropy and that Colombian fund managers have recently started investing in entrepreneurs who generate solid financial returns as well as a significant positive impact.

In Latin America, that impact can be the creation of a new generation of entrepreneurs creating positive social change, through better work cultures and tech-driven services for the vast majority of the region's people.

If you're curious about impact investing, please reach out on Twitter:

@nathanlustig or @magmapartners and I'd be happy to discuss!

Endnotes

1   *World Economic Forum.* https://www.weforum.org/agenda/2016/01/inequality-is-getting-worse-in-latin-america-here-s-how-to-fix-it/

2   *World Economic Forum.* https://www.weforum.org/agenda/2017/03/latin-americans-are-slipping-back-into-poverty-impact-investing-can-reverse-that-worrying-trend/

3   Ibid.

4   *Aspen Network of Development Entrepreneurs, Latin American Private Equity & Venture Capital Association, and LGT Impact Ventures.* https://www.lgtimpact.com/.content/downloads/general-information/LatAm_ImpInv_Report_en.pdf

5   *Bain.* http://www.bain.com/Images/BAIN_REPORT_State_of_impact_investing_in_Latin_America.pdf

6   https://www.lgtimpact.com/.content/downloads/general-information/LatAm_ImpInv_Report_en.pdf

7   *Entrepreneur.* https://www.entrepreneur.com/article/268267

8   https://www.lgtimpact.com/.content/downloads/general-information/LatAm_ImpInv_Report_en.pdf

9   *Acritica.* http://www.acritica.net/editorias/geral/ford-anuncia-apoio-a-startups-brasileiras-para-propostas-de-mobilidade/217313/

10   https://www.lgtimpact.com/.content/downloads/general-information/LatAm_ImpInv_Report_en.pdf

11   *Capria VC.* https://capria.vc/updates/fund-manager-spotlight-odiseo-to-invest-in-nearly-25-colombian-impact-startups-and-generate-over-4000-jobs/

20 Top Latin American Startups

I n 2018, I got a call from an investment banker in London who wanted to know more about later stage Latin American companies. She'd searched Google and Crunchbase, but she was perplexed to only find a few. Although many of Latin America's most successful tech startups have already made a name for themselves in the region, only a few have done so internationally.

Companies like MercadoLibre and Despegar have become household names across Latin America and are being recognized across Asia, Europe, and North America as stable brands that are competing on a global scale. My goal is to give you a first look at some of the most successful and up and coming startups in the region so you can get get an idea of what's going on in the region. In no particular order:

1. DESPEGAR (ARGENTINA)

Founded in 1999 by Alejandro Tamer, Federico Fuchs and Martin Rastellino, Despegar is Latin America's answer to Expedia: an online marketplace for flights, hotels, rental cars, vacation packages, and cruises. Currently, Despegar is the fifth-largest online travel agent in the world and raised more than US$332M in its IPO in 2017. The company has a market cap of US$1.85B in 2018.[1]

2. GLOBANT (ARGENTINA)

Globant was founded in 2003 by Guibert Englebienne, Martin Migoya, Martín Umaran and Néstor Nocetti as a software company that works with major US and UK companies. Since its IPO in 2014, Globant has seen its share prices quadruple with a market cap of US$1.5B in 2018.[2]

3. MERCADOLIBRE (ARGENTINA)

MercadoLibre, founded by Hernan Kazah and Marcos Galperin, is one of Latin America's best-known startups and operates across the region as an online marketplace for goods, much like Amazon or Alibaba. As of 2018, MercadoLibre had a market cap of US$14B.

4. MOVILE (BRAZIL)

Movile, founded by Fabricio Bloisi and six others, is the market leader in all things mobile. With more than $100M in revenue and 120M users, Movile is one of the region's biggest tech companies, getting investment from Naspers. They're also one of the most active investors in startups in the region. iFood, one of their subsidiary companies raised $500M in 2018 and delivered more than 12M orders in November 2018.

5. OPENENGLISH (VENEZUELA)

OpenEnglish, founded by Andres Moreno, Nicolette Rankin and Wilmer Sarmiento, is the leading edtech company teaching English to native Spanish speakers in Latin America and the U.S. Founded in Venezuela in 2006, OpenEnglish offers live classes at all hours and has enrolled over 500,000 students in 40 countries.

6. OLX (ARGENTINA)

Inspired by Craigslist, OLX, founded by Alec Oxenford, Fabrice Grinda and Jordi Castello, is an online consumer-to-consumer exchange platform that is used in emerging markets. It was acquired by Naspers in 2014 and is one of the largest Internet brands to be developed outside of Silicon Valley.[3]

7. PEDIDOSYA (URUGUAY)

Founded in 2009 in Montevideo, Uruguay by Alvaro Garcia, Ariel Burschtin and Ruben Sosenke, PedidosYa is Latin America's answer to UberEats or GrubHub, an online food ordering and delivery platform.

German delivery company, Delivery Hero acquired PedidosYa in 2014 but kept the name.[4]

8. Netshoes (Brazil)

Netshoes, founded by Marcio Kumruian, is a Brazilian e-commerce conglomerate that acts as the official distributor for several major sporting goods brands in Latin America. Netshoes was founded in 2000 and recently made US$148.5M in a 2017 IPO with a market cap of US$251.4M.[5]

9. Rappi (Colombia)

Rappi is a last mile delivery service that may morph into a Fintech company. They've raised more than $380M at a $1B valuation from funds like A16Z and are a powerhouse in Colombia, Mexico, Argentina and Chile. Competitors Cornershop, Mercadoni and Glovo are also battling it out in this market.

10. InvertirOnline (Argentina)

IntervirOnline, founded by Facundo Garreton, is an online stock-trading company, like Etrade or Charles Schwab, for the Latin American market.

11. Wizeline (Mexico)

Wizeline is a software platform that helps developers and companies build technology faster. Based in San Francisco and Guadalajara, founder Bismarck Lepe is showing how technology companies can straddle the US, Latin American and Asian markets.

12. CargoX (Brazil)

CargoX is the Uber for trucks in Brazil. After quitting his finance job in London, Federico Vega and team has built CargoX into $200M in annual revenue, securing investment from Goldman Sachs and other top venture capitalists and investment banks.

13. Satellogic (Argentina)

Satellogic, founded by Emiliano Kargieman, is a space tech company founded in 2010 to democratize access to satellite data. In 2017, they raised US$27M from Chinese internet company Tencent and CrunchFund, a Silicon Valley VC, and launched their sixth micro-satellite into orbit.[6]

14. ArchDaily (Chile)

ArchDaily, founded by David Assael and David Basulto, is an online platform covering architecture news, events, interviews, products, and competitions for and by architecture professionals. ArchDaily is the largest architecture website in the world in English, Spanish, Portuguese and Chinese.

15. Psafe (Brazil)

Psafe, founded by Marco DeMello, develops apps that maximize mobile security, privacy, and performance. With over 100 million installations and 20 million monthly users, Psafe is the largest cloud-based mobile security platform in the Americas. In 2013, Psafe raised a US$30M Series C Round from Qihoo 360, Redpoint e.ventures, and Pinnacle Ventures.[7]

16. Nubank (Brazil)

Nubank is the leading digital financial services company in Brazil, providing online banking solutions for Brazilians through a "no-fee" credit card that is managed through a mobile app. Nubank raised a US$80M Series D round led by DST Global, Sequoia and Goldman Sachs in 2016. In 2018, DST led a $150M round, which allowed Nubank to join the unicorn club,[8] and Tencent's $180M investment a $4B valuation in late 2018 cemented it as Latin America's most valuable fintech startup.

17. 99 (BRAZIL)
99, founded by Ariel Lambrecht, Paulo Veras and Renato Freitas, is Brazil's second popular rideshare platform that operates much like Uber or Lyft. In January of 2018, China's platform Didi Chuxing acquired 99 for a reported $1B.[9]

18. CORNERSHOP (CHILE/MEXICO)
Founded by Daniel Undurraga, Oscar Hjertonsson and Juan Pablo Cuevas in 2015, Cornershop is an online grocery delivery business. It was acquired by Walmart in 2018 for $225M.

19. UALÁ (ARGENTINA)
Ualá, founded by Pierpaolo Barbieri, is an Argentine neobank that has clients in every province of Argentina. After raising $10M from US investors including George Soros, Ualá is poised to become a large player in the Argentine and Latin American ecosystems.

20. OMNIBNK (COLOMBIA/CHILE)
Omnibnk, founded by Diego Caicedo, is a Colombian/Chilean fintech platform that helps companies with invoice-backed financing. OmniBnk works with large financial institutions and small businesses to help finance working capital loans. OmniBnk is a Magma Partners portfolio company.

While many of Latin America's top startups are still coming from traditional hubs like Argentina and Brazil, countries across the region are producing exciting, innovative companies that are gaining global attention. This is not a fully inclusive list and there are many more companies that deserve to be highlighted. We'll go into deeper detail with many of these founders in later country focused chapters.

Endnotes

1   *Bloomberg.* https://www.bloomberg.com/news/articles/2017-09-20/tiger-global-s-despegar-marks-first-argentine-ipo-of-2017

2   *Financial Times.* https://www.ft.com/content/687f5a58-5807-11e6-9f70-badea1b336d4

3   *Fortune.* http://fortune.com/2014/10/29/olx-emerging-markets/

4   *LAVCA.* https://lavca.org/2014/06/26/online-food-delivery-moves-in-latam-delivery-hero-acquires-pedidosya-en-espa/

5   *Marketwatch.* https://www.marketwatch.com/story/netshoes-raises-1485-million-in-ipo-expected-to-trade-wednesday-2017-04-12

6   *TechCrunch.* https://techcrunch.com/2017/06/23/satellogic-raises-27m-for-affordable-high-resolution-imaging-satellites/

7   *TechCrunch.* https://techcrunch.com/2013/12/03/brazilian-antivirus-start-up-psafe-raises-30m-series-c-from-chinas-360-and-redpoint-e-ventures/

8   *TechCrunch.* https://techcrunch.com/2016/12/07/dst-leads-80m-round-in-brazils-nubank-to-take-on-the-big-boys-in-financial-services/

9   *TechCrunch.* https://techcrunch.com/2018/01/03/didi-confirms-it-has-acquired-99-in-brazil-to-expand-in-latin-america/

Jie Hao: How China Sees Latin America

This section is the first of 31 interviews with entrepreneurs and investors who do business in Latin America. They share their unique perspective in their own words in interview format. Most of these interviews are excerpted from episodes of my podcast Crossing Borders. If you want to learn more about an individual entrepreneur or investor, you can listen to the podcast or read a summary on my blog, linked at the end of each interview section. China is an important part of the Latin American technology ecosystem and Jie shares his perspective on this trend in this section of the book.

Jie Hao is a partner at Magma Partners who previously built and sold two companies before heading to Chile to look for deals to invest into in 2012. We had this conversation while I was in Shanghai for the launch of the partnership between Kr Space and Magma Partners to create the Sino-Latin American Accelerator. Jie Hao has helped foster Magma Partners' relationship with Chinese businesses, investors and government, including helping raise Magma Fund II in early 2018, and managing the China-Latin America accelerator partnership with Kr Space.

How did you get involved with Magma Partners?

I studied my PhD in math in Texas, then started a wealth management fund for Chinese people living in the US. After that, I went to Chile in search of business opportunities and met [you]. I was really interested in investing in startups in Latin America, so I invested in some Fund I companies, then went on to help build Fund II in China. In January 2018, we opened a Magma office in Beijing and created a partnership with Kr Space, the Chinese version of WeWork, to create the Sino-Latin American Accelerator.

How did Chinese investors react when you pitched the idea of venture capital in Latin America?

Every single investor rejected me when they first heard my pitch because they didn't know enough about Latin America. Luckily I had a connection at 36 Kr, a Chinese tech publication similar to TechCrunch, and they agreed to publish a weekly column on doing business in Latin America that was very well-received. It was such a big hit that [we] founded Global Huntrepreneur, a company that helps Chinese investors do business globally. I believe China's experience with development and adopting new technology can be a model for Latin America to follow. Partnering with China can help Latin American entrepreneurs find funding, gain access to technology, and learn from China's success.

What is the opportunity for Chinese investors in Latin America?

I am very optimistic about the growing relationship between China and Latin America. In the past 3-6 years, the US has taken a step back from its traditional relationship with Latin America and China has stepped in to fill the void. There is an opportunity for Chinese investors and entrepreneurs to take their knowledge from their local market and bring it to Latin America. There are still a lot of problems that need fixing in Latin America, and Chinese entrepreneurs could borrow tech solutions that are already working back home to solve these issues. Right now, the opportunity in Latin America is open to both China and the US, but China is doing a better job taking advantage. While some big US investors, like Andreessen Horowitz, have made investments in Latin America recently, there are currently no US rivals to corporate investors like AliExpress and Didi Chuxing.

You can listen to our entire conversation on the *Crossing Borders* podcast on Itunes, Stitcher or wherever you get your podcasts, or on my blog:

https://www.nathanlustig.com/2018/05/15/ep-40-jie-hao-how-china-sees-latin-america-startups/

David Lloyd: Why Remote Work in Latin America is A Trend Worth Watching

I n 2011, I met David Lloyd on a Chilean soccer field and we've been friends ever since. David left his job at Merrill Lynch to cofound The Intern Group, an international education program helping college students find internships abroad and then moved to Chile for the Start-Up Chile program.

Founded with the idea of helping talented students get work experience in Latin America and across the world, The Intern Group now has offices in 12 countries, including in Chile and Colombia. David understands the challenges of having a distributed team, but he's also on the cutting edge of a new generation of technology companies that turn these difficulties into opportunities for growth. Because Latin America is on the same time zone as the US and has a highly talented workforce, I believe we'll see huge growth in US companies with Latin American offices.

Why do you have offices in Chile and Colombia?

Our first internship program was in Medellin, Colombia for the FIFA Youth World Cup, where my cofounder Johanna Molina is from originally. After a successful pilot, we first came to Chile because of Start-Up Chile, after our Argentine lawyer sent us something about the program. It seemed too good to be true, but we had to check it out. I personally had always been interested in coming back to Latin America after I previously lived and worked in Argentina, Chile, and Brazil after graduating from university. That international experience marked me and helped me stand out in the rest of my career, so The Intern Group was originally meant to replicate that experience for other students.

Companies around the world can see the value of getting work experience abroad, learning another language, and getting out of your comfort zone. I did that in Latin America, so it was my focus when we started TIG, but we eventually realized Latin America was a bit of a niche market. We still have offices here but we have gone global.

How do you manage people across 12 countries and why is it important?

The easy answer is through technology. Technology lets you sell almost anything globally, at low cost. We bootstrapped this business from the start because we were able to set it up for under US$4K. There are a lot of advantages to this way of doing business, in terms of service and in terms of staff retention.

For our kind of business, it is important to have on-the-ground representation in each country where we have programs to ensure students are happy, doing well, and having a good time. The local expertise is invaluable.

From the employment side, this generation of workers is interested in flexibility - in hours, location, work style. We are totally results-focused, not presence-focused. We provide options for people to work out of any of our offices and have a chance to travel the world. We may not be able to compete in terms of salary, but our employees can work from almost anywhere. This system also allows us to do geographical arbitrage, since a decent US salary can go a lot further in Latin America or Asia than in the US or Europe.

What do you tell investors and other stakeholders about distributed teams?

Most people in London are pretty skeptical when they hear about this scheme. They are mostly worried about accountability and time zones. Time zones are definitely an issue because we have offices in Europe, Latin America, Asia, Africa and Australia, but we find ways to get around it. It can be harder to get the whole team aligned, but these issues are balanced out by the advantages. There is a growing percentage of people that are seeing that this system is working and that younger generations prefer the distributed, flexible model.

On one hand, remote work and distributed teams help with staff retention, since we can offer benefits people are looking for. On the other hand, just do the math. How much does it cost to hire 100 people in New York vs. Medellin or Santiago? Most investors will be convinced by one of these two arguments that distributed teams are an excellent option for a growing international company.

You can listen to our entire conversation on the *Crossing Borders* podcast on Itunes, Stitcher or wherever you get your podcasts, or on my blog:

http://www.nathanlustig.com/2017/05/31/ep-1-david-lloyd-intern-group-crossing-borders-nathan-lustig/

III

Chile

T his chapter is the first of fifteen country or region specific chapters that are designed to give you a primer into each country. Every chapter starts with an introduction into the country's history, macroeconomic climate and entrepreneurial activity. Countries like Chile, Brazil, Mexico, Colombia and Argentina that have more developed entrepreneurial ecosystems have additional sections where we'll go into detail about important cities in the ecosystem, industries like e-commerce and even more economic history. These more in depth overviews have been omitted from smaller country sections.

Every chapter ends with sections featuring between one and four entrepreneurs or investors sharing their experience doing business in their country. The sections are in their own words and are excerpted into question and answer format from episodes of my podcast, *Crossing Borders*, and have been edited for clarity. Others are from original interviews that I conducted and two are excerpts from entrepreneurs' interviews in other news sources. Each interview ends with a link to the original source so that you can go deeper into the country and the entrepreneur's story.

This Chile chapter is no different. It starts with an overview of the entrepreneurial ecosystem, how Start-Up Chile jumpstarted the ecosystem, how e-commerce has grown into a big business and closes with four sections with questions and answers. David Basulto and David Assael share their story of how they bootstrapped ArchDaily into the largest architecture website in the world. Maria Paz Gillet, cofounder of Jooycar, tells us what it's like to start a second startup after a failure. Rocio Fonseca shares her story of starting a biotech company as a female founder in the 2000s, before becoming the director of Start-Up Chile. We close the chapter with Chile-based Korean entrepreneur Sean Park who explains what it's like to run the Latin American office of GroupRaise, a US startup with offices in Santiago, Chile and Houston, Texas.

Chile Overview

Chile, a long, thin country that runs along the western edge of South America, is widely considered one of the best countries to do business in Latin America. Across several indicators in the World Bank's Doing Business Report, Chile beats out the regional competition. In 2018, Chile ranked 55th in the world on the World Bank's Doing Business report, coming in just after Mexico, which ranked 49th./ However, in recent years, Chile's business-friendly reputation has slid from 34th to a controversial and potentially politically manipulated 55th.[1]

Still, Chile is undoubtedly one of the most influential economies in the region, despite its small size. Chile's population is 17 million people and is extremely centralized. The capital, Santiago, is home to 7 million people, or ~40% of the total population. By comparison, São Paulo, the biggest city in Brazil, has over 21 million inhabitants – more than the entire country of Chile.

Chile's overall GDP was US$247B in 2016, 28% of which was made up of exports.2 Chile is the world's largest exporter of copper, and also exports lithium, fish, and wine. While Chile's overall GDP appears small beside giants like Brazil (US$1.8T with 15x higher population) and Mexico (US$1.1T with 8x higher population),3 when measured per capita, Chile's GDP is the second-highest in the region after Uruguay.

Chile also boasts robust institutional stability, quality higher education programs, and the lowest rate of crime in Latin America.[2] Despite high levels of bureaucracy in some areas, the government runs smoothly and efficiently, with relatively low levels of corruption. Chile ranked 26th out of 180 countries surveyed by Transparency International's corruption survey in 2017, right after France and Uruguay, who are tied for 23rd.[3] By comparison, Argentina ranks 85th and Brazil ranks 96th.

It costs approximately 25% less to live in Chile than in the average city in the United States.[4] Rent in Santiago is 83% lower than in New York or San Francisco. The cost of living in Chile is on par with Tupelo, Mississippi, one of the most affordable cities in the US.

Santiago struggles with high levels of pollution, especially in winter, and traffic, like many other Latin American cities, and Chileans work some of the longest hours in the world for relatively low wages. The Chilean work week is the sixth-longest in the OECD, after Mexico, Costa Rica, Korea, Russia, and Greece.[5]

The Start-Up Chile Effect

Since 2010, innovation has been an official priority of the Chilean government. Start-Up Chile was one of Latin America's first accelerator programs and ranked first in the region and fourth in the world on the 2015 Global Accelerator Report.[6] Start-Up Chile is also the reason I first arrived in Chile in 2010, to participate in the pilot round of the program.

Start-Up Chile is a government-funded accelerator program that incentivizes entrepreneurs to use Chile as a launch pad for their startups. The program provides US$40K in equity-free funding, as well as a year-long work visa, to bring companies to Santiago from all over the world. Since 2010, Start-Up Chile has helped more than 1,400 startups which have generated more than US$420M in additional funding, or ten times the original investment made by CORFO, Chile's economic development ministry.[7]

Start-Up Chile is helping Chile transition to a knowledge- and technology-based economy in order to decrease its reliance on minerals such as copper and lithium, which are depleted each year. Chile has one of the most mature entrepreneurial ecosystems in Latin America and has served as a model for the region.

To incentivize innovation, Chile is working to decrease the bureaucratic friction for immigrants who want to start businesses in Chile. In 2017, Chile debuted a new Tech Visa, which allows entrepreneurs or professionals that work in technology to receive a visa in just 15 working days. It is also relatively easy to start a business in Chile, taking an average of 5.5 days.[8]

Dozens of international startups have sprouted out of Start-Up Chile. A few of these companies include:

CargoX: Brazil's "Uber for Trucks," CargoX is a smart freight broker that uses technology to make shipping logistics more efficient.

Doist (Start-Up Chile 2011): Doist has created a variety of online platforms that make working online more productive and less stressful. Its most popular apps are Todoist, an online to-do list, and Twist, a corporate messaging system that rivals Slack.

The Intern Group (Start-Up Chile 2011): The Intern Group provides international summer internships for university students across Latin America, Europe, North America, and Australia. It is based in Medellin, Colombia and Santiago, Chile.

Viajala (Start-Up Chile 2013): Viajala is Latin America's largest travel metasearch company, which aggregates flight and hotel information from dozens of sites for easy searching.

Many of the companies Magma Partners has invested in participated in Start-Up Chile, including GroupRaise, PropertySimple, Slidebean, Keteka, PayForm and many more. However, Start-Up Chile is no longer the only entrepreneurial program active in the country. Chile's largest newspaper, El Mercurio, reported in 2018 that there were over 80 programs – ranging from VC funds to small incubators – supporting entrepreneurship in Chile.[9]

The Drawbacks of Doing Business in Chile

Chile has flourished under a free market regime since the mid-1980s when dictator Augusto Pinochet implemented a neoliberal agenda to drive growth, averaging around 5% per year until a recent drop to 1.6% in 2016.

Chile is the most unequal of all OECD countries, coming in 15th in the world in 2017.[10] This statistic has had an unusually heavy impact on financial inclusion, with Chile ranking 90th on Doing Business rankings for obtaining credit, one of the lowest in the region.

While Start-Up Chile is a highly visible result of government spending on innovation, Chile still relies heavily on mining, which only employs 2% of the population. Other extractive industries, such as logging and fishing, also dominate Chile's economy. Compared to other OECD countries, Chile continues to invest very little in research and development: just 0.4% of the 2017 budget.[11]

As in other Latin American countries, doing business in Chile can be slower and more conservative than in the United States. Finding a job is frequently about who you know, and socioeconomic class continues to be a significant divider in society. It can occasionally be easier in the tech industry, especially with the new visa.

Chile is well-placed to grow. In 2016, 45% of Chileans had smartphones, and three-fourths of the population had access to mobile devices.[12] In the same year, 66% of the population had access to the Internet, and those numbers are multiplying quickly[13] By 2018, 75% of Chileans had access to smartphones. While the economy has took a small dip in 2015-2017, Chile's long-term economic growth and stability will allow it to hold on to a position of power in the regional economy. Having recently elected business-friendly President Sebastian Piñera in 2018, Chile is open and ready for investment.

Endnotes

1   *Bloomberg.* https://www.bloomberg.com/news/articles/2018-01-15/chile-weighs-impact-of-alleged-manipulation-of-world-bank-report

2   *UNDP.* http://hdr.undp.org/en/content/citizen-security-human-face

3   *Transparency International.* https://www.transparency.org/country/CHL

4   *Numbeo.* https://www.numbeo.com/cost-of-living/country_result.jsp?country=Chile

5   *World Economic Forum.* https://www.weforum.org/agenda/2018/01/the-countries-where-people-work-the-longest-hours/

6   *Global Accelerator Report.* http://gust.com/global-accelerator-report-2015/

7   *Start-Up Chile.* http://www.startupchile.org/impact/

8   http://www.doingbusiness.org/data/exploreeconomies/chile

9   *LatAm List.* https://latamlist.com/2018/02/24/chile-had-more-than-80-programs-supporting-entrepreneurship-in-2017/

10   *Council on Hemispheric Affairs.* http://www.coha.org/the-inequality-behind-chiles-prosperity/

11   *OECD.* https://data.oecd.org/chile.htm

12   *Emarketer.* https://www.emarketer.com/Report/Mobile-Chile-2016-Updated-Forecasts-Key-Growth-Trends/2001820

13   *Statista.* https://www.statista.com/statistics/209108/number-of-internet-users-per-100-inhabitants-in-chile-since-2000/

Chilean E-commerce Overview

C hile is a Latin American economic powerhouse. Rapid technology infrastructure development paired with a business-friendly political climate and high levels of Internet penetration have helped Chile's e-commerce market stand out among its larger neighbors.

With a population of ~17 million, Chile has a disproportionate 9% share of Latin America's e-commerce market, despite having only 2% of the region's population. The Chilean e-commerce market was worth US$3.7B+ and targeted to grow at 35% in 2018, reaching US$5B by the end of the year.[1]

Chileans tend to buy internationally. Since its partnership with Correos de Chile, AliExpress (owned by Alibaba) has taken off as the single largest distributor of Chinese and Asian products in Chile.[2] Chile receives over half of its e-commerce purchases from Asia, so Aliexpress has a firm grasp on the Chilean e-commerce market, directly competing with Amazon and MercadoLibre.[3]

Amazon & AliExpress have contributed heavily to this enormous growth by drastically reducing delivery times, making e-commerce more accessible. In 2017, national shipping company Correos de Chile partnered with AliExpress to reduce delivery times from China and the US from a maximum of 60 days down to a window of 16 to 38 days.[4]

Much like in Brazil and Argentina, delivery logistics and mobile commerce development have been the largest hurdles that Chile's e-commerce market needs to overcome. However, by comparison, Chile's e-commerce logistics are already much more streamlined. Currently, Chile ranks 42nd in the world for delivery logistics, Argentina ranks 60th, and Brazil ranks 65th.[5]

Chilean mobile e-commerce still needs improvement. 45% of Chileans owned a smartphone as of 2016, but only 15-20% make online purchases via mobile.[6,7] By 2018, 75%+ owned a smart phone an even more people are making online purchases, especially via Uber, Cornershop, Rappi, Cabify and more.

Still, Chile's population is intensely tuned in to the importance of e-commerce. 40% of Chileans are e-commerce users, while 80% have access to the Internet[8] Since 2014, Chile has held an annual "Cyber Day" in late May to encourage online shopping, similar to "Cyber Monday" in the United States. Chile's Cyber Day 2017 saw record numbers: online sales increased by 24% compared with 2016, revenue exceeded US$145M, and sites with discounts received 45 million visits.[7]

While brand names like ViajesFalabella, Paris, and Walmart dominated Chilean e-commerce during Cyber Day 2017, new startups have begun making a name for themselves thanks to private and public support. I wrote an article for TechCrunch that discussed how the Groupon Mafia, the alumni of Groupon Latin America, have started and financed multiple startups, much like the PayPal Mafia did in the United States.[9] For example, Cornershop, a Chilean grocery delivery service that broke into m-commerce, was founded by the founders of ClanDescuento, the predecessor to Groupon Latin America. In September 2018, Cornershop was acquired by Walmart for $225M.

Chile's government has a long history of supporting the private sector, especially in entrepreneurship. To foster e-commerce growth, the Santiago Chamber of Commerce holds an annual e-commerce Day, to which they recently added an e-commerce startup competition.[10]

While it's clear that big names continue to dominate the e-commerce scene, events like these are showing smaller businesses the importance of reaching their customers through the Internet. Currently, only 56% of small- to medium-sized companies in Chile have e-commerce capabilities, making it hard to compete for consumers' attention.[11]

Portuguese startup Jumpseller (founded by Tiago Matos and Felipe Goncalvez, Start-Up Chile grads with a Chilean office), is making e-commerce simple for more than 50,000 businesses across the region using an intuitive platform, like Shopify. Brands like Karcher, Chilota, and Ttanti are using this service to reach a wider audience, across Latin America and beyond. While small businesses in Chile are still running to catch up with the e-commerce trend, Jumpseller is making the process a little easier.

Chile's e-commerce market has not yet reached its full potential, but its skyrocketing growth and strong international standing put Chile among Latin America's top e-commerce ecosystems. While big names, including Amazon, Walmart, and Aliexpress, continue to dominate, smaller startups are popping up to compete. As more Chileans go online, mainly through their smartphones, the next challenge will be providing faster deliveries across the entire country and making mobile commerce more accessible.

To learn more about e-commerce in Chile and Latin America, please see my case study on the Latin American e-commerce market which is available on my blog,

http://www.nathanlustig.com/2015/08/16/case-study-ecommerce-opportunities-in-chile-and-latin-america/

Endnotes

1   *Cooperativa.* http://www.cooperativa.cl/noticias/sociedad/consumidores/
aliexpress-se-convirtio-en-el-principal-proveedor-de-marcas-chinas-
para/2017-08-28/100500.html

2   http://www.adnradio.cl/noticias/economia/correos-de-chile-se-asocia-
con-aliexpress-para-reducir-tiempos-de-envio-en-un-mes/20160921/
nota/3252330.aspx

3   *ADN Radio.* http://www.adnradio.cl/noticias/economia/correos-de-
chile-se-asocia-con-aliexpress-para-reducir-tiempos-de-envio-en-
un-mes/20160921/nota/3252330.aspx

4   *B2C E-Commerce Report.* https://www.ecommercewiki.org/wikis/www.
ecommercewiki.org/images/5/56/Global_B2C_Ecommerce_Report_2016.pdf

5   *eMarketer.* https://www.emarketer.com/Report/Mobile-Chile-2016-Updat-
ed-Forecasts-Key-Growth-Trends/2001820

6   https://www.ecommercewiki.org/wikis/www.ecommercewiki.org/
images/5/56/Global_B2C_Ecommerce_Report_2016.pdf

7   https://www.ecommercewiki.org/wikis/www.ecommercewiki.org/
images/5/56/Global_B2C_Ecommerce_Report_2016.pdf

8   *E-Commerce Day.* http://www.ecommerceday.cl/2017/2017/04/05/abier-
ta-la-convocatoria-al-ecommerce-startup-competition-chile/

9   *TechCrunch.* https://techcrunch.com/2017/12/29/latin-americas-grou-
pon-mafia/

10   http://www.ecommerceday.cl/2017/2017/04/05/abierta-la-convocato-
ria-al-ecommerce-startup-competition-chile/

11   Pulso. http://www.pulso.cl/
empresas-mercados/e-commerce-chile-oportunidades-las-pyme/

ArchDaily: Bootstrapping a Global Business From Chile

I first met David Basulto and David Assael, the co-founders of ArchDaily, the largest architecture website in the world in Spanish, English, Portuguese, and Chinese, in 2010 at an *asado* in Santiago, where they're based. ArchDaily has followed the two Davids' visions from the start and grown into a global business. Even more impressive, they're completely bootstrapped, never taking investor capital.

They started Plataforma Arquitectura when they were still in university in 2005 and grew the company to millions of monthly viewers, 3M+ Facebook fans, and 80+ employees in six countries. The following Q&As were excerpted from my conversation with David and David at their Santiago, Chile office on the *Crossing Borders* podcast.

How did you start a business while you were in university?

From the start, we never felt like it was a business. It's a project, a hobby, that happens to be a business. One day in university, while we were studying architecture, we had a conversation where it became clear that by spreading information through the internet, we could improve architecture on a global scale. In 2006 we started with the Spanish version, Plataforma Arquitectura, and with ArchDaily in English in 2008. After graduating, we started teaching in university and started putting our energy into ArchDaily because it started to grow very fast. Architects were spreading the word to their friends and colleagues that they could be inspired and learn about architecture online on our website.

We were writing the content that we wanted to have access to. At the time, all architectural knowledge was in expensive books and magazines that weren't published in Chile. They featured architecture from far off places and weren't relatable to us and our peers. We thought we could reinvent this content through a digital platform that would allow people to share it, for free.

When did you know ArchDaily would take off?

One day, we found out that our website was the most read architecture website in Spanish. We were really surprised, because Mexico and Spain had large media companies that were much bigger than us. We thought about moving to Mexico because we couldn't understand how we'd been able to grow so quickly from Chile and wanted to understand our growth.

In 2008, we featured a project by a Colombian architect. A few days later, he told us there were 14 international publications wanting to share his work in countries like Japan, USA, Italy, and China. And we were still only publishing in Spanish! People were reading important architecture knowledge in Spanish, and making the effort of translating, because the content was worth it. We started thinking about publishing in English, because the magazines at the time were not publishing online, so we had little competition. At that time, we went from Plataforma Arquitectura to ArchDaily in 2008.

How has the Chilean or Latin American tech ecosystem changed since you founded ArchDaily?

At the beginning, we started ArchDaily because we were building something we wanted for ourselves. As we grew, we realized what was happening in Silicon Valley and around the world, and we found out that we could be considered a startup. At the time, there was not a big ecosystem in Chile. It was certainly not sexy to be the founder of a startup.

It was risky and did not bring you any status. But now after ten years, it has changed a lot, mostly because Chile has become a lot more open. Start-Up Chile's creation was an inflection point because they brought a big network of people from around the world that expanded the ecosystem very quickly to build on the already growing local ecosystem.

What are the advantages and disadvantages of running a global business from Chile?

One of the main advantages is that everything is harder in Chile, which gave us good training for launching globally. We don't have access to the talent pool or the network that exists in Silicon Valley. We even occasionally struggled to get a good Internet connection, which means we became very efficient at sharing our content. We basically turned all the disadvantages into advantages. Everything is so hard that we have had to invent many things. Maybe this struggle made us grow more slowly than if we had been abroad. But we really value being here, because being outside the network makes you think more globally. If you are in the US, your market is US first. For us, everyone is our customer.

You can listen to our entire conversation on the *Crossing Borders* podcast on Itunes, Stitcher or wherever you get your podcasts, or on my blog:

http://www.nathanlustig.com/2017/05/31/ep-4-crossing-borders-david-assael-david-basulto-archdaily/

Daniel Undurraga:
Advice from Selling Cornershop

D aniel Undurraga never thought he would sell a Latin American company to a US company once, let alone twice. After the US$225M acquisition of Cornershop by Walmart, he has officially sold two startups from Latin America to the US. His first company, Needish, pivoted to become Clan Descuento, which was quickly acquired by Groupon in 2010, when Chile's startup ecosystem was just getting started. Originally a software engineer, Daniel has been an entrepreneur since he was 14, when he built websites for his friends' parents. Fast forward to 2018, and Daniel and is cofounders are behind two of Latin America's most significant exits.

What insights can you share about doing business in Chile after living abroad?

Coming back to one's country after living in other places makes you see it with new eyes. You feel like a foreigner in your own country. What I've noticed about Chile is that it is very conservative and homogeneous. The ruling elite all thinks the same, lives in the same neighborhood, vacations on the same beach, and sends their kids to the same schools. I think we need more immigration and more Chileans need to leave the country to bring in new ideas and new ways of seeing problems. That's one of the great things about Silicon Valley: the immigration.

I also think that if you're in a small country like Chile, you need to have a regional focus for your business. You cannot build a US$1B business in a country as small as Chile; the market just does not exist. You must see yourself as a global company from the start.

What would you change about the Latin American ecosystem if you could?

In Latin America, we have great talent; we have fantastic engineers, brilliant product managers, great people for almost any position. What we don't have are enough founders. We are missing founders who can pull all these pieces together and build something. Historically, we also haven't had very many good VC funds; this industry is just getting started and we still have a lot to learn. It feels like we are stuck in a chicken and egg problem; it takes great companies to have great VCs. We are making a lot of progress, though. There was more VC investment in September/October 2018 than in all of 2016. Things are changing fast.

What advice do you have for founders launching and scaling in Latin America?

I think there are five main reasons why Cornershop succeeded that founders can take as an example. First, we always try to solve problems with software. Second, we focused on international on day one. We coded the app to be multinational, multicurrency, multi-time zone from day one. That forced us to think regionally and we launched in Mexico and Chile from the start.

Focus on excellence. We need to be better and deliver an amazing experience to our users. We believe having software people running key departments is one of the reasons we're successful. It helps us solve problems with code, be more efficient and expand more quickly. Finally, raise internationally, especially in Silicon Valley.

By doing this, it becomes much easier to scale and attract capital. If you are incorporated in the US from the start, for example, you will begin to think of yourself as a global company. Since it's easier to buy and invest in a US or other foreign domiciled company than a Chilean or Mexican company, you already have a leg-up in receiving funding.

You can listen to our entire conversation on the *Crossing Borders* podcast on Itunes, Stitcher or wherever you get your podcasts, or on my blog:

https://www.nathanlustig.com/2018/12/17/daniel-undurraga-the-story-behind-the-cornershop-acquisition-ep-65/

Maria Paz Gillet: Learning Lessons To Create Jooycar

M aría Paz Gillet Martín is a lifelong entrepreneur and technophile who loved technology from a very young age. After creating the first online art gallery in Latin America, chilearte.com, while still in university in the early 2000s, María Paz went on to become an intrapreneur, an entrepreneur inside of a big company, at Cencosud, one of the largest retailers in Latin America, and created a digital presence for giant retail stores Jumbo and Easy in the mid 2000s. She eventually left to create Latin America's first mobile rewards app, HappyShop, which raised US$6M and went viral, but eventually failed.

She took everything she learned and founded Jooycar, Latin America's first Usage Based Insurance (UBI) company and focused on customers first. She quickly closed a deal with insurance giant Sura, helping Jooycar become one of the world's most innovative IoT companies. In 2016, Magma Partners invested to help support Maria Paz's vision of improving access to insurance in Latin America. This Q&A is excerpted from my conversation with Maria Paz in her Santiago office from my Spanish podcast *Cruzando Fronteras*.

What is Jooycar?

Jooycar is the first connected-car platform in Latin America. We use IoT technology that plugs a small device into the car to turn the vehicle into a smart car, which provides insights into people's driving habits to help insurance companies sell more effectively and help people drive better. Jooycar was born from an opportunity we saw at the intersection of the IoT industry, the insurance industry, and the car industry.

How did you get involved in technology?

I've loved technology since I was young. Instead of asking for dolls [as presents], I wanted people to give me computers. I always loved innovation, so I studied business, and in my fourth year of university I discovered the internet and became obsessed. I founded an online art gallery called chilearte.com, which was the first in Latin America, and ran it during my last two years of college. When I graduated, I worked for Cencosud on their digital presence and had to set up jumbo.cl and easy.cl. I was there for nine years as an intrapreneur, before leaving to start HappyShop.

How did you raise funding for HappyShop?

I never really saw myself as an entrepreneur; I just loved to create. But then I started thinking about how I would raise the money to start prototyping my idea for HappyShop. I ended up talking to someone at CORFO, Chile's public innovation entity, who told me I should head to an incubator to get some seed funding, which I ended up doing through the Universidad Católica, where I studied.

When I decided to quit my job, my boss asked if he could join me, so he ended up becoming our first angel investor. We went on to raise US$6M in 1.5 years from Chilean investors, which was a bit of a double-edged sword. Although it was great to be recognized for raising so much capital, we also lost sight of who our customers were and what our business model really was. Although I am grateful for the investment, I feel like we weren't really ready to use that capital to grow, expanded too fast and ended up having to close the company.

When Jooycar asked Magma Partners for an investment, you were already at break-even. What did you do to get to break even so fast?

This time, I didn't waste any time doing pitches and traveling around meeting investors. I focused on building the platform and improving it, and actually finding clients that were willing to pay. To me, the best dollar you can make is the one you make from your clients.

What is the best and worst part of being an entrepreneur?

The best part is that I can invent things for myself. I love to create. And I love sharing the vision with my team, spreading the vision and the optimism that goes with it. The worst part, I'm not sure yet, because I love it so much. I don't really see any negative side.

What advice would you give to women entrepreneurs, especially those who are thinking small instead of building a global product?

As a woman, imagining yourself as a global entrepreneur can be challenging because there are several limits on your time, especially if you want to be a mom or have a family. So my advice is to think big, but also to think smart. In our case, with Magma, I was always clear.

I told you: I am a woman, I have a family, so I can't always be in a plane and we designed our team so that we could still build a successful business without compromising my family.

So when a VC asks how they can help you, we as women have to put all that on the table. We need practical help so we can become global leaders and not burn out.

You can listen to our entire conversation on the Spanish language podcast *Cruzando Fronteras* on Itunes, Stitcher or wherever you get your podcasts:

https://youtu.be/grRpc3E2q-k

Rocio Fonseca: From Biotechnology to Running Start-Up Chile

Rocio Fonseca does not consider herself as fitting the stereotype of the traditional Chilean woman. After studying biotechnology, working for several years as an intrapreneur at Fundación Chile, and starting several of her own companies, she decided to study at MIT. She then spent a year networking in Silicon Valley before returning to Chile to become Executive Director of Start-Up Chile, Latin America's top accelerator program. Rocio has seen over 1700 startups pass through the Start-Up Chile program and helped scale the S-Factory program, started by Start-Up Chile team member Patricia Hansen, which empowers early-stage female entrepreneurs.

Why did you go to the United States?

I used to work in Chile and I was very bored with my position. I felt like my future was really limited and I wanted to do something different. I told my husband that I wanted to quit my job and travel the world and he told me that we should start by studying in the US. We applied to different universities, then I studied at MIT while he studied at Boston University and he studied at Stanford while I worked. While he was at Stanford, we were living in Palo Alto and I had the opportunity to work at the UC Berkeley Center for Entrepreneurship. I also had the chance to network and meet incredible people in Silicon Valley.

What did you learn in Silicon Valley that you brought to Chile?

The most important thing is to have a clear message. In Silicon Valley, people don't have time for you. You have maximum fifteen or twenty minutes to get your message out. You learn to do things very simply and tell people exactly what you want, directly, and tell them what you can give in return. When I got back here, I was so frustrated by the slow, traditional method of getting things done, with one-hour meetings. I always try to push that Silicon Valley method in our Start-Up Chile meetings.

How does Start-Up Chile support entrepreneurs?

At the beginning, we were bringing in entrepreneurs who would advocate for innovation and get the ball rolling. Now we are looking for businesses that want to start here in Chile and really grow our economy based on technology and innovation. Startup Factory is specifically for female founders that are in an early stage, even just prototyping their idea. We give them US$15K for four months to develop a Minimum Viable Product (MVP). We also have a US$10K follow-on fund for the best companies. Our other program is the Seed program, which was our original program, where you have to start with an MVP and you receive US$40K to develop a product and a follow on fund for another US$40K for the best companies to continue to scale.

What is your advice for female entrepreneurs?

Believe in yourself. Trust yourself. You are going to fail at some point, but you just have to move forward and do it faster than others. Changing our mindsets and convincing ourselves that we can do it is the hardest part. That's why we bring other women here, to show them that this problem [the exclusion of women from entrepreneurship] is a global one and we can resolve it together.

Why do you think US investors should look at Latin America?

I think one of the main assets that startups in Latin America have is that we solve real problems, global problems like water scarcity, energy issues, transportation, smart cities. We are not trying to invent a flying car. In Latin America, these are problems that still need to be solved. It is a part of our reality here that entrepreneurs across the region are fighting to solve. When I look at VC portfolios in the US, sometimes I wonder what problem they're really solving. It would be smart for them to invest in Latin America because the startups here are attacking global problems worth solving.

You can listen to our entire conversation on the *Crossing Borders* podcast on Itunes, Stitcher or wherever you get your podcasts, or on my blog:

http://www.nathanlustig.com/2017/08/24/ep-21-rocio-fonseca-empowering-female-entrepreneurs-and-startups-in-latin-america/

Devin Baptiste & Sean Park: Running GroupRaise from Chile & Houston

Paul Kwiatkowski, Sean Park, Devin Baptist & Kevin Valdez, GroupRaise founders

Devin Baptiste who knows what it takes to build a business across borders. His journey has been marked by business and family milestones: his application for Start-Up Chile was due the day his first child was born. Most people would not move to a brand new country with a three-month-old child, but Devin didn't hesitate at the opportunity. He took GroupRaise to Santiago alongside his three co-founders, and the startup has maintained an office in Chile ever since. Devin now manages an diverse team of over 70 people spread across Houston, Chile, and the Philippines, supporting GroupRaise's mission of helping groups raise money for the causes that matter to them while eating at their favorite restaurants.

His cofounder Sean Park moved to Canada from South Korea when he was just 14 years old so he could learn English. After staying in Canada through university, he moved back to Korea to serve Korea's compulsory military service, then joined as co-founder of GroupRaise shortly after. GroupRaise, the tastiest way to change the world as its cofounders describe it, is a service which helps large groups make reservations at restaurants online, with restaurants pledging to donate a portion of the check to a charity of choice.

Sean now manages 15 people in GroupRaise's Santiago office, having moved to Chile four years ago to participate in Start-Up Chile.

What is GroupRaise?

SEAN PARK: GroupRaise helps groups raise money at restaurants by eating. We help groups make a large reservation and then the restaurant sets aside a portion of the bill to donate to the cause of the group's choice. For restaurants, it is a way to reach new customers and increase sales, since a lot of people are coming to the restaurant for the first time. We now working in over 15,000 restaurants in the US.

Why did you establish a GroupRaise office in Chile?

DEVIN BAPTISTE: We got into Start-Up Chile while I was living in Hawaii and my wife was in grad school. We had just had a baby, so this opportunity was something we hadn't really factored in. I knew absolutely nothing about Chile when we moved down there to participate in Start-Up Chile. All the credit goes to my wife for being willing to move to a country we had never visited while raising a newborn baby.

At the end of the program, they invited us to stay in the country for some follow-on funding, so we maintained the office there. We saw the competitive advantage in terms of talent, and the original idea for GroupRaise was that the work could be done from anywhere - for the

US market. We've kept the office in Chile because Latin America is unbeatable in terms of affordable talent. We have an almost unlimited pool of really great people looking for the experience we can give. Having a Chile office even helps with recruitment in the US, since we can provide people with an opportunity to travel internationally and work at a growing startup.

What should foreign entrepreneurs know about doing business in Chile?

DB: Most people have the wrong impression about Chile. Santiago is more metropolitan than Houston. You can hire people from all over the world in Chile; our team there has representation from 5 countries!

However, Chile's business sector is full of long-running monopolies and established corporations that don't treat their employees very well. This situation makes it easy to compete for talent, even as a startup. We are able to provide great jobs while also doing geographical arbitrage from Santiago to Houston. While communication can sometimes be a challenge, Chile is on a similar time zone to the US and new digital tools make it relatively easy to collaborate. We are not a fully distributed team; we are remote, based in two hubs.

What is it like to run the Latin American office of a US company?

SP: I think businesses make decisions based on what makes sense. Those decisions come from people that can make a difference. That doesn't change based on where you are. As long as the team is self-sufficient and is creating business value, it works. It helps us to operate in Chile because the salary is around half of what we would pay in the US, and we get the same or better work for lower cost. If you can have that, it is an advantage, not a disadvantage. We were able to put together an incredible team here because we could offer work at an American company with a clear professional growth path, and a lot of people were looking for that.

How did VCs in the US react to you raising a round for a company based in Chile?

DB: We realized there were a lot of misconceptions about Latin America in the US. We were getting really basic, ignorant questions about whether Chile had internet, talent, electricity etc. Some partners just never understood our model. They couldn't see why it made sense to have a low cost center in Santiago; they saw the distance as a risk because it could make employees less accountable.

I think the Valley might get disrupted in the next decade by the rise of global entrepreneurship. It might not get displaced by just one hub, but there are innovation centers rising all over the world.

What advice do you have to help other leaders across cultures?

SP: It is important to never get tired of reading books about leadership, communication, and how to improve yourself at work. I tend to think a lot about what I've learned over time and how I can maximize that. I think in my early years, I just didn't know how to learn. You have to learn how to learn. You have to search for the resources you need and be diligent about your learning, and when I was younger, I didn't do that. If you're starting out a company and you feel inexperienced, one of the best tips is to spend time around entrepreneurs that are your friends and will share things with you. You will learn the most if you learn from each other.

You can listen to our entire conversations on the *Crossing Borders* podcast on Itunes, Stitcher or wherever you get your podcasts, or on my blog:

http://www.nathanlustig.com/2017/10/25/ep-31-sean-park-how-groupraise-became-the-tastiest-way-to-change-the-world/

https://www.nathanlustig.com/2017/05/31/ep-5-crossing-borders-devin-baptiste-groupraise/

IV

Brazil

B razil is the fifth largest country by area in the world and the second most populated in the Americas behind the United States, with a population of 210+ million people. In this chapter, we'll cover some Brazilian history, its economy, a deep dive into the startup ecosystem and and over of the e-commerce industry. We finish up with Q&As where Federico Vega tells us how he created CargoX, Brazil's Uber for trucks. Fabricio Bloisi, cofounder of Movile, tells us how he helped build a startup into a company with more than 100M users. Marco DeMello shares how he built Psafe into a top five app in the Brazilian app store. Brian Requarth shares his journey from California to Colombia to Brazil to build Vivareal, the Zillow of Brazil.

Brazil Overview

Brazil's 210M population is largely middle class and based in urban environments, which creates a consistent demand for new goods and services, despite Brazil's roller coaster economy, high regulations, seemingly endless political scandals, high taxes, and notoriously difficult business climate.

Operating a business in Brazil is no easy feat. But for companies that do take the leap, capturing a piece of this incredibly large and tech-savvy consumer base can be the ultimate prize for anyone doing business in Latin America. There are many opportunities for entrepreneurs and investors to generate Silicon Valley style returns if they enjoy taking risks and are willing to slog through Brazil's ecosystem.

Brazil: A Brief History of Opportunities and Challenges

Brazil is the largest economy in Latin America and a key gateway for doing business in its neighboring countries. It is the world's fourth-largest democracy and boasts an abundance of diverse wildlife and natural resources. Brazil borders more countries than any other in South America, and its extensive coastline covers 7,491 kilometers. The largest port on the entire continent is located in São Paulo, and is the main point of access for most imports from Europe. Other ports like Paranagua and Vitoria are also important and boast tax incentives for businesses.

Brazil's economy has constant booms and busts. Just 25 years ago, 66% of Brazil's rural population and 38% of its urban residents lived below the poverty line.[1] Government mismanagement was the primary cause. During this time, excessive borrowing and spending and high inflation, coupled with over-reliance on volatile export markets, caused Brazil to stumble every time the rest of the world changed its purchasing habits.

But throughout the 20th century, Brazil thrived on gold, coffee, rubber, and soybean production and did so while under governments that continued to borrow extensively and devalue the currency to encourage foreign trade. This generated double-digit GDP growth up until the 1970s, where Brazil's heavy industrialization peaked.[2] Unfortunately, around 1981 the country entered the worst recession in Brazil's modern history, known as the "Lost Decade." [3] That recession has been eclipsed by the current recession and economic instability since the commodities bust of the financial crisis and beyond.

Brazil re-emerged on the global scene in the 1990s with the introduction of the Real Plan, a series of policies that introduced a new currency, the Real, and other measures to combat the country's rampant hyperinflation.[4,5] By the 2000s, Brazil experienced another boom for its commodities like cotton, coffee, beef, sugar cane, ethanol, iron ore, soybeans, corn, woodpulp and steel, which continue to be the primary drivers of economic growth today.

Brazil is now one of the largest agricultural producers and exporters in the world. Investments in the country's sizable oil deposits are also responsible for nearly 20% of the country's economy. During the 2000s, nearly 30 million Brazilians emerged from poverty.[6] This change was driven by President Lula's policies from 2002-2010 that promoted social inclusion. This was also before he was sentenced to nearly ten years in jail for, of course, corruption.[7]

Brazil won the bid to host the 2014 World Cup and 2016 Olympics, further driving infrastructure investments and tourism, although not without massive corruption and cost overruns that likely could have been invested into higher priorities. Brazil still couldn't escape the effects of the U.S. financial crisis in 2008. Despite corruption and scandals mostly surrounding Brazil's national oil company Petrobras that have dominated the headlines since 2008, the economy is slowly recovering.

As of 2018, despite the ongoing corruption scandals and economic uncertainties, there seems to be an optimism that persists regardless of what happens. Another take on Brazil's corruption is that it's nearly impossible to tell if Brazil is more or less corrupt than other emerging markets like China, Russia, Indonesia and others, but that Brazil's corruption stands out because its institutions are fighting it, rather than letting corruption become forever ingrained in political process. Some believe this difference could be a turning point for Brazil going forward. Jair Bolsonaro, a far right law and order nationalist, won the 2018 primary election, plunging Brazil into even more uncertainty.

Brazil boasts exciting untapped opportunities, so if you're thinking about doing business there, or are just interested in learning more about these opportunities, here are a few things to keep in mind.

Investor-Friendly Initiatives

For foreign investors, one of the most exciting opportunities in Brazil is the Brazilian Investor Visa Program.[8] It provides the opportunity to gain permanent resident to anyone in partnership with a Brazilian company, as well as anyone that invests in an Internet-based business, real estate, or purchases a government bond.

Once the visa is granted, investors can easily travel throughout the rest of South America and even gain full Brazilian citizenship after four years of residency. Other benefits of the investor visa include the ability to live and work in Brazil for both the individual and their family, access to the same rights and benefits as a Brazilian citizen, and no restrictions on the amount of time one must remain in Brazil for these residency benefits.

E-Commerce Opportunities

For those in the e-commerce space, Brazilians spend a considerable amount of time online, which presents some exciting opportunities for companies in this rapidly developing market. Brazilians spend roughly 32-38 hours per month online, and more time on social media than anyone else in the world.[9] 37% of Brazil's online consumers are over the age of 35, providing unique opportunities for retailers interested in reaching an older demographic online.[10] A majority of Brazilians are also accessing the Internet through their smartphones, driving innovative opportunities for mobile-friendly shopping and online payment solutions.

For a quick and low-cost route into the Brazilian market, retailers should consider setting up on MercadoLivre, the "eBay" of

Latin America, or Dafiti.com, Brazil's most popular marketplace for clothing, accessories, beauty products, and housewares. Dafiti.com receives over 50 million visits per month.[11] While setting up on a marketplace comes with its own challenges, such as registering and handling the logistics of delivering the goods, these websites can be a much easier way to navigate and test the Brazilian market before expanding into the country.

If you plan to sell and ship directly to Brazilian consumers from abroad, you are not required to register a local company in Brazil. However, you will need to consider how you will clear customs and take care of any duties involved with importing your goods from abroad. Currently, customs duty is around 10.7%, and import duties can range from 10% to 35%.[12]

If you plan to establish a local Brazilian website (with a .com. br domain) or sell on a Brazilian marketplace, you will need to register as a local company in Brazil. In that case, working with a local representative to help you incorporate your entity and operate in Brazil is strongly recommended because of the complexity of local operational and potential political challenges. Be careful to fully vet your local partners, as I've seen cases of local partners taking advantage of naive foreign investors.

The Startup Ecosystem

It wasn't too long ago that Brazilian startups had little to no access to financing for their ventures. However, new government initiatives and a growing interest from foreign investors are steadily building momentum for the country's entrepreneurial ecosystem.

São Paulo is Brazil's largest city and the hub of the country's startup activity. Companies like VivaReal (a real estate marketplace), Dafiti (an e-commerce marketplace), and Kekanto (a social network for recommendations), are based in the city. The largest banks have

141

also set up entire divisions devoted to fueling São Paulo's thriving fintech sector.

Coworking spaces like plug.co, CUBO, and Impact Hub are easy to access. There's also no shortage of accelerator programs and investment firms helping Brazilian startups launch and grow their companies. Monashees, Kaszek Ventures, Associação Brasileira de Private Equity & Venture Capital (ABVCAP), Instituto Inovação, Ideiasnet, Confrapar, Warehouse Investimentos, and Astella Investimentos are just a few of the most notable investment firms. International players, like Microsoft and Visa, have also set up shop in Brazil to help fill the gap between early capital and larger rounds.

Brazil can be a complicated, but rewarding location for anyone up to the challenge. As Carl Farrell, Chief Revenue Officer at data analytics powerhouse SAS, puts it, "Brazil is very resilient, it will weather the crisis and continue to prosper — it's an economy that's got lots of resources, people, and all the geographic connections that it needs."

Endnotes

1   *ThinkProgress*. https://thinkprogress.org/looking-at-brazils-economic-fall-from-the-top-e8c7f7c84206/

2   Ibid

3   *Mises Institute*. https://mises.org/wire/brazils-lost-decade-we-must-free-our-economy

4   https://thinkprogress.org/looking-at-brazils-economic-fall-from-the-top-e8c7f7c84206/

5   *Country Studies*. http://countrystudies.us/brazil/79.htm

6   https://thinkprogress.org/looking-at-brazils-economic-fall-from-the-top-e8c7f7c84206/

7   *Reuters*. https://www.reuters.com/article/us-brazil-corruption-lu-la-idUSKBN19X2FO

8   *Passport Reviewer*. https://passportreviewer.com/review/brazil-citizen-ship-investment-program/

9   Web Retailer. https://www.webretailer.com/lean-commerce/ecom-merce-brazil/

10   Ibid

11   Ibid

12   Ibid

The Brazilian Startup Ecosystem: São Paulo, Rio de Janeiro, Belo Horizonte, and Florianópolis

B razil's economy experienced ups and downs over the past decade. Almost immediately after Forbes published an article raving about Brazil's entrepreneurial potential in 2012, Brazil entered one of the most disastrous economic crises in the region.[1] Since 2015, stories of political corruption, monetary deflation, and falling commodity prices have plagued Latin America's largest country.

Brazil is a country of contradictions. In the first three months of 2018, Brazil produced three new startup unicorns. The first was 99, acquired by Didi Chuxing for a rumored US$1B.[2] Then in quick succession, PagSeguro reached a US$2.7B valuation with its January 2018 IPO (the fifth-highest IPO ever), and Nubank became the third unicorn of 2018 with a US$150M Series E round in March 2018 and reached a $4B valuation after Tencent's $180M investment in late 2018.[3,4]

As the largest market in Latin America, with a population of over 210 million people, Brazil is still the most attractive country for investment and growth in the region for many investors. Despite the economic downturn, international investors often look to Brazil first when they want to enter the Latin American market. Many tech giants, such as Google, Uber, Airbnb, and Amazon, have opened offices in São Paulo before moving into other Latin American markets. Many entrepreneurs look to invest in Brazil for their long-term growth strategies, as well.

Despite Brazil's dynamic entrepreneurial ecosystem, the Brazilian government can be unreliable in its support of business development.

While former President Dilma Rousseff received praise for her support of entrepreneurship, Brazil is famous for its cumbersome bureaucracy that can inhibit business growth.[5] Brazil ranks 125th out of 190 countries on the World Bank's 2018 Doing Business report, with processes like starting a business, receiving construction permits, and filing taxes ranking even lower.[6] In fact, Brazil's corporate tax system is so complicated that Brazil ranks 184th out of 190 countries on the difficulty of tax filings report.[7] It can take an average of 101.5 days to start a business in Brazil.[8]

Brazilian entrepreneurs are scrappy, determined, and innovative. They're building global businesses that are already receiving millions of dollars, despite the bureaucracy. Four main cities lead Brazil's entrepreneurial ecosystem: São Paulo, Rio de Janeiro, Belo Horizonte, and Florianópolis. While São Paulo is by far the largest hub – the city holds more people than the entire country of Chile – Brazil's other big cities are making their contributions to the Brazilian startup ecosystem as well.

São Paulo: The heart of Brazilian innovation

São Paulo is not only the largest city in Brazil, but it is also the fifth-largest city in the world and the most populous city in the Southern hemisphere. With over 22 million inhabitants, São Paulo has traffic that would make even Los Angelinos cringe. Although rents have gone down because of the recession, as recently as 2012, renting an office in São Paulo was often more expensive than in Manhattan![9] So what makes this city such a hub for business?

São Paulo is the financial center of Brazil; companies in the city alone contributes 50% of the value to Brazil's banking sector. It is also the location of the Brazilian Stock Exchange. Even before Google chose São Paulo for its first Latin American office in 2002, the megacity was home to TOTVS, the biggest IT company in Latin America and the first to IPO in 2005. Tech giants like Uber, Airbnb, and MercadoLibre built offices in São Paulo, inspiring the next generation of entrepreneurs.[10]

Startups in São Paulo receive support from a host of public- and privately-funded entrepreneurship initiatives located in the city, including the Google Campus accelerator, Innovatech, SEBRAE, and Startup Farm. Most local and international venture capital firms that invest in Brazil have an office in São Paulo, including Monashees, Kaszek Ventures, Valor Capital, Redpoint eVentures, and Canary.VC.

Because of the sheer size and importance of São Paulo, many of Brazil's most-recognized startups call this city home, including three of its unicorns (99, Nubank, and PagSeguro), Movile, VivaReal, DogHero, InstaCarro, QuintoAndar, and CargoX. However, São Paulo's sky-high property prices have pushed many startups to work out of the coworking spaces that dot the city, such as ImpactHub, CUBOS, ACE, and Google's Campus.

São Paulo is by far Brazil's largest, most dynamic, and most innovative city. If you can survive the commute, São Paulo is the place to be for startups in Brazil.

Rio de Janeiro: Center for social entrepreneurship

Rio is Brazil's second-largest city and one of its most popular tourist destinations. It's easy to see why; Rio has a stunning cityscape, set alongside white sand beaches and towering verdant mountains, with a world-renowned culture of music and dance. While the city has struggled with violence in the past, mostly due to extreme inequality between the wealthiest inhabitants and people who live in slums, some of Rio's tech scene focuses on resolving social issues.[11]

Social inequality in Rio has always been a problem, but it was highlighted during the 2014 World Cup and 2016 Summer Olympics, rightly causing controversy and protests. As a result, initiatives like the

Igarape Institute and Meu Rio have popped up to create tech solutions to issues like transparency, corruption, political agency, and transportation.

While it may be harder to access capital in Rio than in São Paulo, several VC firms and government programs have made their way to Brazil's second largest city. SVB Capital, Valor Capital Group, Start-Up Brazil, Startup Rio, and Accel Partners are all actively supporting startups in Rio de Janeiro. Start-Up Brazil is a US$78M government initiative that invests up to US$100K in local and foreign startups to help them get started. Investments from private companies, including Microsoft (US$100M), Cisco (US$500M), and Siemens have expanded access to workspaces for startups in Rio de Janeiro, as well. The most-downloaded taxi app in the world, EasyTaxi, and fintech startup, Zoop, which was recently acquired by Movile, launched their businesses from Rio.[12]

Belo Horizonte: The Up-and-Coming Hub

Belo Horizonte, also known as San Pedro Valley, is located inland from Rio de Janeiro in the state of Minas Gerais. As Brazil's sixth-largest city and the founding place of several startups, Belo Horizonte is a major player in the local startup ecosystem. The Brazilian Startup Association, a lobby group and support community for entrepreneurs with over 4,000 startups and 38,000 entrepreneurs across the country, was born in Belo Horizonte.

The founder of the Brazilian Startup Association, Gustavo Caetano, is the CEO of Samba Tech, an online video platform with two offices in the US. Other notable startups that began in Belo Horizonte include Sympla (acquired by Movile), Smarttbot, and Mercado de Residuos, which won third place in Brazil's 2017 Open Startups Competition.

Some of Belo Horizonte's fame as a tech hub comes from its four universities, including Minas Gerais Federal University, which consistently produces some of Brazil's top IT talent. As a result, the local government has pushed to turn Belo Horizonte into a startup hub using programs like BH-tec and Minas Digital. The government of Minas Gerais wants entrepreneurs to see Belo Horizonte as an attractive alternative to São Paulo with less traffic, lower rent, and higher standard of living; similar to how Guadalajara compares with Mexico City.

Florianópolis: Sun, Sand, and Startups

Rio de Janeiro is not the only Brazilian beach destination looking to boost innovation. Florianópolis, located in southern Brazil, is home to at least 600 startups. The Open Startups competition recognized ten of them in 2017 as contributing more than US$350M per year to the city's GDP.[13,14]

Compared to Rio or São Paulo, Florianópolis is a much smaller and more peaceful place to launch a startup; Florianópolis has only ~450,000 inhabitants and is the second-safest city in Brazil. With 60 beaches and an island within the city limits, Florianópolis might seem more like a beach vacation spot than a startup hub. However, the city already has two "tech parks," Alfa and Sapiens Parque, and some experts put the ecosystem on par with Rio's.

The state of Santa Catarina, where Florianópolis is located, created a technological association called ACATE in the mid-1980s to consolidate support for tech companies growing in the region. As the ecosystem matures, Florianópolis sees more tech startups calling the city home, including ContaAzul (US$30M Series D), Soluz Energia, and Ozon-In.[15]

While Florianopolis is still relatively small, the government and local actors are taking steps to help the beach town follow the way of Rio to become a center of innovation in Brazil.

Brazil's startup ecosystem is enormous, chaotic, and powerful. This country of 210 million people is the world's biggest Facebook user, the fifth-biggest economy in the world, and one of the most complex places in which to start a business. It is hard to predict how

Brazil's startup ecosystem will continue to develop, but it is safe to say that these cities will play a significant role in its tech economy in the next decade. If you want to read more about Brazilian entrepreneurship, see my article on e-commerce in Brazil or my overview of business opportunities in Brazil.

Endnotes

1   *Forbes.* https://www.forbes.com/sites/alexisglick/2012/08/22/dilma-rousseff-brazil-entrepreneurs-power-women/#5f6adf437d95

2   *TechCrunch* https://techcrunch.com/2018/01/03/didi-confirms-it-has-acquired-99-in-brazil-to-expand-in-latin-america/

3   *LatAm List.* https://latamlist.com/2018/01/29/brazils-pagseguro-raises-us2-7b-in-ipo/

4   *LatAm List.* https://latamlist.com/2018/03/02/nubank-raises-us150m-becomes-brazils-third-unicorn/

5   *Forbes.* https://www.forbes.com/sites/alexisglick/2012/08/22/dilma-rousseff-brazil-entrepreneurs-power-women/#5f6adf437d95

6   World Bank. http://www.doingbusiness.org/data/exploreeconomies/brazil

7   Ibid

8   Ibid

9   *Forbes.* https://www.forbes.com/sites/kenrapoza/2012/07/16/the-20-most-expensive-cities-to-have-an-office/#33a072fa2ffa

10   *TechCrunch.* https://techcrunch.com/2017/01/19/brazil-a-look-into-latin-americas-largest-startup-ecosystem/

11   *The Guardian.* https://www.theguardian.com/world/2014/feb/09/rio-de-janeiro-tech-hub

12   *LatAm List.* https://latamlist.com/2018/04/06/movile-invests-us18-3m-in-payments-startup-zoop/

13   *ACATE.* https://www.acate.com.br/noticia/100-open-startups-conheca-10-selecionadas-em-sc

14   https://techcrunch.com/2017/01/19/brazil-a-look-into-latin-americas-largest-startup-ecosystem/

15   *LatAm List.* https://latamlist.com/2018/04/20/brazils-contaazul-raises-us30m-series-d-from-tiger-global-management/

Brazil: Latin America's
E-commerce Powerhouse

B razil is already a global player in the e-commerce industry. It is the only Latin American country to crack the top ten retail e-commerce markets in the world. Despite Brazil's recent economic slowdown, e-commerce grew by 11.5% in 2017 and is predicted to grow 10% in 2018.[1] While these statistics show a significant drop from the 28% growth in 2013, it is safe to say that Latin America's e-commerce powerhouse will continue to dominate the region for the foreseeable future.[2]

Brazil's size has been a double-edged sword for its e-commerce industry. On the one hand, with approximately 140 million Internet users in a country of 210 million people, Brazil presents an enormous market for e-commerce.[3] On the other hand, much like Argentina, Brazil struggles with complex land shipping logistics, low credit card penetration and high sales taxes, which slows down the growth of this industry.

Nonetheless, the mood was optimistic at the 6th *E-commerce Brazil* conference in 2017, with retailers viewing Brazil as an opportunity rather than a challenge. Fifty-two percent and growing of Brazilian shoppers already research products online before purchasing.[4] Global e-commerce giants have taken notice of Brazil. Already, Brazil accounts for more than half of MercadoLibre's global revenue.[5] Netshoes, a popular Brazilian online sports retailer, managed to launch a US$157M IPO in 2017.[6] Alibaba, which has been operating in Brazil since 2014, has recently explored offering credit options to help streamline payments on the site.[7]

In October 2017, Amazon made good on a much-speculated promise to expand their Brazilian operations.[8] While Amazon has been selling books in Brazil since 2012, it has recently added electronics and appliances to their offerings, along with a no-hassle return policy that has Brazilian retailers reeling. Both MercadoLibre and Netshoes's stocks fell after Amazon announced it was launching in Brazil.[9]

Given the enormous size of the potential e-commerce market in Brazil, dozens of homegrown e-commerce startups have appeared over the past 15 years. Dafiti, launched in 2010, is an online shoe and fashion retailer based in São Paulo, and has since joined Rocket Internet's Global Fashion Group in a merger worth an estimated US$1B+[10]. In 2012, Brazilian e-commerce startup Baby.com.br was voted Startup of the Year and is now considered the leading online baby products retailer in Latin America. With so many options available to Brazilians, startup Buscape helps online shoppers compare across multiple sites. Buscape was acquired by Naspers in 2009 for US$342M.

Online payments continue to be a major challenge for the Brazilian e-commerce industry. Many Brazilians are still focused on domestic sites because it can be hard to pay abroad with Brazilian credit cards and most do not have international credit cards. All international payments are subject to a 6.38% tax, which disincentivizes many Brazilians from buying on Amazon or Alibaba.[11] Furthermore, Brazilian credit cards issued by local banks only issue payments in Brazilian Reais, meaning international e-commerce retailers have to figure out how to convert currency if they want to operate there.

Up to 90% of Brazilian online shoppers do not own credit cards and instead pay through a bank slip called a Boleto Bancario.[12] Boleto Bancarios are the most popular online payments method in Brazil, making up 25% of all online transactions.[13] Customers can pay with cash at participating drugstores and ATMs, then send proof of payment to the eCommerce company. Usually, these bank slips take 2-3 business days to process, slowing down the pace of business.

Over 22% of online purchases in Brazil came from smartphones in 2016, up from 12% in 2015.[14] In 2017, 40% of the population (81.4 million people) use mobile Internet services, with that number predicted to rise to over 50% by 2021.[15] Brazilians have a strong social media presence – and many retailers consider social media to be in the top three customer acquisition strategies for this region.[16] With over 90 million social media users in the country, there's opportunity for well-placed digital marketing to grab consumers' attention.[17] Though online payment challenges and delivery logistics continue to hold the industry back, the arrival of Amazon and Alibaba in Brazil speaks to its regional importance as an online retail leader. Brazil is currently poised to stay in the lead of Latin America's e-commerce market, beating out Mexico and Argentina, because of the size of its market, its history as an e-commerce giant, and new innovations that are reducing delivery and payment barriers.

Endnotes

1   *eMarketer.* https://www.emarketer.com/Article/Brazil-Ranks-No-10-Retail-Ecommerce-Sales-Worldwide/1011804

2   Ibid

3   *CGTN.* https://america.cgtn.com/2017/11/11/brazil-ecommerce-economy-online-shopping

4   Ibid

5   *Seeking Alpha.* https://seekingalpha.com/news/3300700-mercadolibre-falls-amazon-considers-brazil-push

6   *NASDAQ.* http://www.nasdaq.com/article/buy-brazil-for-the-long-run-netshoes-sets-terms-for-157-million-us-ipo-cm767665

7   *Reuters.* https://www.reuters.com/article/us-alibaba-brazil/alibaba-may-provide-brazil-credit-services-paper-reports-idUSKBN17S1SL

8   *Bloomberg.* https://www.bloomberg.com/news/articles/2017-10-18/amazon-expands-in-brazil-making-worst-kept-secret-official

9   Ibid

10   *TechCrunch.* https://techcrunch.com/2016/04/27/rocket-internets-gfg-pockets-340m-at-1-1b-valuation-down-from-3-5b-a-year-ago/

11   *Crunchbase.* https://www.crunchbase.com/organization/buscape

12   *Export.gov.* https://www.export.gov/article?id=Brazil-e-Commerce

13   Ibid

14   *PagBrasil.* https://www.pagbrasil.com/market-insights-brazil/
 https://www.export.gov/article?id=Brazil-e-Commerce

15   https://www.export.gov/article?id=Brazil-e-Commerce

16   *Forrester Consulting.* https://go.forrester.com/blogs/17-06-23-the_state_of_retail_ecommerce_in_brazil/

17   *EShopWorld.* https://www.eshopworld.com/blog-articles/brazil-ecommerce-insights-2017/

Federico Vega: Building CargoX into the Uber for Trucks

F ederico Vega is an entrepreneur from Argentine Patagonia who created CargoX, the "Uber for Trucks" in Brazil, reaching an over US$200M run rate revenue in 2018. His journey took him from a tiny town in Southern Argentina to the UK, where he worked in finance, to Chile for the Start-Up Chile program, back to Argentina, and finally to São Paulo, Brazil. From the start, Federico has demonstrated the dedication needed to build a large business in Latin America. He even lived in his car for a months in Brazil to help build the businesses, leading to CargoX becoming Goldman Sachs, Soros, Farallon and BlackStone's first direct technology investment in Latin America. This Q&A is excerpted from our conversation on the *Crossing Borders* podcast.

What is CargoX?

CargoX is an online freight broker; we are a trucking business that does not own any trucks. We are the Uber for Trucking, meaning that we help drivers connect with clients quickly so that their trucks are never running empty.

The opportunity we saw in Brazil was that trucks were running empty 40% of the time, which was very inefficient. We connect drivers who have excess space with clients who need to move freight, which is much cheaper and faster, and results in better pay for the driver.

How did a guy from small-town Argentine Patagonia end up running one of the biggest trucking companies in Brazil?

I wonder the same thing every day. I never set out to run a trucking company, but this is where I ended up. After studying in Patagonia and then Buenos Aires, I traveled to the UK and ended up studying economics there. I started working at the Investment Bank J.P.Morgan at an entry level job and worked my way up over eight years to V.P level trading, but I always wanted to start a company so I started looking for ideas.

I knew there was less space to innovate in developed economies, like the US and Europe. Since I am from Latin America I knew how inefficient it is and how much space there was in the market. I thought I could solve a real problem and have a real business opportunity there, especially with my knowledge from abroad. I also realized Latin America's two main problems were online payments and improving logistics.

Did you go straight to Brazil to found CargoX?

If you ask any Latin American, they will tell you Latin America includes everything except Brazil, because the market there is much more complicated than the rest of Latin America and the people speak a different language. I decided to launch CargoX in the rest of Latin America before moving into Brazil as every other non brazilian entrepreneur in Latin America. But after going through Start-Up Chile, I realized that if the intention was to build a multi billion dollar business I should focus on large markets to attract the capital and type of investor needed. Brazil is by far the largest market in Latin America.

What's your advice to someone raising money outside of Silicon Valley or New York?

At early stage of the business you need to move very fast, so don't waste time on networking events, specially in events for entrepreneurs. What I do is spend one-one time with people from my industry. You have a very limited amount of time and you need to use that time to develop a strong network; you don't do that at networking events. I know the CEO of every company who could acquire CargoX in the future and every possible strategic partner, but none of them were met at networking events.

Knowing what you know now, what would you tell yourself before you founded CargoX?

I wasted time trying to "reinvent the wheel" rather focus on solving an existing problem. Building a new market is really hard. It might have big returns, like Facebook or Twitter, but it is almost impossible to pull off, especially outside of Silicon Valley or a main international tech hub. The other kind of company you can build is something that brings efficiency to a market that already exists. We combined a traditional industry that hadn't been disrupted [in Brazil] with new technologies, like machine learning, to make CargoX take off.

You can listen to our entire conversation on the *Crossing Borders* podcast on Itunes, Stitcher or wherever you get your podcasts, or on my blog:

http://www.nathanlustig.com/2017/07/21/ep-12-federico-vega-transforming-transport-logistics-latin-america/

Fabricio Bloisi: How Movile Will Help One Billion People

Fabricio Bloisi cofounded Movile in the early 2000s as an SMS-messaging company. Since 2008, Movile has expanded aggressively, specializing in mergers and acquisitions of competitors to become the largest mobile platform in the region. Fabricio Bloisi's leadership has helped the company grow by following one mantra: Dream Big. He sees Movile becoming one of the largest companies in the world, with the goal of serving over one billion people in the next five years. This Q&A is excerpted from my conversation with Fabricio on the *Crossing Borders* podcast.

How did Movile make the shift from a mobile company to a tech and innovation company?

I believe Movile's strongest asset is not its investment capacity or the technology, but the people, our values and our culture. First, we have a very high capacity to innovate. Movile today is a very different company than it was three years ago, and I'm sure it will be a completely different company in two years. Every year, we change our structure, our innovation areas and the people in charge of those areas. We are a company that accepts that if the world has changed very fast over the past few years, in the next years, it will change even faster. Most big companies can't change fast, but this is something we do quite well.

When I tell the story of the company in three minutes, it looks like success, but in reality, we test hundreds of innovation projects every year. We test 10 or 15 products, and I can be honest that 90% of them will fail. We are good at learning fast and growing, at scale. Maybe 10% of our projects succeed and because of that, we grow, sometimes 10 times.

Where did you get the idea to rapidly innovate and test products, much like in Silicon Valley or China's Tencent?

I was first inspired by Silicon Valley, specifically Google. But now my inspiration is coming more from China, I think Chinese companies are doing amazing work. We learned about the ecosystem approach from Chinese companies like Tencent and Alibaba, which is the approach we are using to house all our apps on a single platform. We are also inspired by AB Inbev, because they have a company culture that is obsessed with results and meritocracy. This is not the Brazilian prototype of a company, but that is why we are outperforming our counterparts here and abroad.

Could you elaborate on your interest in China and their tech companies' approach?

I think everyone in the US and Latin America should pay closer attention to China. They have approached problems differently, with amazing results. Tencent has pioneered a better messaging system than we have in Latin America or the US. We believe we are the best placed company to do what Tencent has done in Asia in Latin America.

Tencent also has payment layers that have really reduced the barriers to people making a purchase. Most companies here still have a large barrier to purchase, which is lowering mobile payment penetration. We have 150 million customers, and we want them all to be able to buy through Movile products, and eventually through any mobile product - with one click.

What is your advice to other founders in Latin America?

Think big. Everything at Movile started with a very big dream, which continues to push us every day. Our vision keeps us on track, even when smaller projects fail. We need to be obsessed about results. That is what will, after many mistakes, allow us to succeed.

I really like the chart that says "What people think success looks like" and it's a straight line, but then on the other side, it's "what success really looks like" and the line on the graph is chaotic, up and down. If problems make you crazy, don't even get into the entrepreneurial world. Welcome the problems - let's solve them!

As an active investor in the region, do you have a piece of advice for other venture capital investors?

The people in the companies we invest in are more important than anything else. The Movile approach to investment is very collaborative, we try to work together with the founders and build something great. My advice would be, put fewer lawyers in the room and really focus on building something with the founders.

You can listen to our entire conversation on the *Crossing Borders* podcast on Itunes, Stitcher or wherever you get your podcasts, or on my blog:

http://www.nathanlustig.com/2018/02/16/fabricio-bloisi-movile-has-a-plan-to-make-life-better-for-1-billion-people/

Marco DeMello: Cybersecurity From Brazil, USA and China

M arco DeMello is the cofounder of PSafe, a mobile security app that has gotten more than 100 million downloads worldwide. Originally from Brazil, Marco joined the Brazilian Air Force before studying computer science and being accepted to MIT. After university, he joined a tech company, then moved to Microsoft, where he was responsible for projects such as the acquisition of Hotmail, the restructuring of the Windows security infrastructure, and the development of Microsoft Exchange 2007. Next, he joined SpotRunner as CTO before raising a Series A in Silicon Valley. He moved back to Brazil to found PSafe, now a top five app in Brazil, and has raised more than US$90M from investors in the US and China. Here's the start of our Q&A excerpted from the *Crossing Borders* podcast.

What are you doing in San Francisco?

This is our new headquarters for PSafe Technology. We are building a strong staff here to focus our growth in the US. We already have a very strong and dominant position in Brazil and we are the biggest company offering Android security solutions in LatAm. Now we are operating in the US on a very fast growth curve.

We started PSafe over 6 years ago in Rio de Janeiro and expanded to two offices in Sao Paulo and Florianopolis. We were well-timed to ride the wave of the Android explosion in Latin America and reached 100 million downloads of our app over the past 4.5 years. As of August 2017, we have over 5 million monthly active users in the US.

What was the advantage of testing your product in Brazil first?

Brazilian mobile users turned out to be much more forgiving than US users. Android technology was also just beginning to flourish when we were also growing. That gave us an opportunity to reach out to early users, almost one-on-one, and learn about what they liked and didn't like about the product. We were able to build up the company and test it, even though we were in a space that is not sexy at all. As a result, we were able to make it to the US as a profitable company that can compete with well-established leaders there.

Why did you decide to go to the United States?

I got accepted to a program at MIT, which brought me to the US in the first place. Things quickly evolved from there: I got a job and got an H1B visa. What started as one year in the US became twenty. I became a US citizen and moved to Redmond to work for Microsoft in the heyday when we were building the internet. It was a fantastic time to be in Redmond, and I had the opportunity to work personally with Bill Gates on more than three of my projects. I went from being the smartest fish in the tank to being the dumbest fish in the tank, and that was really humbling.

What did you learn at Microsoft?

I learned to always ask the questions you think are stupid questions because there are no stupid questions, there are stupid assumptions. If you assume something you think is right, you will inevitably be making a mistake.

I've also learned to document things. If you don't write it down, it never happened. Documenting things is one of the least appreciated things about being a successful company.

What are the top misconceptions people have about digital security? One is that security doesn't matter, that it's somebody else's problem. Your digital security is your problem. Another one is that mobile devices are safer than PCs. That is not true. If it's digital it's hackable, period.

What advice would you give to LatAm entrepreneurs looking to raise money in the Bay Area?

I usually tell them to think very long and hard about who they are going to raise capital from because those investors will be partners for the life of the company. You want to find someone who will be a partner and not just a check, so do your homework. Finding investors that are rowing with you in the boat -- instead of screaming for you from the shore -- is essential. Make sure they are really worth the equity you are giving them.

You can listen to our entire conversation on the *Crossing Borders* podcast on Itunes, Stitcher or wherever you get your podcasts, or on my blog:

https://www.nathanlustig.com/2017/08/31/ep-23-marco-de-mello-building-a-digital-security-company-in-brazil-that-serves-the-world/

Brian Requarth: Building the Zillow of Brazil

V ivaReal is the largest property portal for real estate search in Brazil. You can think of it as the Zillow of Brazil. Originally from California, Brian always had a taste for adventure and entrepreneurship. His journey started by taking a road trip from California to Costa Rica and ending up in Colombia. Brian started working as an English teacher in Bogota, he started his own business, getting his first clients by knocking on doors in a used suit that he bought for less than $5.

After starting several businesses across the US and Latin America, he realized he needed to stick to a single big market to scale, and moved to Brazil. He went on to raise US$74M in venture funding to scale VivaReal, the leading real estate platform in Brazil with over 5 million listings, 20,000 customers advertising on the site, and 20 million visits a month from people looking for properties across the country, which recently merged with its largest competitor Zap.

Why did you launch VivaReal in Latin America?

We actually started with VivaReal.us because I didn't have the domain, and we went after the Spanish-speaking US market. This was about the time Zillow and Trulia were raising a lot of funding, so we wanted to focus on that niche, and we did well. We started just before the housing crisis and launched VivaReal.us for the US Hispanic population and then we made VivaReal.net for the expat population in Mexico, Panama, and Costa Rica.

After operating for a few years, I read a Stanford case study about MercadoLibre which showed that that Brazil was really the market to hit. We wanted to emulate MercadoLibre, working across multiple markets, so we launched three websites: in Mexico, Colombia and Brazil. Brazil really took off and was growing much faster. Within two years after that, we decided to go AAB, "all about Brazil," and relocated from Colombia to Brazil.

How did you raise money in Brazil and abroad?

I think of capital raising as a formula that includes four buckets. The first bucket includes angel investors that can bring things like operational expertise or CEO experience and [the second] can help reach later stage financing. Those two buckets help set the foundation.

Then the next bucket is to have a local investor. There are certain challenges when you're from the US and doing business in Latin America and having a local investor was really critical to overcome them. It is really important for a local fund to be involved, because a lot of US funds will prefer to co-invest and will feel more comfortable if there is a local fund as well. I was lucky to find good partners with Monashees and Kaszek, which are top tier funds in Brazil and Latin America.

The fourth bucket was institutional capital that had deep pockets, hedge funds and bigger VC funds. Although we didn't expect more than money from them, we actually got a lot of operational help, as well.

Why should US investors look at Latin America?

I think this ecosystem presents an incredible opportunity that is still in its infancy. Currently, there isn't as much competition from mature companies as you might find in the US. It's kind of a frontier market. However, in Brazil, Argentina, Chile, Colombia, and Mexico, you are starting to see bigger and more mature startups, like 99Taxis, Nubank, MercadoLibre. There is definitely activity in the region and from an investor standpoint there is less competition to getting involved. I will say, if you're going to invest, you should commit to the market you're entering. But it is clear it is just a matter of time before it takes off. Over the next ten years, I'll be investing a lot more in Latin America.

You can listen to our entire conversation on the *Crossing Borders* podcast on Itunes, Stitcher or wherever you get your podcasts, or on my blog:

http://www.nathanlustig.com/2017/07/31/ep-15-brian-requarth-building-online-portal-real-estate-brazil/

V

Mexico

M exico's business opportunities rival those of any other emerging economy in the world. Despite a complicated history with violence and corruption, the country is starting to transform its negative reputation into new opportunities. New initiatives, especially to boost Mexican innovation, and an ever-expanding middle class with disposable income have opened a new era of business opportunities for residents and foreigners alike.

To attract new investment, the Mexican government is making significant improvements to its infrastructure to compete globally in sectors like telecommunications and transportation. According to a recent PWC report, Mexico will become the seventh largest economy in the world by 2050.[1]

But to understand how Mexico will get there, it's important to understand Mexico's history and some factors that led it to become what it is today.

A Brief History

In the early 1930s, Mexico began its recovery from the Great Depression and its manufacturing sector started to accelerate. This upturn included the nationalization of the petroleum and railroad industries as well as land reforms into the late 1930s. This strategy helped the country sustain economic growth from the 1940s until the late 1960s. Government initiatives fostered the growth of the consumer goods industry and many Mexican major cities saw significant growth.

Following WWII, the Mexican government undervalued the peso to reduce costs of imported capital goods and further expand its productive capacity. Mexico's economy remained strong into the 1960s, and by 1970, Mexico was largely self-sufficient in food crops and most consumer goods, and was also a significant exporter of oil and petroleum.

This growth was not sustainable, and the peso became increasingly overvalued, hurting non-oil exports. In 1982, Mexico entered a strong recession, from which it recovered slowly. Growth rebounded in the 1990s in conjunction with the ratification of the North American Free Trade Agreement (NAFTA). Yet another peso collapse followed in 1994, creating another economic crisis.

At the turn of the 21st century, with China becoming a cost-competitive manufacturing alternative, Mexico turned its manufacturing industry toward more valuable products, such as automobiles and aircraft, to stay in the game. During the 2000s, with the help of NAFTA and its proximity to the U.S., electronic exports also increased by 73% and automotive exports increased by 152%.

Mexico Today

In 2013, Mexico created the National Institute of Entrepreneurship (INADEM), which has been a critical component of developing Mexico's thriving startup ecosystem. In 2014, the organization distributed over $650M to 500,000+ entrepreneurs and small businesses, leading to 70,000+ new jobs. Up to 2018, INADEM supported 20+ seed funds and participated in another 8-10 funds as an investor. Business schools across the country are also promoting entrepreneurship and the next generation of business leaders to embrace the knowledge economy.

While there are still challenges one must overcome to do business in Mexico, big technology successes are opening the doors to exciting new opportunities for new products and companies "Hecho en Mexico."

The Opportunities

Thanks to the North American Free Trade Agreement (NAFTA) and the renegotiated replacement in 2018, owning and operating a business in Mexico is relatively straightforward – though this may still change with Donald Trump in the White House. You don't need to be a Mexican resident or travel to Mexico to open a Mexican business. A few industries, such as gas and oil, are highly restricted, but for the most part, registering a business is not all that difficult. According to The World Bank and International Finance Corporation (IFC), Mexico currently ranks 36th in the world for ease of starting a business.

Even though you do not have to be a Mexican resident to start a business, you will need to obtain a visa if you'd like to work in the country. Depending on the type of visa you need, this process may be more complicated than in other Latin American countries like Chile or Colombia.

Mexico's economic output, as measured by Gross Domestic Product (GDP) was $2.2T in 2015 – less than the United States ($17.9T), but greater than the other NAFTA partner, Canada ($1.6T). Geographically, Mexico is roughly the same size as Saudi Arabia, but has five times as many people! Mexico manufactures and exports the same quantity of goods as the rest of Latin America combined. Mexico has 44+ free trade agreements, the largest of those trade partners being the United States, China, and Japan. This means that any company interested in manufacturing in Mexico has duty-free access to 60% of the world GDP.

Mexico's number one export is manufactured products, but it also exports considerable amounts of fruits and vegetables, silver, coffee, and cotton. In recent years, Mexico has become a major hub for electronics manufacturing – producing most of the flat-screen TVs sold in the U.S. Mexico's emphasis on trade has given Mexican companies a key competitive advantage. For example, Gruma is the world's largest tortilla maker, and Bimbo (which acquired U.S.-based Sara Lee) is now the largest bread maker in the world.

Mexico's financial sector is well-developed. However, compared to more developed nations, it is still quite difficult to obtain credit. Fintech companies are filling the gap in the market to serve the largely unbanked population in Mexico and the rest of Latin America. More than 40% of venture capital dollars went to Fintech companies in 2016, up from 29% in 2015.[2] Companies like online lending company Kueski and Konfio along with payments company Clip have closed large Mexican Fintech rounds in 2017.[3]

The funding scene in Mexico is now one of the most mature in all of Latin America. The connection between Mexico and Silicon Valley strengthened in 2012 when 500 Startups acquired Mexican.vc, and it continues to solidify.[4] Alta Ventures, Mountain Nazca, ALLVP, Angel Venture, Variv, Mita Ventures, and Wayra are also investing heavily in Mexican startups. Programs like Hackers/Founders are helping Mexican entrepreneurs. Startups like Clip, Konfío and Cornershop are making international headlines, raising US$70M+ combined. Since 2014, my fund, Magma Partners, has invested in five companies founded by Mexicans including neobank Albo.

Lately, all eyes are on Guadalajara which is growing into one of the leading tech outsourcing, manufacturing, and service centers in the world. Due to its proximity to the U.S. (a four-hour flight from San Francisco), major U.S. tech companies have set up back offices in the city. Hewlett-Packard, General Electric, IBM, Intel, and Oracle all have offices in Guadalajara and are creating an influx of direct foreign investment.

But there are also U.S. startups, like Wizeline, setting up back offices in Mexico to cut operations costs.[5] Mexican developers are out-competing Eastern European and Indian developers and as an added bonus, are on US central time.

This influx of investment is also helping the city build a reputation as the home of some of the best engineering talent in all of Latin America. As the city continues on its path to becoming an important tech hub, and the government continues investing in its infrastructure, Guadalajara will continue to boast exciting opportunities for those interested in technology and innovation in Mexico beyond its capital city.

The Challenges

One of Mexico's biggest challenges is violence related to organized crime and corruption both in the government and the local police. Outgoing President Enrique Peña Nieto has been focused on increasing security spending from 1.5% to 5% of GDP (the same level that worked for Colombia).

In recent years, however, the crackdown has only led to more distrust in the government and an increase in violence, leaving more than 200,000 dead since 2006. While the violence is mostly isolated in specific parts of the country, it's something to keep in mind for anyone interested in doing business in Mexico as it is a complex issue that will require many more years to resolve. Additionally, it's led to political instability and uncertainty, especially around every national election.

In general, Mexico's business culture tends to be slow-moving. It's common to discuss important issues at the end of meetings, rather than diving into the problem from the start. There are also large cultural and wage gaps between executive-level employees and other workers.

Recent political events in the U.S. are also generating many uncertainties in Mexico's business environment. Trump recently referred to NAFTA as one of the "worst trade deals in history" and threatened to terminate the agreement, sending shockwaves waves throughout industries in the U.S. and Mexico alike.

The 2018 renegotiation of NAFTA could have significant consequences for businesses on both sides of the border and is an issue to watch carefully.[6] Talks of imposing a 35% tariff on Mexican imports as well as encouraging Mexico to end its maquiladora program are just a few of the issues Trump wants to bring to the negotiation table.[7] As of September 2018, both sides have announced a deal, but the details have not come out.

If you compare Mexico and South Korea's manufacturing sectors, which started around similar times, South Korea created value added processes, which led to home grown companies, whereas Mexico mostly did lower level assembly of other countries' goods. If Mexico had focused on high level, value add industries, it might be more competitive on a global scale and more of the wealth generated from this industry would stay in Mexico. It remains to be seen if Mexico will learn the lessons of the past to continue to build for the future.

The lack of competition in Mexico is also a barrier to growth in some key sectors of the economy. For example, Carlos Slim, a Mexican telecom tycoon and the world's richest man in 2007, owns three companies which control 70% of mobile phones, 80% of home phone lines, and 70% of broadband in Mexico. This makes it incredibly challenging for companies in these sectors to compete. There are other near-monopolies in industries like television (dominated by Televisa) and industries like retail, oil and gas and others are highly concentrated.

Another issue is paying taxes, which can be a laborious process in Mexico. Corporate income tax is currently 30% and takes ~155 hours to file. VAT and social security filings can take a long time to process.

Uncertainties around President Andrés Manuel Lopez Obrador's government that was elected in 2018 and Donald Trump's 2016 election continue to persist, causing some damage to both business and consumer confidence in Mexico. Governmental initiatives to put Mexico's technology sector on the global map are generating an exciting new wave of opportunities and hope that Mexico can one day move forward as a global powerhouse, but may be derailed by national politics and its past reputation. Tech companies are trying to do their part from Mexico City to Guadalajara and Monterrey to continue to build the technology ecosystem.

Endnotes

1   *The Baja Post.* http://www.thebajapost.com/2017/02/14/espanol-mexi-co-sera-7o-lugar-economico-mundial-en-20150/

2   *Anna Diaz.* https://medium.com/draper-network/viva-m%C3%A9xico-mexicos-startup-ecosystem-on-the-rise-e6ec3809bb30

3   *BusinessWire.* https://www.businesswire.com/news/home/20160421005166/en/Kueski-Secures-Largest-Capital-Funding-FinTech-Startup

4   *TechCrunch.* https://techcrunch.com/2012/08/07/500-startups-mexican-vc/

5   *San Francisco Chronicle.* https://www.sfchronicle.com/business/article/Border-is-no-barrier-at-Wizeline-11059164.php

6   *Lexology.* https://www.lexology.com/library/detail.aspx?g=39387bf2-2f64-4633-8be6-c1522a018f80

7   *The Balance.* https://www.thebalancesmb.com/export-process-ing-zones-epz-2221273

Mexico E-commerce: The Battle for Marketshare Begins

M exico has all the right ingredients for an e-commerce boom: a young, tech-savvy population, rapidly-increasing Internet penetration, and access to the world's biggest e-commerce retailers, namely Amazon, Walmart, and Alibaba. In fact, Amazon and Alibaba have been vying for territory in Mexico's e-commerce space for the past three years, betting on explosive growth.

While Mexico accounts for 12.6% of Latin America's online purchases, only 1.6% of Mexico's retail spending is conducted online, which means that there's massive room for growth.[1] Currently, only about 50% of the population has access to the Internet, and the enormous economic disparities between the urban and rural areas are holding the market back from exponential growth.[2] As Latin America's second-largest e-commerce market, Mexico is poised for an online retail boom as Internet services reach more of the population.

Mexico's strategic location close to the United States has a lot to do with this market's growth potential. As one of three partners in the US$1.2 trillion NAFTA trade deal, Mexico is uniquely well-connected to the US and Canada, making international e-commerce much more available to the population.

Amazon set up its first distribution center in Mexico in 2015 and debuted Prime membership there in early 2017, taking bold steps to capture the market before it takes off. Already 60% of Mexican online shoppers are using international retailers, taking advantage of a simplified clearance process for low-value commercial goods at the border.[3]

In comparison with Brazil and Argentina, shipping logistics in Mexico are considerably simpler, with Amazon already conducting one-day delivery. However, extremely low levels of financial inclusion in Mexico, especially in rural parts of the south, make online payments tricky. More than 60% of Mexicans do not have access to credit cards, and many international retailers do not yet accept payments in pesos via Mexican debit cards.[4]

A few creative companies have gotten around this barrier already; Walmart offers cash payments on delivery, and beer retailer Anheuser-Busch-InBev allows customers to make payments in cash at local convenience stores. Clip, a Mexican startup similar to Square, is helping small vendors accept payments via credit and debit card, and online, so they can compete with the e-commerce giants. Albo, a Mexican Neobank, is helping people access the financial sector.

Mexico's business environment also presents fewer barriers than Argentina's or Brazil's, meaning homegrown e-commerce startups are plentiful. Companies like El Puerto de Liverpool, have been selling online since 1997, opening the market for newer retailers like Linio, Andrea.com, and Cinepolis.com.[5] The popular delivery startup, Rappi, has also expanded to Mexico, joining the race to provide Mexican consumers the goods they need on-demand, competing with companies like Cornershop.

Other innovative startups have popped up in Mexico's e-commerce space, including Luuna, selling budget-friendly mattresses, AZAP, a flower delivery company, and Rigs, an online auto parts retailer that is helping Mexicans buy auto parts online. You can listen to my conversation with Nestor de Haro, Rigs' founder, on the *Crossing Borders* podcast. **https://www.nathanlustig.com/2017/12/11/ep-35-nestor-de-haro-building-alibaba-auto-parts-mexico/**

With up to 70% of Mexican shoppers buying online, large international retailers like Walmart are investing heavily in their online platforms as well. In 2016, Walmart spent up to 10% of its Walmex budget on creating its online platform, targeting smartphone users specifically.[6] Alibaba is also building relationships in Mexico, signing an agreement with the Mexican government in 2016 to sell more Mexican goods on the platform.[7] Nonetheless, the biggest share of the e-commerce market still belongs to regional giant MercadoLibre.[8]

These online vendors are beginning to displace smaller brick-and-mortar vendors in Mexico who cannot compete with the convenience of credit and faster shipping options. With Mexico ranking 49th on the World Bank's Doing Business report, compared to Brazil at 125, and Argentina at 117, the e-commerce market does not face as many barriers as it does in the Southern Cone.[9] Even though the online retail market is still far from maturity in Mexico, both international and domestic companies are taking a bet on Mexican e-commerce, projecting high growth over the next decade.

Endnotes

1   *ILifeBelt.* https://ilifebelt.com/e-commerce-en-mexico/2017/06/

2   *eShopWorld.* https://www.eshopworld.com/mexican-ecommerce-insights/

3   *Export.gov.* https://www.export.gov/article?id=Mexico-ECommerce

4   *Fortune.* http://fortune.com/2015/11/13/amazon-mexico-ecommerce/

5   *Bloomberg.* https://www.bloomberg.com/quote/LIVEPOLC:MM

6   https://ilifebelt.com/e-commerce-en-mexico/2017/06/

7   *Reuters.* https://www.reuters.com/article/us-mexico-alibaba/mexico-signs-e-commerce-deal-with-chinas-alibaba-group-idUSKCN1BH2DQ

8   *Bloomberg.* https://www.bloomberg.com/news/articles/2017-12-01/amazon-s-arrival-leaves-mexican-e-commerce-pioneer-in-the-dust

9   *World Bank.* http://www.doingbusiness.org/data/exploreeconomies/mexico

Mexico Startup Hubs: Mexico City, Guadalajara, Monterrey

With startup hubs across Latin America vying to become the next Silicon Valley, Mexico may be ahead of the game, and carving out its own niche south of the border. In 2015, TechCrunch published an article arguing that Mexico's transition over to the innovation economy might just turn it into one of the world's biggest economies in the next decade.[1] Bismarck Lepe, a Mexican-American entrepreneur who pioneered Mexico-Silicon Valley cross border companies with Ooyala and Wizeline, contends that Mexico will be one of the most interesting countries in which to do business.

Mexico's unique geographic and cultural positioning allows it to capture both the US and the Latin American markets, while its size and natural resources allow it to compete with South American giants like Brazil. Three major cities in Mexico – Mexico City, Monterrey, and Guadalajara – are at the forefront of the innovative movement and each city is contributing to Mexico's growing startup ecosystem.

While Mexico City is the most powerful hub due to its size and the availability of private and federal capital, Guadalajara and Monterrey are important second cities that are vying for technology and startup leadership. Here's a deeper look at the startup ecosystems in each of these Mexican cities.

Mexico City: Mexico's Business Capital

Mexico City, DF (Distrito Federal) or CDMX (Ciudad de Mexico) as it's known, is one of the largest cities in the world, with a population of 21 million people. In the past two decades, Mexico's enormous capital has started to overcome a reputation of violence and is now the center of cultural, political, and economic activity in Mexico.

Mexico is one of the first countries in Latin America to begin regulating the Fintech sector via a law passed by the Mexican Senate in December 2017.[2] This law was considered a victory for the cryptocurrency and crowdfunding sectors, as it put Mexico on par with advanced countries' Fintech regulations.

The Mexican government went already gone all-in on funding innovation through the Instituto Nacional del Emprendedor (INADEM), a semi-autonomous branch of the Secretary of the Economy based in CDMX. INADEM committed over US$600M to funding startups across the country, but was closed down by the Lopez Obrador government in late 2018.

Mexico's government has prioritized investing in innovation. The national development bank, Nacional Financiera (NAFIN), also based in Mexico City, recently refocused its investment efforts to support technological innovation and the needs of small businesses as well. Mexico City is one of Latin America's private investment hubs. Early-stage international investors like Mountain Nazca and Telefonica's incubator, Wayra, have offices in Mexico City where they invest in promising startups in Mexico City.

Local early-stage VC funds like Alta Ventures, ALLVP, Angel Ventures, Jaguar Ventures, Variv and 500 Startups invest into local entrepreneurs. Startup Mexico, Arkfund and Startup Weekend Mexico are based in the capital and direct a significant portion of their resources toward developing the local startup sector.

Because of market size, venture capital funds and government support, Mexico City is the birthplace of a majority of Mexico's international startups. Aventones, a ride-sharing app that helps people avoid Mexico City's terrible traffic, was acquired by Europe's BlablaCar after becoming Latin America's most successful rideshare app.[3] Mexico City is also the birthplace of Clip, a phone attachment similar to US-based Square. Clip raised an US$8M round from American Express in 2015 and a follow on in 2017.

Mexican scooter sharing startup Grin, founded by VCs turned founders, raised a $28M seed round in 2018 and Cornershop, a Mexican-Chilean grocery delivery startup, raised a US$21M round in 2017 led by U.S. venture capital firm Accel with participation from Creandum, ALLVP, and Jackson Square Ventures.[4] Cornershop was acquired by Walmart for $225M in 2018.

Mexico City's importance and economic dominance make it a prime location for startups. With exciting coworking spaces like The Pool and ImpactHub dotting the city, it's not difficult for entrepreneurs to find a niche here. However, Mexico City's size can also be a disadvantage. The traffic can be crippling, and entrepreneurs can avoid commute headaches by staying in buzzing startup areas like the Roma, Condesa and other neighborhoods with a high density of startups.

Guadalajara: An Up-and-Coming Engineering Hub

Guadalajara, GDL for short, is already well-established as a hub for international tech manufacturing. Companies like Hewlett-Packard, IBM, General Electric, and Kodak have invested heavily in Guadalajara since the mid-1990s, reinforcing its reputation as a center for engineering talent in Mexico.

The University of Guadalajara, one of the best universities in Mexico, is churning out talented professionals that have the potential to become Mexico's next generation of entrepreneurs or to support Guadalajara-based startups.

The Government of Guadalajara recently stepped in to shift the city's focus from production for foreign export to local innovation. Through initiatives like Ciudad Creativa Digital Guadalajara (CCDG) and Reto Zapopan, the local government is providing direct investments in the innovation sector. The CCDG campus is located in downtown Guadalajara and aims to strengthen Mexico's position in the global economy through creative industries like television, technology, video games, and interactive media. Reto Zapopan is a government-funded incubator and coworking space for high-impact startups working in Guadalajara.

In response to President Trump's increased restrictions on immigration, cities like Guadalajara are trying to attract top tech talent from abroad to settle in Mexico instead of the US.[5] Nonprofit StartupGDL has already brought five startups to the city and other tech companies are following suit, with some looking specifically at Dreamers in the US, who may need to search for jobs abroad as Trump lets DACA expire.[6] Just a four-hour flight from San Francisco, Guadalajara is also attracting Silicon Valley tech companies to set up back offices there since Trump restricted access to foreign talent by tightening regulations on the H1-B visa.

VC firms and angel investor networks are also finding a niche in Guadalajara. Angel Ventures, the most influential angel investor network in Mexico, has offices in Guadalajara and Mexico City. Guadalajara also has its own network of angels, the Guadalajara Angel Investor Network, or GAIN for short. Although the venture capital system in Guadalajara is still nascent, startup builder Agave Lab has chosen Guadalajara as its home.

The Mexico branch of international startup accelerator Hackers & Founders, called the H/F Co-Op, was founded in Guadalajara, placing bets on Mexico's becoming the world's fifth-largest economy in the next 35 years. Hackers & Founders Mexico now operates in 23 cities and has over 300,000 members. If you want to hear more about Guadalajara and Hackers and Founders check out my *Crossing Borders* podcasts with Mak Gutierrez and Jonathan Nelson. **https://www. nathanlustig.com/2017/09/18/ep-26-mak-gutierrez-supporting-makers-and-startups-in-guadalajara/**

The supportive environment of Guadalajara is fertile ground for some of Mexico's most successful startups. Guadalajara-based online money-lending service Kueski closed a US$35M round in 2017 in what was the largest round ever raised by a fintech startup in Mexico.[7] San Francisco-based startup Wizeline has its largest office in Guadalajara, both because the founder is a Guadalajara native and because the company wants to capitalize on the tech talent coming out of the city.

Unsurprisingly, the warm climate, low cost of living, and thriving art scene make Guadalajara one of Mexico's most attractive cities. As a result, Guadalajara has seen dozens of coworking spaces pop up in the past few years, such as Nevermind Coworking, HackerGarage, and Epicnest.

Guadalajara is also the headquarters of several digital startups such as Rigs, an auto parts marketplace, Fullbox, a furniture rental company, and VoxFeed, an influencer marketing marketplace.

Monterrey: The International Business Hub

Located just a few hundred miles south of San Antonio, Texas, Monterrey is a well-positioned hub for international entrepreneurship across the US – Mexico border. Several university programs, such as the University of Texas' Center for Global Innovation and Entrepreneurship, are located in Monterrey to foster cross-border knowledge transfer and bolster tech innovation in Mexico. Also situated in Monterrey is a Startup Grind Community powered by Google that brings together entrepreneurs working in the city.

Monterrey is home to some of Mexico's most dynamic venture capital firms, which have helped place this city on the map. Monterrey is the headquarters of Alta Ventures, a VC firm with offices in

Monterrey and Utah, which invests between US$2M and US$10M in Mexican startups.

Other investors in the city include Naranya, an early-stage investor in digital startups across Latin America, and ImpactHub, a social impact accelerator with a network that spans across Latin America and the rest of the world. Startup Mexico, a private incubator and accelerator, also has an office in Monterrey.

Monterrey is the home of one of Latin America's top universities, Tecnologico de Monterrey, which is renowned for turning out talented, hardworking professionals. Monterrey is also the headquarters of startups like DeCompras.com, Mexico's first e-commerce site, and EnviaFlores, Mexico's flower delivery app.

Monterrey is one of Mexico's most modern and fastest-growing cities, with an exciting restaurant scene and infrastructure. There are many places for entrepreneurs to work, including El Cowork, Taller.C, and Parvada Cowork & Co.

The downside is many residents find that the city is growing at an uncontrollable rate, driving prices sky high and bringing in smog. Furthermore, Monterrey is located far from any other major Mexican city, making transportation to and from the city frustrating.

Conclusion

Mexico is one of Latin America's most important economies and quickly becoming one of the region's most promising startup ecosystems. The major cities of Mexico City, Guadalajara, and Monterrey are leading the charge; however, Mexico's enormous size and resources leave space for other smaller cities to follow suit. Mexico has already seen the benefits of supporting entrepreneurship and will likely continue developing new initiatives to boost its growth. It will be interesting to watch these nascent startup hubs continue to grow to support the Mexican startup ecosystem.

Endnotes

1 *TechCrunch.* https://techcrunch.com/2015/03/26/beyond-the-maquiladora-a-look-at-mexicos-startup-scene/

2 *Reuters.* https://www.reuters.com/article/us-mexico-finance/mexican-sen-ate-passes-fintech-law-idUSKBN1E00HX

3 *LAVCA.* https://lavca.org/2015/04/22/aventones-the-most-successful-ridesharing-platform-in-latin-america-is-acquired-by-blablacar-the-french-us100m-funded-global-leader/

4 *TechCrunch.* https://techcrunch.com/2017/05/07/cornershop-a-grocery-de-livery-app-in-chile-and-mexico-raises-21m/

5 *Forbes.* https://www.forbes.com.mx/visa-tech-opcion-para-traer-talento-silicon-valley-mexico/

6 *Reuters.* https://www.reuters.com/article/us-trump-effect-mexico-tech/mexico-tech-industry-benefits-from-u-s-anti-immigration-stance-idUSKB-N1CM1F2

7 *BusinessWire.* https://www.businesswire.com/news/home/20160421005166/en/Kueski-Secures-Largest-Capital-Funding-FinTech-Startup

Bismarck Lepe: The American Dream is Now in Mexico

B ismarck Lepe is one of the most successful Mexican-American entrepreneurs in Silicon Valley. The son of Mexican immigrants to the US, he graduated from Stanford and became one of Google's first 300 employees. Bismarck sold some of the Google stock he earned as an employee to start a video company, Ooyala, which he then sold a few years later for more than US$400M.

He has created hundreds of tech jobs in Guadalajara through his second venture, Wizeline, a project and software management service. Wizeline has offices in Guadalajara, San Francisco, and Ho Chi Minh City. This interview is translated and excerpted from Bismarck's conversation on the Valle de los Tercos podcast, the best Spanish language startup podcast in Latin America, which you can listen to here: http://www.elvalledelostercos.com/episodios/bismarck-lepe-fundador-de-wizeline-como-llevar-silicon-valley-a-mexico

Why are you so passionate about the tech ecosystem in Mexico?

We grew up very poor, but I grew up happy. My parents, who were Mexican immigrants, worked hard picking produce to give us a good life, but I always wanted more. I always thought that making a lot of money would be the way to do it. When I got into Stanford, I thought I was going to be a doctor, because the most successful person I knew was a doctor. But that was 1998, just when the internet bubble was starting. My roommate connected me to the tech scene and I saw that technology was the best way to make a lot of money. I was lucky enough to get to Google before it went public and I got equity. But when we sold Ooyala, I realized money wasn't the most important thing. I realized my impact mattered a lot more. Now, I think that with technology, we can change Mexico's future very quickly. If Mexico can focus on education, and we bring great jobs, we can change Mexico's development for the better.

What did you learn from Ooyala that you can apply to Wizeline?

I left Google after exactly four years. I learned a lot from Ooyala, and there are a lot of similarities with Wizeline. I am still the only director of the company. We have enough capital to be able to think in the long term and conduct experiments. Wizeline has grown a lot faster; we are 3x bigger now than at the same point for Ooyala. Most importantly, we've had a Guadalajara office for Wizeline since the first day. With Ooyala, we didn't have a foreign office until the 3rd year.

What we have in Guadalajara is very strategic. Right now, talent is like the petroleum of the 1900s. If you have it, you can refine it and make incredible products. But if you have nothing, you cannot do anything. In Mexico, we've found lots of under-utilized talent and we're using that to our advantage.

What potential for innovation do you see in Mexico?

I think Mexico really needs the tech giants, Facebook, Google, Amazon, and Microsoft, to open bigger tech offices in Mexico. We already employ 400 people in Mexico and we plan to employ 1000 by the end of 2019. But if one of these giants came in, they could hire 1000 people off the bat. While these companies pay great salaries, offer equity and excellent benefits, the best thing employees learn is how to be entrepreneurs. They learn how to identify problems that really have a large market behind them, and how to build solutions to those problems that make billions of dollars.

Look at India. India used to be like Mexico, providing many services, but not creating many products. Then in 2005, Amazon opened an office in Bangalore and started making products. All of the unicorns from India have come from alumni of one of the tech giants. That's what we're trying to do in Mexico.

We started a fund called Wizefund, which is around US$5M, for Wizeline employees. Anyone who works for Wizeline for over two years can receive funding from Wizefund to start their own project. We know that this model works, because Ooyala employees created over 30 companies, 19 of which raised capital and created more than 600 jobs. Those jobs pay over 10x more than a factory or service wage. That is the impact entrepreneurs can have on this country. That's why I like to say that the American Dream is now in Mexico.

Alba Rodriguez: Promoting Food Security with Gricha

A lba Rodriguez is the founder and CEO of Gricha, a company that produces high-protein flour and other products using crickets. At 25 years old, Alba became fascinated with the idea of finding a sustainable replacement for meat, fish and other kinds of animal protein. After dozens of attempts to make a cricket cookie that actually tastes good before succeeding, she went on to sell her idea on Facebook and then presented on Shark Tank Mexico. She continues to develop new products made of cricket flour and is passionate about changing people's mindsets so they consider insects as a viable nutrition option.

What inspired you to found a startup based on crickets?

Gricha solves two problems. One is the ecological problem relating to the massive production of animals to create meat and protein. It's not just beef. In Chile, the massive production of fish is causing damage to the sea. Animal production at scale is highly damaging to the environment. As our population grows, we will not be able to continue supplying animal protein for everyone. We really need high-quality protein to survive, and I want to show that insects are an option. A cricket is actually one of the most protein-dense animals on the planet; its body is about 70-80% protein. That's much higher than cows, pigs or fish.

What is it like living and working in Guadalajara?

I think it is awesome. Guadalajara is growing fast. There are a lot of companies starting here, and the entrepreneurship community is very supportive. There are many people making startups and they are more than willing to help you. They all want to help turn Guadalajara into a global innovation center.

What is it like to start a business in Mexico?

I think it is hard obviously, but I also think starting a business is hard anywhere. Even Facebook and Google had their rough moments. Mexico does have a lot of bureaucracy, but in our industry we haven't run into it much yet. The people are very open to new ideas and trying new products, so I think society is getting better with the help of young entrepreneurs.

What is it like being a female founder in Mexico?

We are outnumbered. When I go to meetings, 85-90% of people there will be men. In a way, I feel that men believe a man more than a woman just because they are both men. Men often assume that women are just doing this project between university and getting married and having kids. They assume as soon as we start a family we'll just leave the project. I want to believe that it is not because they believe that we are not smart enough, but because they believe we are going to quit when we have a family. But there are plenty of strong women that have companies and they are an example for everyone that women can do business, too.

You can listen to our entire conversation on the *Crossing Borders* podcast on Itunes, Stitcher or wherever you get your podcasts, or on my blog:

http://www.nathanlustig.com/2018/02/02/ep-36-alba-rodriguez-gricha-using-insects-to-solve-food-insecurity-and-improve-nutrition/

Santiago Zavala: From Entrepreneur to Investor with 500 Startups

S antiago Zavala is a Mexican entrepreneur turned venture capitalist who now runs 500 Startups Mexico. Santiago grew up just outside of Mexico City in an entrepreneurial family that was in on the ground floor of the Latin American tech scene. He started programming and built his first business, a guitar forum with millions of users, when he was just 12 years old. He founded a startup in university, then worked at a startup in Silicon Valley, before co-founding a network of hackathons across Latin America. Next, Santiago created Mexican.VC and merged with 500 Startups, where he and his team have invested in over 79 companies. With a recent exit, they confirmed an 8x return on their first fund, with more room to continue generating returns from additional companies.

How did you get involved in the Latin American tech scene?

I was very lucky because my father was always very involved in the tech scene. In the 90s, he started making some of the first websites in Latin America and probably one of the first e-commerce sites in Mexico.

I started to code when I was very young because my father was so passionate about it. I was lucky to find something that is both useful today and something I love to do. When I was about 12, I used HTML and open source code to build an online forum about learning to play guitar, which ended up having millions of viewers. It really took off when I was 15, and I had contributors adding sections from all over Mexico and Latin America.

What advice would you give to entrepreneurs who are still in school?

I think that building your own portfolio by doing small projects is really important. You also have to believe in yourself. You have to send those emails and follow up. If you have an opportunity, you need to be on top of it. It is also really important to keep learning, so that you don't feel like you're making it up as you go along.

Did you always want to invest in Latin America?

I never imagined myself investing. When I was doing my job in Mexico, I started a hacker community here, and kept working on it from the Bay Area. In 2011, we started to look at this hackathon community that was spread across 16 cities in Mexico and we were asking ourselves how to get these really capable people working on startups. We realized the challenge was that they had no access to funding to even get started. There was a real need for access to capital. We also knew that no one would do it for us, so we started doing it ourselves. We eventually raised enough money for a fund we called Mexican.VC and we were able to invest in 7 companies. The rest is history.

What did you learn from Mexican.VC?

The teams that were able to move on to the next stage and reap more investment had founders that could walk through walls. They would definitely not stop because of a simple problem. They were usually able to put other emotions and ego aside and really focus on solving the problem. Both of our portfolio companies that have succeeded have founders that are very strong. They are unstoppable and won't necessarily take advice from everyone. I definitely look for that now when I am investing.

How has entrepreneurship in Latin America changed since you started working with 500 Startups?

We've really seen startups and entrepreneurs become more sophisticated. At the beginning, we met with lots of companies that just had a prototype. Now when we have the pitches, entrepreneurs already have their product on the market and are making sales. We are getting more people coming to us that already had previous investors. I also see fewer "copycat" businesses and more companies that are targeting the specific culture and environment of Latin America.

How can governments and VCs support Latin American entrepreneurship?

For the governments, I think there is a lot that they can do to support the efforts of people that have already started helping. Focus less on the noisy events and competitions that don't have much to do with making startups successful. For VCs, I suggest working closely with entrepreneurs to see where they are struggling and provide a solution to that. If you feel like you don't have enough deal flow, change your offering.

You can listen to our entire conversation on the *Crossing Borders* podcast on Itunes, Stitcher or wherever you get your podcasts, or on my blog:

http://www.nathanlustig.com/2017/08/07/ep-16-santiago-zavala-seeking-funds-investing-latin-american-startups/

VI

Colombia

C olombia has come a long way as a country and as a place to do business. The sensationalized version of Colombia that Netflix's Narcos depicts is no longer accurate, though the reputation lives on.

Colombia's history is long and complicated, filled with violent groups trying to control the country's lucrative drug trade. But there's so much more to Colombia than drugs. 2017's historic peace agreement between the Colombian government and Revolutionary Armed Forces of Colombia (FARC), the largest guerrilla group, is a potential inflection point in Colombia's history.[1] And if I had to bet on a single Latin American country for the next 10-15 years, Colombia would be my pick.

Though many think of coffee, Colombia's largest export is actually petroleum, which makes up over a third of the country's exports, followed by coal, coffee, cut flowers, and gold.[2] Coffee, however, was responsible for pushing Colombia toward a manufacturing-based economy. After the War of a Thousand Days ended in 1902, Colombia's coffee boom pushed the country to seek better transportation and manufacturing mechanisms.

Coffee production consistently grew in the 20th century, employing more than 500,000 families. While the government managed Colombia's economy conservatively, the political atmosphere turned increasingly unstable, corrupt and violent from the drug trade.

In 1991 the country adopted a new constitution in order to make peace and bring drug lords to justice. Colombia remained relatively stable economically until the late 1990s when fiscal deficits caused higher public debt which resulted in the country's first economic recession in over 60 years. But by the early 2000s, the economy began to recover buoyed by high petroleum prices and stable coffee prices.

Some credit former President Uribe, who led from 2002 – 2010, for his stand against terrorist groups disrupting the peace in Colombia. Though now marred by scandals, Uribe began to reform the country. In 2016, under President Santos, Colombia signed a peace agreement FARC. As Colombia has stabilized and gotten safer, tourism has boomed, growing 250% since 2006, for backpackers, expats and digital nomads taking advantage of great quality of life and lower costs of living.[3] Colombia's luxury tourism market has grown exponentially, highlighted by companies like Amakuna Travel, a luxury service provider based in Medellin.

Colombia's safety has drastically improved, which means more stability and more opportunities for doing business. Medellin was named the most innovative city in the world and the murder rate is down 95% from its peak, putting it on par with some of the larger cities in the US.

Advantages

Colombia's GDP is steadily growing. 2017 saw a 2.8% bump, and while inflation remains at 4%, it's expected to drop to 2-3% in 2018.[4,5,6] Especially compared to its volatile neighbors, Colombia's economy remains steady and ranked #53 in the World Bank's 2017 Doing Business Report.[7]

In the last ten years, Bogota has received US$16.77B in Foreign Direct Investment (FDI), and that number is expected to increase due to the 2016 peace agreement with the FARC guerrilla group.[8] Cartagena is booming, and is cleaning itself up. Barranquilla is going through a construction boom. Other major cities now have affordable direct flights from New York, Miami and more.

Investor confidence in Colombia is also growing. Thanks to political stability and steady economic growth, over 700 multinational companies have launched Colombian investment programs.[9] Colombia is also a relatively open, free market economy, with several free trade agreements with partners such as the United States and the European Union. Furthermore, having ports on both the Pacific and Atlantic Oceans makes the country a strategic location to do business.

Colombians are qualified and entrepreneurial. The country has a literacy rate of roughly 95%, and the population encourages entrepreneurial opportunities.[10] 71% of adult Colombians view entrepreneurship positively, and 60% of adult Colombians are potential entrepreneurs, according to Global Entrepreneurship Monitor.[11] A study by the World Economic Forum and Global Entrepreneurship Monitor found that only Colombia and Chile had a high amount of early-stage entrepreneurial activity and an unusually high proportion of ambitious and innovative entrepreneurs.[12]

The government is helping entrepreneurs. Ruta N, a federally-sponsored organization, offers early-stage companies support such as promotion, classes, finance opportunities, and vast networking in the city of Medellin. iNNPulsa, the Business Growth Management Unit of the National Government, promotes entrepreneurship, innovation, and productivity in all of Colombia. The organization's goal is for Colombia to be one of the top three most innovative economies in the region by 2025 and one of the most competitive economies in Latin America by 2032. By offering grants, iNNPulsa gives Colombians the tools to generate economic growth and prosperity in the country.

The government wants to bring over 65% of the country online by 2018, a realistic goal since the country already has a smartphone adoption rate of 69%(the US rate is 75%).[13] The Colombian government passed Law 1014 in 2006 that creates a national and regional network for entrepreneurial development. And in 2009, they passed Law 1286 to create a national system of science, technology, and innovation and to support high-technology, high-impact entrepreneurship.[14]

The Ministry of Information Technology and Communication started Apps.co, seeking to create a new generation of digital entrepreneurs in Colombia. They nurture the connection between ideas, talent, and the market, offering collaborative work with entrepreneurs to turn ideas into businesses.

The support paid off as startup successes such as delivery service Rappi received an investment from big names including Andreessen Horowitz at a $1B valuation in 2018.[15] Mercadoni, also in the delivery space, raised $30M from the Brazil and the US.[16] Travel metasearch website Viajala has already raised $500,000 and is on its way to toward being the Kayak of Latin America.

Funds like Firstrock Capital, Torrenegra Labs, Wayra and company builders like Polymath Ventures are helping seed the ecosystem. Companies like Authy have been acquired by US startups and the ecosystem is starting to grow. My fund, Magma Partners, made our first three investments in Colombia in 2016 and 2017, including OmniBnk, the winner of our Latin America-wide Fintech competition.

Setting up a business is relatively easy and has improved since 2016. In the Doing Business Report, Colombia ranks #61 for starting a business (up from 80 in 2016). Many international bodies, such as Standard & Poor's, Moody's & Fitch and the World Bank, identify Colombia as a trustworthy partner. So with high investor confidence, a relatively stable economy, and a strong entrepreneurial spirit, Colombia has many advantages.

Disadvantages

There are a few areas where Colombia falls short and needs to improve. Of course, the drug trade is alive and well, though Peru has overtaken Colombia as the largest producer of cocaine. While the violence that follows the drug trade has drastically decreased, it is not gone completely. The peace agreement with FARC should reduce violence country-wide, but especially in the countryside that has previously been more violent.

Colombia also has poor management of intellectual property rights and was put on the United States Trade Representative's Priority Watch List of countries with insufficient copyright legislation and enforcement.[17] We recommend that most companies doing business from Colombia incorporate in the US and hold their IP there, and have a local subsidiary to accept payments and hire locals. This structure should help the company protect IP, while giving local employees the stability they require.

Many Colombian corporations do not pay their full share of taxes, which leads to underinvestment in infrastructure and distrust of companies. Colombia ranks #139 in the Doing Business Report for paying taxes and a very low #174 for enforcing contracts.[18]

Corruption and poor infrastructure still plague Colombia. Though the government has pledged US$70B to improve infrastructure, the results are still years, if not decades, away.[19] Major cities generally work well, but connections between them are still not well developed.

Colombia still has issues with corruption and a lack of transparency, according to Transparency International, and bribery is still part of doing business in certain sectors of the economy.[20] While not anywhere near the levels of Brazil, Venezuela or Argentina, Colombia needs to improve if it wants to continue to grow into a mature economy.

Colombia still has work to do in dealing with oligopolistic sectors of the economy, where competition is low, which can make starting a business difficult. However, with an economy that's more stable than some other Latin American countries and a highly qualified and entrepreneurial population, I'm very long Colombia because of its people, their ambition, and Colombia's location and commitment to the global economy.

Endnotes

1   *PRI.* https://www.pri.org/stories/2017-03-01/colombias-farc-rebels-begin-disarming

2   *Observatory of Economic Complexity.* https://atlas.media.mit.edu/en/profile/country/col/

3   *Colombia Reports.* https://data.colombiareports.com/colombia-tourism-statistics/

4   *World Bank.* https://data.worldbank.org/indicator/NY.GDP.MKTP.KD.ZG

5   *Trading Economics.* https://tradingeconomics.com/colombia/inflation-cpi

6   *OECD.* https://www.oecd.org/eco/outlook/colombia-economic-forecast-summary.htm

7   *Doing Business.* http://www.doingbusiness.org/rankings?lien_externe_oui=Continue

8   *Santander Trade.* https://en.portal.santandertrade.com/establish-overseas/colombia/investing

9   Ibid

10   Ibid

11   *Global Entrepreneurship Monitor.* https://en.portal.santandertrade.com/establish-overseas/colombia/investing

12   *World Economic Forum.* http://www3.weforum.org/docs/WEFUSA_EntrepreneurialInnovation_Report.pdf

13   *Comscore.* https://www.comscore.com/Insights/Market-Rankings/comScore-Reports-January-2015-US-Smartphone-Subscriber-Market-Share

14   https://www.gemconsortium.org/country-profile/52

15   *LAVCA.* https://lavca.org/2016/12/01/entrepreneur-profile-simon-borrero-co-founder-ceo-rappi/

16   *TechCrunch.* https://techcrunch.com/2017/06/06/colombian-grocery-delivery-app-mercadoni-raises-6-2m/

17   *Colombia Reports.* https://colombiareports.com/us-calls-colombia-implement-intellectual-property-laws/

18   http://www.doingbusiness.org/data/exploreeconomies/colombia

19   *WorldFolio.* http://www.theworldfolio.com/news/colombia-thinks-big-with-70-billion-infrastructure-program/3959/

20   *Transparency International.* https://www.transparency.org/country/COL

Medellin, Bogota, Cali and Barranquilla

T he Colombian entrepreneurial ecosystem has grown quickly the past few years. While the two most prominent cities, Bogota and Medellin, are often in the spotlight for their startup successes like Rappi or Fitpal, the third- and fourth-largest cities, Cali and Barranquilla respectively, are edging their way into the ring as well. These two strategically-placed cities, Cali near the Pacific and Barranquilla on the Caribbean Coast, are drawing attention from investors and beginning to develop the infrastructure they need to start to compete alongside Bogota and Medellin.

Looking deeper into the Colombian startup scene, you'll notice many differences between the cities. Here's a look at what each has to offer and how they contribute to Colombia's growing entrepreneurial spirit.

Bogota

As the political and economic powerhouse driver of the Andean nation, Bogota is also the headquarters for many of Colombia's fastest-growing startups, as well as a significant hub for investment. Two of Colombia's top three universities are located in Bogota, leading to a highly educated local talent pool for growing companies.

Innovation in Bogota has surged partly as a result of the Colombian government's efforts to revitalize the country and the capital through the innovation economy. For example, in 2012, the National Government founded INNPulsa to promote business development in Colombia. In partnership with INNPulsa, the startup accelerator

HubBog has invested in many innovative startups in Bogota. Also headquartered in Bogota is the Ministry of Technology and Communications' brainchild Apps.co, an online learning platform that helps turn digital business ideas into fully-developed enterprises.

With all this support from the Colombian government, it is unsurprising that many of Colombia's most innovative startups were founded in the capital. The now-international delivery service, Rappi with a $1B valuation, got its start in Bogota, as did the Colombian answer to Classpass, Fitpal, and invoicing backed finance company, OmniBnk.[1] These companies have already flown beyond Colombia's borders into Mexico and are set to reach the rest of Latin America, as well. Two-factor authentication technology, Authy, also comes from Bogota and was acquired by cloud communications platform Twilio, representing one of the more interesting exits in Latin America.

Even the booming capital of Colombia suffers from the perceptions of violence and corruption that still plague the nation. Some startups have found it challenging to get funding. Luckily, more US funds have started to invest in the region. Bogota hosts most of Colombia's largest investors, so startups looking to work with international venture capital firms with a Latin American focus might find Bogota to be a strategic location to start a company. Firms such as Firstrock Capital, Wayra Colombia, or Polymath Ventures and Magma Partners have offices in Bogota.

As the most innovative and cosmopolitan city in Colombia, Bogota does not lack for places to work, with many coworking spaces, including Carpe Diem House, Colabora, El Cluster Coworking Hub, House Lab, and Seedspace (in Bogota and Medellin) enabling entrepreneurs to work from any part of the city.

Some entrepreneurs find Bogota a challenging city to live in, due to urban sprawl, high amounts of traffic, high altitude and unpredictable weather. Those who do choose to call Bogota home, however, have an easy time traveling, as Bogota is a mere three-hour plane ride to Miami or Mexico City, five hours to Chile or New York, and seven hours to Los Angeles. Entrepreneurs living in Bogota can enjoy direct flights to major hubs, which eases the burden of travel.

Bogota is still unquestionably the economic and political capital of Colombia, outperforming its smaller counterparts. While Medellin, Cali, and Barranquilla are quickly emerging startup hubs in Colombia, Bogota is still the place to be for business.

Medellin

The second biggest city in Colombia is already competing fiercely with the capital to become the innovation center of the country. With government initiatives like incubator Ruta N and university startup accelerator Parque del Emprendimiento, Medellin is becoming well-known as a hub for international entrepreneurs. Located about 3000 feet lower than Bogota (8300 ft.), Medellin (4980 ft.) has perfect sunny weather year-round and boasts a significantly lower cost of living, making this city the ideal place to bootstrap a new startup.

Medellin, known as "the city of eternal spring," draws in many entrepreneurs simply for the enjoyable weather. Medellin also has a lower cost of living than Bogota, where rent is 20-30% higher.[2] More airlines now offer flights directly in and out of Medellin, eliminating the once necessary stop in Bogota. People in Medellin enjoy direct flights to Miami, New York City, and other major hubs across the United States.

Growing tech companies like Viajala, a platform for comparing airfare in Latin America, and SiembraViva, an organic produce delivery service that supports small farmers, have found a niche for themselves in Medellin. Even delivery giant Rappi has a center of operations in downtown Medellin, as this city has boomed in the past ten years.

Medellin's miraculous turnaround has put it on the map as an emerging hub for entrepreneurship, bringing in investors looking for explosive growth. Venture capital firms like Firstrock Capital (with offices in Medellin and Bogota) and Capitalia are already capitalizing on the innovation coming out of Medellin, and these investments will undoubtedly grow in the coming years. Much like in Bogota, Medellin's reputation sometimes holds the city back from receiving substantial investments that would allow the startup ecosystem in Colombia to compete with innovation heavyweights like Argentina, Brazil, and Chile.

Still, as digital nomads and entrepreneurs have flocked to Medellin, the city has become replete with high-quality coworking spaces to suit any startup. Some of the best include La Casa Redonda, NODO Coworking, Quokka Cafe Coworking, and AtomHouse Medellin (also found in Bogota).

As Antioquia, the province where Medellin is located, tries to transition Medellin to the innovation economy, this city has become one of Colombia's largest centers of entrepreneurship. Second only to Bogota in innovation, Medellin boasts newer infrastructure, a lower cost of living than the capital, and is quickly coming to the attention of international entrepreneurs as an ideal place to launch a new venture.

Cali

Cali is the capital of the Valle de Cauca region and the economic center of southwestern Colombia. It is also the only major Colombian city located near the Pacific Coast and has free trade zones that are helping build the local economy. In 2016, Colombia's third-largest city hosted a successful Startup Weekend that showed that Cali's entrepreneurial ecosystem was starting to grow.

This nascent community has gained the support of a few small investors, namely Creatic, a tech incubator and education center for the Valle de Cauca region. They have partnered with coding boot camp Coderise to train 800+ people in digital skills and to train 26 teachers to teach students programming. The tech education support from Creatic is empowering entrepreneurs from Cali to create innovative online platforms that help the people of Cali solve pressing pain points.

Another Cali-based initiative is ParqueSoft, a social entrepreneurship initiative. ParqueSoft acts as an incubator for marginalized individuals in Colombia and is led by innovators in digital art, science, and IT. This organization allows new entrepreneurs to learn skills and gain experience needed to succeed.

Cali is predicted to follow soon in the footsteps of Medellin and is quickly attracting real estate investment from speculators betting on Cali's rise. However, Cali still lags behind Medellin and Bogota when it comes to quality of life and ease of doing business, even though the government of Cali has tried to advance investment in the Valle de Cauca region through Invest Pacific. The regional government is also redoing the infrastructure to turn Cali into a "smart city" to put it on par with Colombia's larger innovation hubs.[3]

Coworking is catching on in Cali as well, with El Lab Coworking and Enfoque Lab providing varied options for entrepreneurs and digital nomads. With its strategic location just an hour from the Pacific Ocean and signs of initiative from the regional government to promote innovation, Cali could quickly become a key startup hub.

Traveling can be an issue, as getting to the United States or another Latin American country takes more time and is more expensive than flying out of a hub like Bogota. New flights to south Florida allow for more flight options via Miami and Fort Lauderdale. While the cost of living in Cali is much lower than Bogota, the city's infrastructure isn't as well developed and can be more dangerous than other large Colombian cities.

Barranquilla

Colombia's fourth-most populous city and home to its largest port, Barranquilla is another burgeoning startup hub located on the Caribbean Coast. Barranquilla is one of Colombia's oldest cities and was once the second largest city in the country. While Barranquilla's startup scene is still in its beginning stages, the government of Barranquilla is actively working to improve the city's poorly planned infrastructure to put Barranquilla back on the map as an innovative city.

Barranquilla's new accelerator, Macondolab, is starting to empower startups on Colombia's Caribbean coast with support from government initiative, Apps.co. Macondolab, founded at the Simon Bolivar University, has supported the growth of 30+ startups with mentorship, office space in their downtown Barranquilla campus, and seed capital. At the moment, Macondolab is the only well-known startup accelerator in Barranquilla but its founders have big ambitions of making a name for themselves in Colombia and Latin America as a whole. CaribeTIC, a Barranquilla based organization, brings the Caribbean IT sector together to promote tech company competitiveness.

Venture capital is still scarce in Barranquilla, although Corporacion Ventures (based in Bogota) has partnered with the Barranquilla Chamber of Commerce to make strategic investments in social entrepreneurship in this port city. The regional government of the Atlantico State has yet to make any significant tech investments, but they are trying to encourage investment in Barranquilla through ProBarranquilla, meant to make the city more attractive and open for business.

The most notable startup to come out of Barranquilla is Koombea, a B2B digital product development company that was founded in 2007 and has since gone on to build apps across five continents. Other Barranquilla-based startups include Appetit, a social network for foodies, and Joonik, a full-stack software development startup.

For those looking to work in Barranquilla, the coworking scene is already well-developed, which makes finding an office relatively easy. Standout options include the Cubicus Workspaces located all over the city, Monokuko Space, a creative, open office environment, and Construconceptos, a flexible, coworking and coliving space in the north of the city.

Barranquilla, like Cali, has lower Internet connectivity and is more difficult for entrepreneurs to travel back and forth to the US compared to Bogota or Medellin. Numerous outsourcing companies set up shop in Barranquilla because of the high level of English spoken in the city and relatively sound infrastructure. Barranquilla, however, is much smaller than Bogota, Medellin, and Cali, so entrepreneurs do not have the same community of resources there.

Overall, with startups already competing on the global market, Barranquilla is poised to become a leader in innovation in the Caribbean, especially considering Colombia's emphasis on entrepreneurship.

Conclusion

The four largest cities in Colombia are growing to become major players in Latin American entrepreneurship. New contributions from Barranquilla and Cali have put these two cities on the map, and their geographic placement may enable them to catch up to better-established hubs like Medellin and Bogota. The Colombian government is pushing hard to promote innovation all over Colombia, and the results are beginning to show, with startups like Rappi, Authy OmniBnk, and others leading Colombian entrepreneurs forward.

Endnotes

1   *Crunchbase.* https://www.crunchbase.com/organization/rappi
2   *Numbeo.* https://www.numbeo.com/cost-of-living/compare_cities. jsp?country1=Colombia&city1=Bogota&country2=Colombia&city2=Medellin
3   *Smart Cities Dive.* https://www.smartcitiesdive.com/ex/sustainablecitiescollective/how-cali-colombia-learned-bogot-s-and-medell-n-s-mistakes/200316/

The Medellin Miracle

B efore my first trip to Colombia in 2012, I didn't know what to expect. I came back in 2015 and 2016 and saw huge positive changes in Cartagena and then traveled to Medellin for the first time, a beautiful city nestled in a mountain valley. Fast forward to 2018, and I believe that Colombia is the country to watch in Latin America. Medellin, Colombia's second city, is a hidden gem that's just starting to get its due both for tourism and as a potential tech hub in South America.

In 2012, a group of Chilean friends and I planned to go to Colombia's north coast for two weeks and hang out on its beautiful tropical beaches. I had studied a bit about Colombia in high school Spanish class, as my teacher was Colombian and wanted to share Colombia's natural beauty with us. Being high schoolers, most of us only wanted to learn about Pablo Escobar, the drug gangs, movies, the violence, the civil war, how someone could murder a soccer star after scoring an own goal (watch the documentary The Two Escobars, it's really good)…pretty much the only news about Colombia we ever heard in the US was bad news.[1,2,3]

In college, I wrote a paper about the drug war, the hunt for Pablo Escobar and the violence that plagued Colombia in the 1980s and 1990s. Medellin was the most dangerous city in the world. Its murder rate was 381 per 100,000, 15x more than 2016 Chicago and 7x more than Baltimore and St. Louis, the US's most dangerous cities as of 2018.[4,5] Medellin's murder rate is down almost 90% from its peak, but would still have one of top 10 murder rates in the US today. The turnaround is called The Medellin Miracle.[6]

In 2012, my friends and I went to the north coast, landing in Cartagena, continuing on to Santa Marta, Tayrona and Isla Baru. Some of my family and friends expressed concern about the trip, but I told them not to worry, Colombia was much safer than in the past and was growing quickly. We didn't have any problems, but saw police corruption, lots of foreign tourists in town for sex or drug tourism and underdeveloped, dangerous roads outside of the city. A few of our group got pick-pocketed, and we noticed that bit of an edge: if you said something to the wrong person, or were unluckily in the wrong place and the wrong time, you might end up in real trouble.

Fast forward to 2015. I spent a few days in Cartagena and the difference was like night and day.[7] There were hundreds of beautiful new apartment towers along the waterfront. Before, the same stretch was filled with run down buildings or nothing at all. The historic colonial era walled city is even more developed, with more restaurants and better lighting. It feels much safer. But the part that surprised me most was the part outside of the walled city, where I'd stayed before.

When I was there in 2012, most of the roads weren't paved, the only accommodations were cheap party hostels. The streets were lined with drug dealers, military police and prostitutes, many of them working together. In 2015, that's mostly gone, at least from public view. The roads are paved, the infrastructure is better. And there are countless boutique hotels and interesting restaurants that have opened up to serve ever increasing numbers of tourists. Even the taxis seemed to have gotten an upgrade, likely from competition with Uber!

On that same trip in 2015, I spent time in Medellin and Bogota, this time for a mix of business and vacation. I hadn't been to Medellin before, but had been watching Narcos to see a bit more about how things might have worked in the 80s and 90s. I didn't really know what to expect and some of my family and friends still had the same idea about Colombia: that it's dangerous, full of narcos, guerrillas and corrupt police. I quickly realized Medellin didn't deserve that reputation anymore when a friend told me about the 90% decline in the murder rate and surging infrastructure development.[8]

Medellin, known as the City of Eternal Spring, is a South American gem that's just starting to get discovered by tourists.[9] Nestled into a lush, green, mountain valley, Medellin has the same weather all year round: 70s-80s and a bit of humidity. The locals say it's a place you can pick your weather: want it a bit colder? Go up into the mountains a bit. Like it really hot? Go farther down the valley. It rains tropically for part of the day during the rainy season, but otherwise has an amazing climate.[10,11]

Cost of living is incredibly low. It would be hard to spend $2500 per month living in a nice part of town with a top notch lifestyle if you lived in Medellin full time. You could certainly have a great lifestyle for $1000. Backpackers have been coming to Medellin for years, but tourism has been booming since 2012. The bourgeoning startup scene supported by top engineering talent, motivated entrepreneurs, smart venture capitalists and RutaN continues to attract more people to the city.

I've been back to Medellin a few times per year since 2016 and the city keeps getting better. New infrastructure, restaurants and bars are opening up, nightlife is continuing to improve, startups, from both Colombia and abroad are expanding and more tourists are coming. Located five hours from NYC, seven from LA and Chicago, three from Miami, and five from Santiago and Buenos Aires, three from Lima, Medellin is uniquely positioned to grow into a tourism and business hub.

While Medellin is still clearly more dangerous than Chile or nice parts of major US cities, I never felt in danger riding public transport, taking taxis, and going to a night time soccer game. There's still petty crime, drugs are readily available if you want them and there's a bit of an edge in some places, but if you don't get completely trashed and keep your wits, you'll most likely be fine, just like in any other big city. There are still potentially dangerous parts of the country, mostly in areas where the ELN, a guerrilla group, still have strong influence near the Venezuelan and Ecuadorian borders, but most tourists don't go there.

The 2016 peace treaty ended the world's longest civil war with FARC. [12]Most Colombians I've talked to are sick of the conflict and ready for peace. They were hopeful that the peace treaty would hold.

I'm really bullish on Medellin both as a bourgeoning tourist destination and also as one of Latin America's startup hubs, and Colombia as a country. It's a large market, close to the US, with interesting, open, fun people and some of the most incredible natural landscapes in the world. It's also a hotspot for digital nomads in Latin America.

Endnotes

1   *The Guardian.* https://www.theguardian.com/cities/2014/apr/17/medellin-murder-capital-to-model-city-miracle-un-world-urban-forum

2   *BBC.* https://www.bbc.com/news/world-latin-america-11400950

3   *Telegraph.* https://www.telegraph.co.uk/sport/football/teams/colombia/10938692/Andres-Escobar-murder-Colombia-prepare-for-biggest-ever-World-Cup-match-on-20th-anniversary-of-death.html

4   *IADB.* https://www.iadb.org/en/topics/citizen-security/impact-me-dellin,5687.html

5   *Pew Research Center.* http://www.pewresearch.org/fact-tank/2014/07/14/despite-recent-shootings-chicago-nowhere-near-u-s-murder-capital/

6   https://www.theguardian.com/cities/2014/apr/17/medellin-murder-capital-to-model-city-miracle-un-world-urban-forum

7   *New York Times.* https://www.nytimes.com/2015/04/30/realestate/house-hunting-in-colombia.html?_r=0

8   *Wall Street Journal.* https://www.wsj.com/articles/five-cities-that-are-leading-the-way-in-urban-innovation-1461549789

9   *Journal Sentinel.* http://archive.jsonline.com/news/opinion/medelln-how-a-murder-capital-became-a-power-child-of-innovation-b99652931z1-366262161.html/

10   *Kauffman.* https://www.kauffman.org/currents

11   *Finance Colombia.* http://www.financecolombia.com/ruta-n-business-incubator-anchors-medellins-innovation-district-driving-business-growth-and-social-inclusion/

12   *World Politics Review.* https://www.worldpoliticsreview.com/articles/18397/a-three-player-chess-game-colombia-s-peace-talks-with-eln-and-farc

E-commerce Overview

C olombia is one of Latin America's biggest economies, yet traditional e-commerce has struggled to take a hold due to complex logistics challenges such as Colombia's mountainous geography and lack of integration with international markets. Many consumers in Colombia are still wary of online retail platforms and until recently, payments systems did not offer any options for the unbanked.

All that began to change when Rappi entered the market. Founded in 2015 as a grocery delivery service, Rappi has gone on to raise millions of dollars from US investors like Y Combinator and Andreessen Horowitz for its intuitive app that allows users to order just about anything to their doorstep.

Rappi gained millions of users in Colombia and Mexico, as its founders quickly tackled issues like delivery logistics and offline payment systems that had long stumped e-commerce companies in Latin America. Rappi deliveries offer an immediacy that has helped skeptical consumers place their trust in online commerce. Their cash-on-delivery payments system democratized mobile and electronic purchasing in Colombia and Mexico, where credit and debit cards remain relatively rare. Rappi closed a $200M investment round at a $1B valuation in late 2018.

While Rappi has become a regional reference point for e-commerce startups looking to operate in Latin America, Colombia's e-commerce market as a whole still faces challenges. Colombia's e-commerce providers are also concerned with the security of online payments. While the level of online fraud is low in Colombia (.45%), international retailers still struggle to operate within Colombian borders, and not just because of Colombia's mountainous geography.[1] Colombia has a negative reputation internationally that has made retailers and payments processors impose controls around money laundering or other illegal activity, despite data that shows most online payments aren't involved in illegal activity. PayPal withdrew from Colombia in 2015, and sites like AliExpress do not yet offer sales in Colombian pesos.[2]

To combat these concerns, the Colombian government has implemented mandatory e-invoicing for all Colombian businesses starting in January 2019.[3] This regulatory measure is meant to aid in tax collection and financial analysis for companies across Latin America's fourth-largest country by having one verified invoice per transaction per company. E-invoicing will reduce fraud and increase tax revenue, leading to more people trusting e-commerce providers.

Colombia's government is all in on e-commerce; it is the only country in Latin America with a fully-dedicated Ministry of E-Commerce. The Ministry of E-Commerce and the Ministry of Technology have created a non-profit E-Commerce Observatory that monitors and measures the growth of the sector.

From 2015 to 2016, the Colombian e-commerce market exploded, growing by 64% in one year.[4] By 2017, it had slowed down to a more manageable 22%, making up just over 4% of Colombia's GDP.[5] In 2016, the Colombian government reported the gross revenue of the industry at US$26B, although this figure might be skewed because Colombia is the only Latin American country to include both tax payments and B2B sales in their industry revenue figures. Visa and Euromonitor reportedly calculated Colombia's e-commerce revenue at ~US$3.1B in 2015.[6]

As Latin America's fifth-largest e-commerce market, Colombia has begun to catch the eye of international retailers. In 2018, eBay partnered with PideloRapido, a delivery service offering US goods to Latin American customers.[7] Most importantly, this service does not require Latin American buyers to have a US billing address or a PayPal account. So far, PideloRapido serves customers in Guatemala, El

Salvador, Panama, and Colombia, with plans for further expansion throughout Latin America in 2018.

Latin American giants MercadoLibre and Linio, are also well/established in Colombia, though the recent arrival of AliExpress has upped the competition. In 2017, Amazon Web Services targeted Colombian companies for the platform, spurring rumors about when Amazon might launch in Bogotá.[8]

Still, these international sellers all struggle with the same challenge: online payments. 57% of Colombian e-commerce users pay via cash on delivery (COD), the payment system that allowed Rappi to explode in Colombia.[9] Other popular payment methods include PayU, Kushki and ePayco, local replacements for PayPal that enable seamless online money transfers. As bank access improves across Colombia, customers are increasingly turning toward credit and debit card payments, helping simplify payments for online sellers.

While lack of stable Internet access still prevents many Colombians from shopping online, large local retailers are still hopping on the trend. Colombia's major grocery store, Exito, and Chilean retail store, Falabella, are among the top companies helping Colombians transition to online shopping.

In turn, homegrown startups are following in these popular e-commerce retailers' footsteps, helping Colombians access more services through the Internet. SiembraViva, an online produce market, assists rural farmers to get their products into urban supply chains. KiwiCampus uses robots to lower food delivery costs drastically. Viajala helps customers across Latin America shop for plane tickets. Ropeo makes on-demand fashion available to Colombians. Dozens of other e-commerce startups are targeting the Colombian market as the population becomes increasingly accustomed to buying online.

Much like Chile, Colombia participates in the regional initiative E-commerce Day which includes an e-commerce startup competition and a networking opportunity to keep a pulse on the industry. Colombia's e-commerce sector continues to face challenges that are holding it back from its potential. However, as Colombians gain stable access to the Internet and online transactions become more commonplace, Colombia is becoming a trusted partner for international retail companies. Latin America's fifth-largest e-commerce market if growing quickly, and Colombia's private and public sectors are well-positioned to seize the opportunity.

Endnotes

1   *PulsoSocial.* https://pulsosocial.com/2017/07/07/asi-evoluciona-el-ecommerce-en-colombia/

2   *El Tiempo.* https://www.eltiempo.com/archivo/documento/CMS-16305735

3   *Observatorio E-Commerce.* https://www.observatorioecommerce.com.co/la-facturacion-electronica-sera-obligatoria/

4   *Export.gov.* https://www.export.gov/article?id=Colombia-eCommerce

5   Ibid

6   *AMI Perspectiva.* https://amiperspectiva.americasmi.com/the-strongest-e-commerce-markets-in-latin-america/

7   *ESeller Cafe.* https://esellercafe.com/ebay-expansion-latin-american-markets-via-pidelorapido/

8   *Cámara Colombiana de Comercio Electrónico.* https://ccce.org.co/noticias/que-implicaria-la-llegada-de-amazon-colombia

9   *Finance Colombia.* http://www.financecolombia.com/nielsen-57-of-colombian-e-commerce-shoppers-still-pay-cod-cash-on-delivery/

Diego Caicedo: Streamlining Loans To Small and Medium Businesses

D iego Caicedo grew up in both Popayan, Colombia and San Francisco, California, a childhood that would prepare him for a lifetime of entrepreneurial pursuits across Latin America and the US. Diego left home at age fifteen after graduating early from high school to go to university in Bogota, then dropped out two semesters before finishing his degree in engineering so he could start an international coffee business.

When the business eventually failed, Diego dusted himself off and became an entrepreneur in the Chilean and Colombian mining industries. While working on his mining business, he realized that businesses across Latin America struggled with financing options, and that banks were not closing the gap. Diego eventually founded OmniBnk, a Fintech company based in Colombia and Chile that helps financial institutions, large companies, and their suppliers optimize invoice-backed financing. I've enjoyed working with Diego and his team since they won the Latin America-wide Magma Partners Fintech competition in 2017.

Why is invoice-backed financing so important in Latin America?

OmniBnk helps SMEs get financing using the information from electronic invoices to provide credit for businesses. Electronic invoicing is much more developed in Latin America than in the US because most Latin American countries have centralized tax systems that require companies to pay social security, health insurance, and pensions for their employees. All revenue and spending information has to be reported monthly to the government to make the appropriate deductions.

Chile was the regional leader in e-invoicing, requiring companies to standardize invoicing in an XML [computer readable] format so it could be processed at scale. Those invoices contain a lot of data that can be leveraged for financing and credit scoring, since they reflect critical internal information about companies and their cash flow. However, many small businesses do not receive payment on those invoices for up to 90-120 days and often struggle with liquidity. Omnibnk uses those invoices to score suppliers and provide them financing so they can operate their businesses smoothly.

What did you learn while raising capital and finding partners in Latin America?

The rules for raising capital in Latin America are different from the US. You need real numbers to raise significant capital in Latin America; if you are not focusing on your key metric, whatever that might be, you will not get the financing you need. I think founders should never take lack of capital as an excuse to not build something big. We have always looked to our clients as our first source of financing and only pursued outside capital to accelerate growth that was already happening. The hustle matters a lot more than the money at the beginning stages of your business.

What tips do you have for other Latin American founders trying to raise capital?

In Latin America, you should always prioritize the network over the capital. One of the most dangerous things for an entrepreneur is to get so stuck in the day-to-day of your business that you don't look up to make sure you are going down the right path. The right investors can be a sounding board for your ideas who can provide fresh eyes and point you in the right direction. Never raise more capital than you need to make it to the next milestone. Having too much capital at your disposal makes you lose focus. Everything becomes shiny when you have money, but it makes it hard for you to focus on building a lean, profitable business. When looking for investors, focus on the network and not so much on the capital.

In our case, although we knew we could help financing companies score their clients and automate their businesses, it was hard to convince established players to change the way they did business. We managed to get a meeting with Latin America's Merrill Lynch, BTG Pactual, through Francisco Saenz, and they only accepted our proposal because we came well-referenced. We managed to close a US$200M deal with them to help fund businesses through OmniBnk. These corporate partnerships are the way to scale our business, but we depended on our network to get started.

You can listen to our entire conversation on the *Crossing Borders* podcast on Itunes, Stitcher or wherever you get your podcasts, or on my blog:

https://www.nathanlustig.com/2018/09/04/ep-53-diego-caicedo-streamlining-small-business-finance-in-latin-america-with-portal-finance/

Antonio Nunes: Building Last Mile Delivery in Latin America

A ntonio Nunes is a Portuguese entrepreneur who has lived his life across borders. At age 19, he started an NGO that is still running today to support entrepreneurs in Mozambique. After returning to Europe, Antonio went on to work for Rocket Internet, building several successful e-commerce businesses in Asia and Oceania. He then jumped at the chance to co-found Linio, Rocket Internet's Amazon for Latin America, which was later acquired by Chilean retail giant Falabella for $138M.

While working on Linio in Bogota he became hooked on solving the last-mile grocery delivery problem for the Latin American market. He took what he had learned at Rocket Internet to launch Mercadoni, a grocery-delivery app that now operates in Colombia, Mexico, and

Argentina. After raising multiple rounds of VC funding from global investors including tech giant Movile, he and his team have continued to expand across Latin America, competing for market share in one of Latin America's fastest-growing industries.

Why is last-mile delivery such a big market opportunity in Latin America?

Going to the supermarket for a lot of people is a huge waste of time. Some people in Latin America spend up to four hours a week buying groceries, when they could be with their families, working on personal projects, or enjoying time with friends. This problem is magnified in Latin America, as compared with the US, because retail penetration is lower, traffic tends to be even more congested, and in some cities, security is a significant issue.

Leaving the house to buy groceries is a huge inconvenience for a lot of Latin American people. When I arrived in Bogota to build Linio, I realized that no one was touching the US$300B Latin American grocery industry. Last-mile delivery in Latin America is an opportunity both from the demand side, that people need the service, and from the unit economics side, since delivery is relatively cost-effective as compared with the US.

What advice do you have for entrepreneurs looking to raise capital in Latin America?

Raising a US$9M Series A round from Bogota required us to be creative. At the time, there were only two VC funds active in Colombia. We were really looking for investors who would share our vision about how to grow Mercadoni regionally and who understood the size of this market opportunity. For our Series A, we looked for three different investor profiles: angel investors from the retail industry who could add value to what we were doing, large Argentine financial players, and tech companies who were interested in helping retailers go online. We received a large portion of our investment from Movile, the

Brazilian mobile giant, who has been a strategic partner in helping us develop and expand our app across the region.

Why is Latin America changing so much faster than the United States?

The rate of change in Latin America is very high. Even since I've been living in Bogota (since 2012), I've noticed a lot of companies opening, startups launching, and there is a lot more to do. Latin America is experiencing the same leapfrogging effect that could be observed in emerging economies in Asia, although a few years behind.

For me, phones are a symbol of the difference between the rates of change in the US and Latin America. While the US is still using landline technology in many areas, Latin America jumped straight to mobile, and then on to smartphones very quickly. With increased macroeconomic stability in the region, Latin Americans are purchasing more and they are using their phones to do so. There is a very high rate of technology adoption in Latin America, sometimes even faster than in the United States.

You can listen to our entire conversation on the *Crossing Borders* podcast on Itunes, Stitcher or wherever you get your podcasts, or on my blog:

http://www.nathanlustig.com/2018/06/19/ep-45-antonio-nunes-delivering-latin-americas-groceries-with-mercadoni/

VII

Argentina

Argentina has the third-largest economy in Latin America (after Brazil and Mexico), and the second-highest GDP per capita in the region in Purchasing Power Parity (PPP) terms, only after Chile. But you may have heard the saying, "As rich as an Argentine," a phrase that was coined to describe Argentina's wealth and prosperity in the 1800s-1929.[1] Argentina had the fourth-highest GDP per capita and was one of the wealthiest countries in the world. Between 1890 and 1930, the capital city of Buenos Aires transformed from a colonial town to the sprawling, mammoth metropolitan area of 13M people that it still is today.

Unfortunately, the Great Depression followed all of that prosperity, which was followed by decades of political turmoil. During the 1940s-1970s, Argentina borrowed from foreign banks and ran hefty budget deficits. In the 1970s, Argentina's credit rating dropped so low that leaders resorted to printing more currency, leading to the Argentinian Peso's steady decline.

Argentina went through a period of hyperinflation and political instability which lasted until the 1990s. By the 1990s and the first dotcom bubble era, the government launched new initiatives to reopen the country, and Buenos Aires became the birthplace of some of Latin America's most successful technology companies. A group of Argentine Internet pioneers founded companies like MercadoLibre, the eBay of Latin America, and OfficeNet, which was eventually acquired by Staples[2,3]

But this boom didn't last long. In 2001, Argentina defaulted on its public debts and faced another currency devaluation.[4] Argentine entrepreneurs who lived through this period became instilled with the understanding that if you want to survive and do business, you're going to need the right combination of patience, resilience and hustle. They also started to look at foreign markets, using Argentina as a base to go global.

The good news is that despite the constant state of uncertainty and political instability, there were Argentine entrepreneurs who persisted, churning out some remarkable companies. During the 2000s, two of the nine Latin American companies which are now in the billion-dollar club were founded in Argentina, OLX (the Craigslist of Latin America) and Globant (a top outsourcing company that IPOed in the US). I've found that Latin America's best entrepreneurs generally have come from Argentina. It makes sense: you have to be a problem-solver with the entrepreneurial spirit who is willing to hustle just to do many basic daily tasks in Argentina!

So what is it like doing business in Argentina today? Argentina has been a hard place to do business in the 2010s, plagued by inflation and corruption. President Mauricio Macri made some changes to make life easier for startups, businesses, investors and consumers, though with mixed results.[5]

Opportunities in Argentina

The Ley de Emprendedores of 2017 allows entrepreneurs to register a business 100% online in 24 hours.[6] Previously, it took 26 days. This fast-track company registration allows entrepreneurs to register a simplified business entity (SAS), bank account, identification number, and a business temporary address.

There is a new governmental push towards Venture Capital Development.[7] The government created a new law to:

» Create and support accelerators and expand venture capital funds.
» Provide tax incentives for investors to invest in new companies or venture capital funds.
» Promote the creation of high-impact Argentine business ventures.

Argentina has the highest Internet penetration rate in Latin America (80.1%). It's one of the largest and most technology-developed populations in the world.

E-commerce is growing in the region. In 2015, the average online store grew sales by 58%. Shipping and logistics startups are also coming in to deal with infrastructure difficulties to make online shopping easier. The government is changing rules so that companies can import goods without the need for import licenses.

Bitcoin and other cryptocurrencies are booming in Argentina, where people were early adopters because of a lack of trust in banks and government. Argentina not only leads Latin America in bitcoin development and adoption of the digital currency, it's also a global leader. As of June 2017, Coinmap lists 145 venues that accept Bitcoin in Buenos Aires alone. For perspective, London lags behind at 90 and New York 87.

According to Bitcoin Market Potential Index, which ranks Bitcoin's potential utility across 177 countries, Argentina is the country with the single greatest potential for digital currency because of rampant inflation and informality.[8] Bitcoin use doubled between mid-2014 and mid-2015 and continues to grow in 2018 as Argentina experience high inflation. Argentina is a hot spot for Bitcoin and blockchain companies, including: Xapo, Ripio, RSK Labs, and Bitex.

Challenges in Argentina

Inflation is still a problem, with a reported annual rate of 40%, which makes doing business in the local market challenging. Employees have it rough; wages aren't keeping up with inflation so it's hard for employees to buy anything imported, making life more difficult for everyone. President Macri has been trying to solve the problem since his election in 2015, but hasn't had much success. Argentina saw a ~50% devaluation in less than a month in mid 2018. Inflation, the commodities bust and economic mismanagement have pushed Argentina into a recession.

Over the last decade, Argentina has received very low levels of foreign direct investment as it isolated itself from the world's capital markets. The new administration removed currency controls and reached a deal with the country's last remaining creditors from the 2001 default, resolving a decade-long dispute, which will help Argentina return to international capital markets.

Navigating Argentina's byzantine tax system is difficult and businesses often need to hire a third party to handle all of their financial reporting. Argentine business taxes are levied at three levels: federal, provincial, and municipal levels. Both the corporate income and capital gains tax rates currently sit at 35%.

Accessing traditional credit is difficult and credit card use is low due to high inflation and interest rates. According to the Central Bank of Argentina, credit card interest rates can range anywhere from 36% to 111%, however websites like elMejorTrato.com and Comparabien.com can help businesses compare interest rates for credit cards and loans from various banks and loan services. Startups like Afluenta have come on the scene to offer peer-to-peer lending to bridge the gap.

Over the past few years, it has been quite difficult to move money out of Argentina, as foreign businesses often need to do. Additional roadblocks, such as requiring companies to balance their imports with an equivalent amount of exports, have also made the country a challenging place to do business. Companies like Porsche resorted to exporting several hundred bottles of red wine for each car it imported.[9] Some companies end up bribing customs officials to look the other way or incorporate in Uruguay or the United States to deal with this issue.

While Macri's government has made progress to make it easier to do business in Argentina, it's still one of the hardest places in Latin America to operate. It's best to have a local partner, whether you're operating in Argentina or opening an office for your US or European based business. I personally still wouldn't operate a business in Argentina targeting the local market yet, as it's still too unstable. But many top foreign investors like George Soros and Steven Cohen have made bets in Argentina in 2018. I would look to Argentina for top technology, design and marketing talent, rather than the local market

Endnotes

1   *Wall Street Oasis.* https://www.wallstreetoasis.com/blog/as-rich-as-an-argentine

2   *New York Times.* https://www.nytimes.com/2008/12/26/business/world-business/26peso.html

3   *Endeavor.* https://endeavor.org/entrepreneurs/entrepreneur-to-entrepreneur-connections-egypts-sasco-group-and-officenet-co-founder-santiago-bilinkis/

4   *Rabo Bank.* https://economics.rabobank.com/publications/2013/august/the-argentine-crisis-20012002-/

5   *BBC.* https://www.bbc.com/news/world-latin-america-34899223

6   *LAVCA.* https://lavca.org/2017/03/30/five-keys-understanding-argentinas-entrepreneurship-law-en-espanol/

7   *ARCAP.* https://medium.com/perspectivas-de-arcap/a-law-that-enhances-the-venture-capital-industry-in-argentina-a4d05d7478bb

8   *London School of Economics.* http://blogs.lse.ac.uk/businessreview/2016/05/12/most-countries-in-the-10-most-likely-to-adopt-bitcoin-are-in-the-developing-world/

9   *Automotive News Europe.* http://europe.autonews.com/article/20111104/ANE/311039835/porsche-importer-uses-wine-sales-to-keep-autos-coming-into-argentina

Buenos Aires, Córdoba and Mendoza

Argentina is a country of paradoxes. Four of Latin America's unicorns come from Buenos Aires and some consider Argentina's capital to be the best-placed city in the world for adopting Bitcoin and other cryptocurrencies.[1] On the other hand, Argentina regularly experiences currency hyperinflation. High levels of bureaucracy can impede even the best entrepreneurs.

MercadoLibre, Despegar, Ualá, OLX, Satellogic, Afluenta, Ripio, and Agrofy are just a few of the successful global startups that have come out of Argentina. One reason why Argentina is an entrepreneurship hub is precisely the challenges entrepreneurs have to overcome. Argentina is also lauded for having one of the best public education systems in the world, and is a net exporter of development talent.[2] Finally, Argentina has the highest English proficiency in Latin America, so it was well-placed to become a global tech hub.[3]

Despite being a 10+ hour flight from New York City, Argentina is on US Eastern time zone for most of the year and is only four hours behind London, making it a strategic outsourcing location. Most of Argentina's entrepreneurs come from three major cities: Buenos Aires, Córdoba, and Mendoza. Here is a deeper look at the startup ecosystems of Argentina's main cities.

Buenos Aires: The Birthplace of Unicorns

All four of Argentina's startup unicorns were founded in Buenos Aires. MercadoLibre, a platform for companies of all sizes to sell products online, much like eBay was Argentina's first success story. Founded in 1999, MercadoLibre has spread across the region and is one of the region's most successful startups.

The other unicorns, Globant, OLX, and Despegar have all been acquired or had a IPO in the 2010s. These companies, founded during the late 1990s and early 2000s in Buenos Aires, have become both symbols of Argentina's entrepreneurial potential and excellent training grounds for the current generation of entrepreneurs. They have also placed Buenos Aires at the center of a global entrepreneurial ecosystem, as many of the city's main companies have reached international acclaim.

The Buenos Aires metropolitan area has just under 15 million people, making it the second-largest metropolitan area in South America after São Paulo. Beyond being the seat of the Argentinean government and the largest city in the country, Buenos Aires holds up to 90% of Argentina's entrepreneurial activity.[4] The city is brimming with incubators, coworking spaces, and tech startups. One article estimated that most of Argentina's 100 coworking spaces are in Buenos Aires.[5]

AreaTres was the first coworking space inBuenos Aires, and it helped catalyze the development of much of the rest of the ecosystem. Two venture capital funds, NXTP Labs and Kaszek Ventures, launched in Buenos Aires in 2011, followed by Quasar Ventures in 2012. Lisa Besserman's Startup Buenos Aires (SUBA), a startup support organization, got its start in 2013. Palermo Valley, a Buenos Aires startup organization, has over 600 members and has brought together a strong group of entrepreneurs from the city. Buenos Aires also has over 7,500 brick-and-mortar businesses that accept Bitcoin, which citizens readily adopted because of inflation and foreign capital controls.[6]

Compared to Santiago, Buenos Aires has much less public funding and yet it has a slightly better track record for taking startups global and for testing cutting-edge technology. In 2015, the city government launched Academia Buenos Aires Emprende to teach basic entrepreneurship skills for free.

In 2016, Buenos Aires also created the accelerator program, IncuBAte to rival Start-Up Chile. The incubator program is open to national and international entrepreneurs with high-impact ideas. Offering a network of mentors and elite connections, Buenos Aires will try to build on its already successful startup ecosystem. Startups that are chosen to participate will receive an equity free US$30,000 grant, mentorship and office space. The tech ecosystem and government officials are excited about the program.

Here are a few Buenos Aires-based startups to watch:

» SATELLOGIC: This startup sends mini satellites into space to democratize access to satellite data. It is now based in Silicon Valley and raised a US$27M Series B led by Tencent in 2016.

» RIPIO: One of Latin America's largest cryptocurrency exchanges that allows Argentines to easily transfer between pesos and Bitcoin.

» ETERMAX: This video game and mobile app company built Trivia Crack, one of the most downloaded apps in the history of the App Store.

» UALÁ: An Argentine neobank that is helping Argentina's unbanked have access to the financial system.

Córdoba: A Hub for Entrepreneurial Education

Argentina's second-biggest city is well-known as a university town. The city is home to the National University of Córdoba, Blas Pascal University, Catholic University of Córdoba and several others, all of which have their own incubators or entrepreneurship programs. Córdoba also hosts one of Latin America's top accelerators, Incutex Company Builders. Overall, this city is coordinating significant efforts to join the Argentinean startup ecosystem.

The local government has pushed Córdoba to catch up with Buenos Aires through programs like Córdoba Acelera, which coinvests with local accelerators, and Programa Emprende Industria, which connects entrepreneurs and industry experts for mentorship opportunities.

These programs are beginning to attract entrepreneurs and investors to the city, which is a significant source of the country's talent.

International funds such as Founder Institute, 500 Startups, Alaya Capital Partners, InnovaSV all have offices in Córdoba, betting on its young, tech savvy population. As a smaller city located far away from the national government in Buenos Aires, the local government and ecosystem has been able create more centralized startup programs in Córdoba. Their efforts have already borne fruit; local startups Aivo, a customer-service chatbot powered by artificial intelligence, and Tambero, a dairy cattle management platform, have received international attention.

Mendoza: Startups in Wine Country

Located a 30 minute plane ride or a ten-hour drive across the border from Santiago, Chile, one of the region's most active tech hubs, Mendoza has received entrepreneurial influence from Santiago, Chile that pushed the local government to prioritize startups early on. While access to capital and credit in Mendoza is still a stumbling block, the local government is openly supportive of tech development through programs like Consejo Consultivo Emprendedor (CCE) and Mendoza Emprende.

These two initiatives are looking to bring 20,000 jobs and 4,000 businesses to the city best known for its wine. Mendoza Emprende offers funding, education, and institutional support for startups and organizations that promote entrepreneurship in Mendoza, and has received backing from the Ministry of Economy, Infrastructure, and Energy, as well as from the Inter-American Development Bank. The Consejo Consultativo Emprendedor, which is a part of Mendoza Emprende, brings together actors from the public, private, and civil sectors to create development initiatives for the city.

Much like Córdoba and Buenos Aires, Mendoza also has a large university population that is being educated in entrepreneurship and tech innovation. Cuyo University's UNCUYO incubator is one of the most active university incubators in the region. Startup Mendoza, the local entrepreneurial community, has mapped out the startups, incubators, and coworking spaces in Mendoza and even organized a US$1M crowdfunding campaign in 2017. Some of the best-known startups from Mendoza include Eventioz (acquired by Eventbrite) and KindApp, which improves transparency in charitable donations.

Argentina is one of the three major startup hubs in Latin America, alongside Brazil and Mexico. While years of government regulations and economic crises have created massive challenges for entrepreneurs in Argentina, Buenos Aires is still a globally-recognized startup hub, with smaller cities Córdoba and Mendoza trying to catch up. However, the future is uncertain for Argentina, as hyperinflation continues to create economic instability in Latin America's second-largest country. Nonetheless, Argentina's entrepreneurs have proven themselves to be resilient to the rollercoaster economy and continue to develop products that quickly reach global acclaim.

Endnotes

1 *Digg.* http://digg.com/2016/argentina-bitcoin

2 *The Next Web.* https://thenextweb.com/contributors/2017/07/04/argentina-a-look-into-latin-americas-most-global-tech-hub/

3 *Education First.* https://www.ef.com/cl/epi/regions/latin-america/argentina/

4 https://thenextweb.com/contributors/2017/07/04/argentina-a-look-into-latin-americas-most-global-tech-hub/

5 *La Nacion.* https://www.lanacion.com.ar/1989877-crecen-las-oficinas-flexibles

6 http://digg.com/2016/argentina-bitcoin

E-commerce Overview

D espite years of sky-high taxes on imports and challenges with online transactions, Argentina is still an important force in Latin American e-commerce. The birthplace of MercadoLibre, Latin America's most popular e-commerce site, Argentina is the fastest-growing e-commerce market in the region, registering up to 28% yearly growth[1]

While Argentina still comes in behind Mexico and powerhouse Brazil, its predicted market share in e-commerce is expected to grow from 8.9% to 14.6% of the region's total sales volume by 2019.[2] So what is driving this meteoric growth?

It's a combination of Argentina's young, Internet-savvy consumer base which is now being aided by President Mauricio Macri's increased openness to cross-border commerce. Argentina is not new to the e-commerce game. Latin American e-commerce giant MercadoLibre was founded in Buenos Aires in 1999 and now operates in 16 countries, with more than 174.2 million active users in Latin America.[3]

China is interested in Argentina, from natural resources to infrastructure to high value produce. In 2017, President Macri signed a Memorandum of Understanding with Alibaba Founder Jack Ma, agreeing to sell more Argentine wine and fresh foods to China through the Chinese e-commerce platform.[4] As a result of the agreement, Argentina declared Alibaba an official e-commerce channel, opening up opportunities for Argentine producers to market and sell their goods abroad.

The Chinese e-commerce titan is not the only online retailer entering the Argentine market. Government officials are beginning to confirm rumors that Amazon is looking to set up an office in Buenos Aires to start providing delivery services in Argentina. Former U.S.

Ambassador to Argentina, Noah Mamet, who is now an investor focused on growing Argentine businesses internationally, confirmed in October 2017 that Amazon is planning to open a 100-person office in Buenos Aires to run its Argentine operations. For now, Amazon is opening an administrative center to answer queries and prepare for its entry into Argentina.

However, to date, the most significant barrier holding Argentina back from becoming Latin America's e-commerce leader is logistics. Most logistics companies in Argentina cannot deliver as quickly and reliably as online retail requires. For example, Avenida.com, an Argentine e-commerce, was running its delivery operations by distributing most products to 11 pickup locations in Buenos Aires, where customers could gather their packages and interact directly with staff, thereby building trust. However, this system is not unique to Avenida. It adds a layer of inconvenience that is keeping some potential customers from buying online. Furthermore, online payments can be extremely challenging in Argentina, with global payment services like PayPal offering unfavorable exchange rates and limited services. MercadoLibre developed MercadoPago, which processes online payments much like PayPal, but with a Latin American focus.

The outlook for Argentine e-commerce is overwhelmingly positive. Internet penetration in Argentina was above 70% in 2017, and almost half the population has access to a smartphone.[5,6] E-commerce as a whole is expected to be used by 44.3% of the population by 2022, while 95% of the population is already at least familiar with MercadoLibre.[7,8] MercadoLibre generated US$262.3M just in Argentina in 2016 – almost a quarter of its total revenue that year. Overall, it has been estimated that up to 20 million people will be shopping online in Argentina by 2021, up from 16.8 million in 2017.

With President Macri prioritizing business growth and trade, and Argentina's well-connected population on board with e-commerce, Argentina is on track to maintain its status as an e-commerce giant in Latin America. Amazon, Alibaba, and MercadoLibre are now all vying for the attention of Argentina's growing online customer base. The next challenge is figuring out how to deliver products quickly and reliably in this large country.

Endnotes

1   *Business Insider.*https://www.businessinsider.com/argentina-will-be-an-e-commerce-leader-by-2019-2016-3

2   https://www.businessinsider.com/argentina-will-be-an-e-commerce-leader-by-2019-2016-3

3   *MercadoLibre.* http://investor.mercadolibre.com/static-files/b4f4df6f-2daa-40a6-8502-ef37308b260b

4   *The Street.* https://www.thestreet.com/story/14114731/1/alibaba-aims-to-bring-argentina-s-wine-and-produce-to-chinese-consumers.html

5   *Statista.* https://www.statista.com/statistics/209111/number-of-internet-users-per-100-inhabitants-in-argentina-since-2000/

6   https://www.statista.com/statistics/621034/smartphone-user-penetration-in-argentina/

7   https://www.statista.com/outlook/243/114/ecommerce/argentina#

8   https://www.statista.com/statistics/730712/mercadolibre-popularity-argentina/

Pierpaolo Barbieri: Banking the Unbanked in Argentina

P ierpaolo Barbieri, the founder of Ualá, is an Argentine entrepreneur who founded a neo-bank that uses prepaid debit cards and smartphones to allow people to deposit and spend money in Argentina. They have raised over US$44M from investors in the US like Goldman Sachs, Ribbit Capital, George Soros and have clients in every province of Argentina. Pierpaolo's goal with Ualá is to increase financial inclusion in his home country, where 70% of millennials prefer to visit the dentist rather than the bank. He wants to make banks redundant by offering more agile services to the Argentine middle class.

What is your goal with Ualá?

My goal is to become the largest issuer of cards in Argentina. This is a market where there are a lot of options for the top 2% of people, but over 50% of the population has never had access to a bank account before, and up to 15% have never had a banking credit line. Most credit cards and banks in Argentina require you to pay a lot of hidden fees, making them inaccessible for a lot of people. However, we live in a highly-educated country where 95% of people have phones and 82% of those are smartphones. That's why we created Ualá as the first fully-mobile, free, online card that is a global Mastercard that works anywhere in the world, and that can be managed completely from your phone.

What is the state of the financial industry in Argentina?

Currently, 75% of people in Argentina have some sort of card, but they don't use them. Many people just take all their money out of the bank at the beginning of each month. Now the regulations have changed because of the size of the unregulated informal economy and all businesses have to accept cards if they sell something over US$1-2. Cards have grown in popularity since then, but most cards aren't serving the market. There's very little availability of credit because up to 30% of the economy is undeclared right now. That's why we are developing a lending line, to offer credit where currently there are only loan sharks. We are also the only card that processes live transactions, so we are helping people learn to trust cards and financial institutions, which is challenging in Argentina.

What advice to you have for US investors or startups looking to do business in Latin America?

Latin America is about to take a giant leap forward in terms of innovation. There is a whole new generation of entrepreneurs coming of age in Latin America right now and they are going to bring significant change. There is still so much opportunity and so many markets where systems can be improved. Latin America has significant, and growing, purchasing power and great demographics. There is a lot to look at when you're thinking of investing in LatAm.

You can listen to our entire conversation on the *Crossing Borders* podcast on Itunes, Stitcher or wherever you get your podcasts, or on my blog:

http://www.nathanlustig.com/2018/05/29/ep-42-pierpaolo-barbieri-how-uala-is-increasing-financial-inclusion-in-argentina/

Lisa Besserman: From NYC to Buenos Aires

L isa Besserman is the founder and director of Startup Buenos Aires. Originally from New York, Lisa was on a traditional startup employee track when she decided she wanted to work remotely. She chose Buenos Aires for a two-month trial, but she fell in love with the city and the entrepreneurial culture. She quit her job to help develop Argentina's startup community and what started as a few entrepreneurs meeting up at a friend's house to talk about startup problems led to the creation of Startup Buenos Aires (SUBA). SUBA is an organization that represents the startup, tech, and entrepreneurial community in Buenos Aires, which has gotten buy-in from locals, expats and even the Argentine government.

How did you end up in Buenos Aires?

In 2012, I was working for a tech company in New York and reached the point where I wanted to escape the New York winter. I looked at a map for places in the Southern Hemisphere that would be warm and would be on a similar time zone to NYC, so I could be in touch with my team. That place turned out to be Buenos Aires. At the time, I spoke no Spanish, but I convinced my company to let me work remotely. I bought a ticket and set off for Argentina for 2-3 months. During that time, I realized there was a lack of support for startups and entrepreneurs in Buenos Aires, so I set out to build that community, and eventually decided to stay in Argentina to see that project through.

Did you have any culture shock when you first started working in Argentina?

My culture shock was more on the business side than on the personal side. Personally, I found Argentinians to be very warm and I had no trouble making friends. But when I started trying to build the community for Startup Buenos Aires, I was failing miserably. I sent out emails to many influencers in the industry to explain my idea and ask if they were interested, and I got zero responses. Eventually, I was told I had to try to build a relationship by meeting people for coffee or at an event before I could try to do business with them. Coming from New York, this way of doing business was a bit of a shock to me. Now I'm working on finding the sweet spot between US-style efficiency and the Latin American business style based on relationships.

What initiatives have helped Argentina develop an entrepreneurial ecosystem?

I think entrepreneurship is embedded in people's DNA in Argentina. These are some of the most resilient entrepreneurs I've ever met; despite the instability and lack of infrastructure, Argentina has more unicorns than any other Latin American country. What really tipped the needle on Argentinian entrepreneurship was the involvement of the government. When the administration changed and started realizing that entrepreneurship and human capital could turn Argentina into a global power, they really began to shape the ecosystem. That change made a big difference for us, as well as for other private actors in the ecosystem. Some of the programs they have created include IncuBAte, which is similar to Start-Up Chile, and BA Emprende, which is a free entrepreneurship education program. On the private side, NXTP Labs, Wayra, AreaTres, La Maquinita, and WeWork are also significant players.

What is next for SUBA and Argentina's startup ecosystem?

We will continue to evolve based on what the ecosystem needs. From the start, we developed our programs based on what entrepreneurs and investors in the ecosystem felt they were missing. We will shape ourselves to be the resource entrepreneurs in Buenos Aires need. Through that work, we want to help turn Argentina into a global outsourcing hub like India or China to change the perception about offshoring. We will also continue to work with the local government and other organizations to strengthen the Argentinian ecosystem over the coming years.

You can listen to our entire conversation on the *Crossing Borders* podcast on Itunes, Stitcher or wherever you get your podcasts, or on my blog:

http://www.nathanlustig.com/2018/06/05/ep-43-lisa-besserman-startup-buenos-aires-building-argentinas-startup-community/

VIII

Uruguay

The small country of Uruguay, wedged between its two much larger neighbors, Argentina and Brazil, is home to 3.4 million people and has been on the forefront of many innovative reforms. Uruguay ranks first in Latin America for democracy, peace, lack of corruption, e-government, press freedom, size of the middle class and prosperity.[1]

Despite its small size, Uruguay has a unique culture and interesting achievements that have inspired Uruguayans to believe that anything's possible. This attitude may be best epitomized by its national soccer team, which has won two World Cups, two Olympic gold medals, and 15 Copa Americas (more than any other South American country).

The Economist named Uruguay 'country of the year' in 2013 for, among many reasons, the country's dedication to personal rights and inclusion.[2] Uruguay has an innovative policy of legalizing the production, sale and consumption of cannabis, and first nation in the world to fully legalize the production and sale of marijuana for recreational use.

Same-sex marriage and abortion are also legal, leading Uruguay to be regarded as one of the most progressive nations in the world. Uruguay has a low crime rate and a high level of English speakers, making it a somewhat unknown but good place to do business.

Uruguay did endure a civil-military rule from 1973 – 1985, but nothing on the scale of its neighbor Argentina. In 1985, Uruguay became democratic again, and the country began to implement social reforms to better the lives of citizens. When Tabaré Vázquez came to power in

2004, he tripled foreign investment, reduced poverty and unemployment, and cut public debt from 79% of GDP to 60%.

Uruguay experienced one of the biggest economic and financial crises in its history around 2002, principally as a cascade effect from economic problems in the region. Inflation, which had been a mere 3.59% in 2001, hit 24% by 2002.[3] The economy contracted by 11%, and unemployment climbed to 21%. The Financial Times reported that Uruguay "will need a miracle similar to its World Cup victory in 1950 to survive" and quoted 100 to 1 odds that they'd get out of it.[4]

Despite this, Uruguay's financial indicators remained more stable than those of its neighbors, a reflection of its solid reputation among investors and its investment-grade sovereign bond rating, one of only two in South America.

After this crisis, the locally-owned banks are more well-capitalized and safe. In 2009, when most of the world's economy was suffering from the global recession, Uruguay posted economic gains and GDP increased 3%.[5,6] In 2009, Uruguayans elected José Mujica, who had spent 15 years in prison during military rule. During his term, the country legalized abortion, same-sex marriage, and the use of cannabis. Many people might recognize Uruguay because of former President José Mujica, often noted as "the world's humblest president," who would donate 90% of his $12,000 USD per month salary to organizations and persons in need.

In 2014, Tabaré Vázquez won the presidency once again. By 2017, inflation was stable around 6.5% and GDP grew by 2%. For startups and entrepreneurs, Uruguay may be small, but it's an interesting place to consider doing business more as a base to attack other markets, rather than in its small local market.

Advantages of Doing Business in Uruguay

Uruguay has a favorable legal system, welcomes foreign investment by individuals and does not discriminate against foreign investors.[7] Uruguay is also a popular place to invest in real estate because foreigners can buy, own, and sell property with the same rights and protections as a Uruguayan citizen. Roughly 130 U.S. firms operate here, and Uruguay provides tax exemptions to software companies that choose to export their products and services, one of the reasons why it's the largest software exporter in the region.[8]

Uruguay XXI promotes imports and exports with the goal of making Uruguay an investment destination. The National Agency for Investigation and Innovation, a state-run organization, hosts conferences and events for the startup community, as well as offers resources and support for entrepreneurs in Uruguay.

Many coworking spaces like Sinergia Cowork and daVinci are popping up. Mostly around Montevideo, they foster an active startup community. Ingenio, the first tech incubator in Uruguay, launched in 2007 and continues to grow.

With improvements to the ecosystem and help from the government, Uruguayan entrepreneurs have more incentives to start a business compared to 15 years ago. They're using this newfound support to produce global products and services. PedidosYa, founded in October 2009, expanded all over Latin America and was acquired by German giant Delivery Hero and is Uruguay's most well known startup.

Tryolabs, which has offices in Montevideo and San Francisco, helps startups and enterprises create natural language processing (NLP) and build AI-based products. The company decided to give back to the ecosystem by creating a scholarship program for Uruguayan students studying computer science.[9]

CityCop, a social GPS application for community watch, originated in Uruguay and has expanded all over Latin America to help individuals take part in curbing crime. Another GPS-startup from the region is GPSGay, the largest network for the LGBT community across Latin America, won a Seedstars competition. Sur3D, which helps retailers offer live custom product creation experiences.

Additionally, Uruguay has high level software engineers who can be hired at a relatively lower hourly rate compared to the US (US$30-$40 an hour). Along with the multitude of Uruguayan startups, many Argentine startups and companies end up based in Uruguay for its economic stability.

Disadvantages to Doing Business in Uruguay

Though it may seem as though this country is a top business climate, there are some drawbacks. The pace of doing business is slower and the market is smaller than the US or even other Latin America countries, which can cause some entrepreneurs frustration when working here. From ATMs running out of cash, to suppliers not showing up, foreigners and Uruguayans alike can have a hard time when trying to work efficiently in Uruguay.

Uruguay ranks 90th out of 190 in the World Bank's Ease of Doing Business Report, but ranks even lower on dealing with construction permits (163rd), registering property (110th), trading across borders (146th), paying taxes (113rd) and enforcing contracts (111th).[10]

Anyone planning on relocating to the region should be aware of the slower pace of doing business and a smaller market, especially compared to the United States. However, the government is putting incentives in place for entrepreneurship and making an effort to keep its anti-corruption, pro-business reputation, which has historically been ranked alongside Chile in the region.

Endnotes

1 *US Embassy, Montevideo.* https://photos.state.gov/libraries/uruguay/19452/pdfs/UruguaysRankingsJune2013.pdf

2 *The Economist.* https://www.economist.com/leaders/2013/12/18/earths-got-talent

3 *Britannica.* https://www.britannica.com/place/Uruguay-Year-In-Review-2002

4 *John B. Taylor.* https://web.stanford.edu/~johntayl/Onlinepaperscombinedbyyear/2007/The_2002_Uruguay_Financial_Crisis_Five_Years_Later.pdf

5 *International Living.* https://internationalliving.com/countries/uruguay/

6 Endeavor. https://endeavor.org/location/uruguay/

7 *US Department of State.* https://www.state.gov/e/eb/rls/othr/ics/2017/wha/270102.htm

8 *Neon Roots.* https://www.neonroots.com/articles/why-uruguay-is-the-tech-hub-for-startups

9 *Tryo Labs.* https://tryolabs.com/blog/2017/06/06/tryolabs-scholarship-for-uruguayan-cs-students/

10 *World Bank.* http://www.doingbusiness.org/data/exploreeconomies/uruguay

Patricio Williams Becú: Funding Latin America's Farmers

P atricio Williams Becú is the founder of DTA and PagoRural, an Argentine startup now based in Uruguay that offers structured debt vehicles to help farmers finance the investments they need to succeed. He left a stable finance job at the height of the financial crisis in 2009 to found PagoRural with only US$10K in his bank account. He went on to issue over US$20M in loans in the first four years, then raised capital from Silicon Valley and Europe. He has served over 15,000 farmers across Argentina, Paraguay, and Uruguay and financed US$120M in loans in from early 2016 to early 2017.

What does PagoRural do?

PagoRural is the first non-banking company to provide financing to farmers in Argentina, Uruguay, and Paraguay. I'm looking to expand to Brazil and probably the US. We want to disrupt the credit markets surrounding the agriculture industry. We do agricultural value chain finance and work alongside vendors like fertilizer companies and seed companies and help the farmers to finance their input purchases for up to a year. We have just launched a US$100M line of credit to fund more farmers in 2017 and hope to continue expanding in 2018.

Why do clients need your service?

We finance everyone from unbanked farmers to giant corporations. I often get asked if we give payments to people that don't have bank accounts. We do. We don't discriminate. We have a very wide variety of clients. We offer secure and agile lending, because our clients don't typically get financed by banks. A lot of them have to finance themselves, so there is a gap in the market where a lot of farmers could have more success if they just had more agile funding options.

Why did you decide to expand outside of Argentina and into Uruguay?

I think as an entrepreneur you always dream about going outside your borders. Our first step was to enter a market like Uruguay or Paraguay. We are still researching expansion to Brazil and the US, but those are big markets and we might have to raise more capital to get involved. Strategically, the US would also allow us to have a counter-season market, since our work is very cyclical in the Southern Hemisphere.

But I'm very humble about reaching foreign markets. It's easy to put a number in a Powerpoint but not very easy to actually act on that promise. We always make sure to keep our model as flexible as it needs to be so that it serves farmers no matter where we are.

What advice would you give to entrepreneurs that are just starting?

We have two ears and one mouth. We should always listen more than we speak. You should always be listening to your market and your clients rather than pushing your idea on them. The most successful companies are constantly learning from their clients.

What would you tell US investors about why they should invest in Latin America?

Latin America is full of good entrepreneurs who have faced every challenge. You have people "running with mud up to their knees" as we say in Latin America. If those entrepreneurs had the chance to work with money, with investors, and with mentors, they would have a chance of building a great business.

I also recently told one of the World Bank's main bankers that what we really need in Latin America is long-term commitment. The environment in Argentina and other parts of Latin America can be very volatile, and that's very different from the US and Europe. In the long-run, we need stability. We need investors who will be in it for the long run, who are willing to wait a little longer for the exit. It could even be more lucrative than in the US. I also think that Latin American entrepreneurs should be less afraid to go abroad to raise money, but should know it won't be easy.

You can listen to our entire conversation on the *Crossing Borders* podcast on Itunes, Stitcher or wherever you get your podcasts, or on my blog:

http://www.nathanlustig.com/2017/07/13/ep-10-patricio-williams-becu-investing-latin-america-funding-farmers/

IX

Peru

M any travelers visit Peru to experience Machu Picchu, and it is incredible, there is much more to this country than its wonder of the world. Known for its gastronomic sector, Peru has some of the most diverse (and delicious) food in the world. Peru is a great place to visit, if only to eat! It has a rich culinary history filled with seafood which later mixed with Spanish, Japanese and Chinese cuisine brought by immigrants, to create some of the best food in the world.

Peru has diverse terrain, from the steeply sloping Andes and dense jungles to the cerulean coastline. About one-third of Peruvian residents live near or close to the ocean. The population is just shy of 32 million, surpassing Chile but falling below Colombia. Monthly wages are on the upswing at 1680 Peruvian Sol (roughly US$519), with a minimum wage of 850 Peruvian Sol.[1]

The capital city, Lima, is experiencing rapid growth and the government is allocating investment towards more infrastructure and improving public transportation. Foreign investors are paying close attention to the new Cuzco airport which offers easier access to Machu Picchu.[2] Peru offers multiple visas for foreigners interested in the business sector, but these visas can come with a significant amount of red tape.

Peru is one of the founding countries of the Pacific Alliance, a free trade agreement between Chile, Peru, Colombia and Mexico. 80% of Peru's trade is through free trade agreements.[3] Despite open international policies and trade agreements, Peru struggles with corruption and an informal economy, although not to the level of Brazil, Venezuela or Argentina. Though there have been anti-corruption movements in the past, Peru still has to fight corruption in business and politics for it to reach its full potential.

Corruption aside, foreign investment and improvements in infrastructure have led to a major push for innovation. The Peruvian government has stepped it up by funding accelerators and incubators to ensure growth. StartUp Peru, supported by Peru's Ministry of Production, and based on Start-Up Chile, incubates new ideas that lead to job growth and international market expansion. The incubator hosts startup contests, offers financing, and connects participants to global entrepreneur networks.

Angel Ventures has an office in Peru and helps early-stage startups find resources and mentors to foster innovation in the country. The organization helps startups with financing, incubation, strategy, and access to the startup ecosystem around the world. Angel Ventures wants to empower high-impact entrepreneurs and help them scale business models that contribute to the sustainable development of Peru.

Wayra has been active in Peru. One of its graduates, Quantico, analyzes audiences on social platforms and provides insight to enhance campaigns. Quantico monitors social media and provides models and performance analytics to consumers. Its CEO Javier Albarracín is a leading entrepreneur in social media intelligence. Crehana, another Wayra alumnus, is an educational platform that allows subscribers to take as many classes as they'd like on the platform. With more than 95,000 users, its mission is to ensure that today's professionals have skills to prepare them for the digital age.

Peru's thriving food scene has been brought to life by world class chefs and new startups like Mesa 24/7, an online platform for restaurant reservations. Along with dining, the entertainment sector is quite popular, attracting both foreign businesses and investors. Cinepapaya, a movie ticket site, was acquired by Fandango. The acquisition expanded Fandango's reach in multiple Latin American countries.

Peru's startup ecosystem is a few years behind countries like Chile and Colombia, but is following in their paths and making improvements that may allow Peru to catch up much more quickly than some people think.

Thank you to Greg Mitchell from Angel Ventures Peru for contributing to this chapter.

Endnotes

1   *Trading Economics.* https://tradingeconomics.com/peru/wages
2   Efe. https://www.efe.com/efe/english/business/construction-of-new-cuz-co-airport-arouses-controversy/50000265-3169201
3   *UK Foreign Office.* https://www.gov.uk/government/publications/overseas-business-risk-peru--2/overseas-business-risk-peru

Pedro Neira: From Real Estate to Dating Apps

P edro Neira is the founder of Mi Media Manzana, the largest dating app in Peru and the most-downloaded dating app built in Latin America for a Latin American market. Before Mi Media Manzana, Pedro had founded three startups, one in Barcelona and two others in Peru. After the failure of his first Peruvian startup, Pedro and his co-founders built AdondeVivir.com, Peru's largest real estate portal, which was eventually acquired by Navent. Pedro didn't take a single day off between leaving AdondeVivir and starting Mi Media Manzana and the app has been growing ever since. Mi Media Manzana has over one million downloads in Latin America and recently received investment from Axon Capital Partners.

How would you describe the Latin American dating industry?

There is a lot of opportunity still in the online dating industry in Latin America. I have been working on Mi Media Manzana for four years, and when I started there were no other apps available in Latin America. The only service that was working here was Match.com, and that was a desktop-only service, which doesn't work well for the Latin American market. We actually started with a desktop version of our site, trying to be the Latin American version of eHarmony, but in 2014 it became clear we needed to switch to mobile. Now over 90% of our traffic is from mobile devices and 80% of those customers use Android. We were the first to go mobile in LatAm and that put us way ahead in terms of serving a Latin American audience that connects to the Internet on their smartphones.

What is it like to raise funding in Latin America vs. in the US?

I think the fundraising process in the two regions is basically the opposite. It was actually easier to raise in the US than in Peru. In the US, investors just wanted to see we had the idea, the traction, and the team, but some of them didn't even ask for our numbers. In Lima, there were hour-long meetings, with dozens of Excel spreadsheets, and partners wanted to hear they wouldn't lose all their money. I think it was valuable to learn to raise money in many different environments. For Mi Media Manzana, we have raised four rounds in Lima, Silicon Valley, South Korea, and New York. I always recommend that founders look for funding at home before heading abroad. Also, start growing your network long before you think you need funding. Once you need the money, it's too late to start networking with US VCs.

What is the future of the Latin American and Peruvian startup ecosystems?

I think Latin America is the next region of the world that is set to grow like crazy. First the US went through its revolution, then Asia, and now it's Latin America's turn. In Peru, there was no ecosystem even just five to eight years ago when I came back from Barcelona. Then Wayra arrived in the country and a lot of people applied and that was really an inflection point for us. Startup Peru has also really supported entrepreneurship. At this point, what we are missing is a few more success stories. With five to ten exits, international investors will start paying attention to Peru. Right now, we just have Cinepapaya, but we need a few more to gain a spot in the conversation. We also need access to Series A level funding in Peru to help scale the current startups. I think overall Latin America will be the most interesting regional market over the next five to ten years.

You can listen to our entire conversation on the *Crossing Borders* podcast on Itunes, Stitcher or wherever you get your podcasts, or on my blog:

https://www.nathanlustig.com/2018/06/26/ep-46-pedro-neira-innovating-for-the-latin-american-dating-industry/

Greg Mitchell: Helping Build The Peruvian Startup Ecosystem

G reg Mitchell moved to Peru seven years ago, leaving a New York finance job to begin managing investments for Angel Ventures in Peru. Having lived and worked in the Dominican Republic as a Peace Corps volunteer, Greg had been looking for the right opportunity to get involved in the Latin American startup ecosystem and make an impact on that community. Angel Ventures is actively investing in high-impact, scalable startups in Peru and helping them reach larger markets in Mexico and the US to continue growing.

What do you do in Peru with Angel Ventures?

I lead the Lima office of Angel Ventures, an early-stage investment firm in the region. Part of my job is sourcing and business development for the Angel Ventures regional fund. However, most of my time is on the ground in Peru, cultivating a network of angel investors. Part of our model at Angel Ventures is to work with local angel investors and filling a role in the ecosystem development by connecting those investors to the best entrepreneurs in Peru and across the region.

Angel Ventures was started in 2008 by two MIT Sloan grads. They started building a network with angel investors in Mexico, then used their track record and execution to raise a US$20M venture capital fund that has been primarily invested in Mexico-based or regional startups. There are multiple gaps in the Latin American funding environment, so we try to fill the post-acceleration, angel, seed, and Pre-Series A spaces.

How would you describe investing in Peru?

We are currently the oldest angel network in Peru, of the five that exist there now. It has taken some time, but in the six years I've been in Peru, it seems like now is the critical time for angel investing to happen here. One thing we talk about as entrepreneurs is that timing is a critical factor, and this seems like the perfect time to build an angel investor network, right as the ecosystem is building up.

How do you get Peruvians to invest in startups?

We try to open their eyes to how great the entrepreneurs in Peru are. Most investors came in with the idea that the ecosystem was less developed than they thought and they considered they were doing a service to the community by sitting down with college kids to mentor them as they built their businesses. That dynamic has really changed. Endeavor, a global startup support network, is now active in Peru. The Peruvian government has been providing access to capital through

Startup Peru. There are now very high-quality entrepreneurs that are starting to attract VC capital from outside Peru and that's validation for the angel investors here. When local angel investors start seeing that, they realize they are a little bit behind and there is an opportunity for them to invest before a VC round and increase their returns.

What do you see as the future of Peru's startup ecosystem?

I think it is going to receive more venture capital. From 2011 to 2015, there was no committed capital directed at Peru. There are now great opportunities, with many entrepreneurs and very little capital chasing after them. One thing I also expect to see happen is for regional startups to start entering Peru. While large startups present in the region are here, like Cabify, Uber, and MercadoLibre, I want to see startups from Mexico, Argentina, and Chile entering the Peruvian market, even if it is after they go to the US. This dynamic is a really important part of attracting VC to Lima. Lima is a big city of ten million people that is filled with traditional, inefficient industries. It is a perfect place to test ideas and validate products.

You can listen to our entire conversation on the *Crossing Borders* podcast on Itunes, Stitcher or wherever you get your podcasts, or on my blog:

http://www.nathanlustig.com/2017/08/28/ep-22-greg-mitchell-funding-startup-business-in-peru-and-regionally-in-latin-america/

X

Ecuador

Ecuador is a geographically small Andean country rich in history and home to 16.1 million people, making it nearly the same size as Chile by population. The capital city, Quito, is officially recognized as a World Heritage Site by the United Nations. In recent years, Ecuador has transformed into a more stable place to do business with one of the best-performing economies in Latin America.

With relatively easy access to the US, many companies are coming to Ecuador to take advantage of its excellent trade routes, sometimes friendly trade agreements, and dynamic workforce. The minimum wage rose to US$375 per month in 2017, ranking as one of the highest in South America.[1] Ecuador's close proximity to bordering countries Colombia and Peru make it a prime location for trade and a source for cheaper materials. Like Chile, Ecuador is a smaller country compared to neighbors like Peru and Colombia.

In 2000, the dollar was named the national currency of Ecuador, which helped to usher in this new wave of stability for the country after years of economic downturn and 60% inflation.[2] After Ecuador retired the "sucre" after 119 years, the dollarization eased transactions and slowly opened the doors to more foreign investment. Oil prices are extremely important to the economy After Ecuador was dollarized, the economy had more stability, but could lead to problems when the dollar is strong and Ecuador may want its exports to benefit from a weaker dollar.[3]

As of 2018, Ecuador's corporate tax rate is 22%.[4] This was reduced from 25% in 2011 as a way to promote more investment in Ecuador. This rate can also be lowered ten percentage points more when companies reinvest their profits. In addition, there is an exemption from income tax for five years when an investment is made in the following sectors: food production, forestry, metal, petrochemical, pharmaceuticals, tourism, renewable resources, logistics in foreign trade, biotechnology, and software. These tax structures have made it easier for entrepreneurs and investors to do business in the country.

Ecuador, with a GDP of $183B, has a petroleum based economy which accounts for 40% of the country's wealth.[5] Additionally, it's a major exporter of crops like coffee, cut flowers, shrimp, fruit and palm oil. The tax, legal, and regulatory environment can be difficult to navigate without a local expert. The World Bank and IFC rank Ecuador 114th for ease of doing business, which is quite low.[6] The process of starting a business can take one month on average, and construction permits can take over 128 days to obtain.[7]

Compared to its close neighbors, Ecuador's startup scene has been slow to take off, but it's starting to pick up. QuitoTech, which started in 2013, is a coworking/incubator space that is paving the way for dozens of other private initiatives.

From Edtech to medical companies, Ecuador is experiencing a new influx of innovative companies. One example is Cuestionarix, an online platform designed to help students prepare for exams by providing interactive tools to help them study. Another, Siplik, is changing the way patients communicate with medical professionals, offering a platform that makes it easy to do consultations and receive results online. And YaEstá is one of the largest e-commerce platforms to come out of Ecuador.

Ernesto Kruger established Kruger Corporation in 1993, with the goal of promoting innovation and leadership in Ecuador. Kruger is a serial entrepreneur and after his company IPO'd in Spain, he decided to give back to the Ecuadorian startup community by creating Kruger Labs, an accelerator founded in 2013. Kruger Labs, based in Quito, specializes in digital startups and offers perks like mentoring, public relations, and legal assistance for local companies.

Ecuador can be a viable option for those looking to invest in or start a business. Over the past few years, there has been a lot of talk about Yachay, a planned city for technological innovation and knowledge-intensive businesses that will help push Ecuador from a commodity-based economy to a knowledge-based one.[8]

As of 2017, Ecuador's new government does not share the same vision for Yachay, so it remains to be seen if the city is ever to be fully completed.[9] Though less developed than its neighbors, as Ecuador begins implementing initiatives to try to turn the country into a hub for high-tech innovation many are starting to explore doing more business in Ecuador.

Endnotes

1   *El Telegrafo.* **https://www.eltelegrafo.com.ec/**
2   *ABC News.* **https://abcnews.go.com/International/ story?id=82666&page=1**
3   *World Atlas.* **https://www.worldatlas.com/articles/the-economy-of-ec-uador.html**
4   *Kreston International.* **https://kreston.com/wp-content/uploads/2017/06/ Doing-Business-in-Ecuador-June-2017-26-june-17.pdf**
5   *Quito.com.* **https://www.quito.com/v/economy/**
6   *Trading Economics.* **https://tradingeconomics.com/ecuador/ease-of-doing-business**
7   *TMF Group.* **https://www.tmf-group.com/en/news-insights/business-cul-ture/top-challenges-ecuador/**
8   *CNET.* **https://www.cnet.com/news/plotting-the-next-silicon-valley-youll-never-guess-where/**
9   *Science Mag.* **https://www.sciencemag.org/news/2017/07/plans-re-search-powerhouse-andes-begin-unravel**

Alejandro Freund: Delivering E-commerce in Ecuador

A lejandro Freund is an Ecuadorian entrepreneur who is the co-founder of YaEsta.com, the leading e-commerce business in Ecuador. Alejandro came back to Ecuador to start his business after studying abroad in Argentina, Italy, and the US. He went on to raise US$2.5M from angel investors and venture capitalists in Latin America and the US and beat out many traditional retailers in the Ecuadorian e-commerce market.

How did you break into the Ecuadorian e-commerce market?

When we got here with my co-founder (who also did his Masters in Europe), we started asking people how they do their shopping and found out nobody was buying online locally. They would buy something on Amazon and pick it up when they went to the States. That was our first trigger. I had been buying online in Argentina since 2004, yet here

I was in 2012 and e-commerce was unavailable in Ecuador. We had to start at zero and create the market ourselves.

We raised US$50K in angel investment, picked up an experienced Board of Directors, and launched a platform by February 2014, with three suppliers and 21 products. It was just me and my co-founder, so we had to do the delivery logistics ourselves. The first product we ever sold was a case of craft beer.

How did you grow to become a leader in the market?

We didn't have a marketing budget to start out with, so we started attending small artisan fairs to convince merchants to place their products on our site. We actually gave them their own link, so they could drive direct traffic to their product on our site. We basically used our whole first year as a trial and error period.

Since then, we have grown significantly. The first year, we closed with US$50K in sales and had a catalogue of 1,000 products from 50 suppliers. We had delivered to 15 out of 24 of Ecuador's provinces, including the Galapagos Islands. In 2015, we raised almost US$500K in venture funding and went on to sell about US$250K that year. That was our validation. It showed that people were willing to buy online if you had good prices and a variety of options. In 2016, we created a C Corp in the US (now the parent company of the Ecuadorian branch), raised US$1M and updated our platform to the latest software. We closed the year with almost US$1M in transactions, 30,000 products, and over 300 suppliers. We expect to surpass US$10M in sales by 2020.

Why are big retailers in Ecuador so far behind on e-commerce?

The big regional players that have dominated other markets have struggled in Ecuador. Local retailers tend to have an oligopoly that is lowering competition and deters other players from entering. These retailers are inflexible and unwilling to invest significant resource to make e-commerce work. I believe they are not willing to sacrifice margins and their bottom line to go into an industry that doesn't make sense for them in the short-term. Also politically, Ecuador has not been an attractive market for investors, since we had the same president for ten years with a socialist agenda that has not been very investor-friendly. That has created a buffer, which allowed us to consolidate before any other player could get in.

What advice would you give to US investors looking at Latin America?

The margins are much better here. The competition is different than in the States, which is a very mature and consolidated market. You have a lot of opportunities, but in very select, niche areas. Building another Spotify or Amazon at this point is impossible.

There is enormous potential to scale regionally in Latin America. We speak one language from Mexico to Argentina, making a very large market of 400M+ people with huge opportunities to solve problems for them. Part of the struggle to scale here has been due to the lack of funding. There are seed funds, but it can be near impossible to raise a Series A or further. There is a big opportunity to do follow-on investment in Latin America in more mature companies.

You can listen to our entire conversation on the *Crossing Borders* podcast on Itunes, Stitcher or wherever you get your podcasts, or on my blog:

http://www.nathanlustig.com/2017/07/18/ep-11-alejandro-freund-pioneering-ecommerce-latin-america/

XI

Venezuela

V enezuela has made headlines for all the wrong reasons. Whether it's hyperinflation, lack of food, or the plummeting economy, theformer Latin American powerhouse's situation is dire.[1] As of 2017, Venezuela was home to 31M people, with the highest concentration in Caracas, the capital. A reported 3.5 million Venezuelans have fled, with 90% coming in the past 15 years as the economy has worsened.[2]

In the past, Venezuela was a shining example of established democracy in South America, but due to political unrest, the economy has taken a turn for the worse. The inflation rate, which might be as high as 1,000,000% annually in 2018, has led to insurmountable shortages of basic goods, and turmoil for citizens.[3] It's to the point where some restaurants ask you to pay your bill when you order your meal, because people might dine and dash and prices will be higher after dinner. The average wage for those lucky enough to have a job is US$11 month as of 2018, of which only US$5 is actual cash.[4] The remaining $6 balance is a food allowance, which makes it nearly impossible to survive.

You can find entrepreneurial, talented Venezuelans on Upwork and other platforms who are working for foreign companies and earning money in dollars just to have enough money to survive. Others have turned to mining Bitcoin using subsidized electricity, but the government has quickly tried to shut down any independent miners.[5] Many of the most talented Venezuelans have left the country. I've run into medical doctors driving Uber in Houston, Santiago and Miami, lawyers and engineers running property companies in Chile and extremely talented people working across all professions all around the world.

Venezuela has the world's largest supply of crude oil and nearly half of government income comes from oil export, but inefficiency and corruption block much of its supply from reaching international markets. It takes an average of 230 days to open a business in Venezuela (unless you bribe someone), compared to the average 31.6 days for the rest of Latin American and the Caribbean.[6] I wouldn't advise doing business in Venezuela at this time.

Many fear that the Venezuelan economy cannot bounce back. However, there is a strong sense of pride among Venezuelans, despite an ongoing political nightmare with lack of access to things to meet their basic needs, leading to the "Venezuelan Diet," a derisive term based on statistics that shows that the average person has lost 19 pounds during 2017 and 33% miss at least one meal per day.[7] Venezuela's rise and fall is a nearly fully self-inflicted wound: reliance of high oil prices to meet government spending, massive corruption, hyperinflation and politicians who care more about staying in power than actually helping their citizens.

Some entrepreneurs are powering through and speaking out about surviving. In a time of uncertainty and volatility, operating a business can be extremely difficult, but it is not impossible. Others have made the decision to leave Venezuela, moving to places like Colombia, Chile, Argentina, Brazil, Mexico and the US.

Tech startups continue to push forward, especially working on companies that help people operate in Venezuela's dire circumstances. A startup called Frigo provides a solution to limited goods. Frigo is a recipe app where consumers can manage shopping lists and receive curated recipes based on the contents of their kitchen. Users can keep track of their groceries, along with their expiration dates.

In some cases, entrepreneurs have audiences in Venezuela and beyond, making it easy to continue international business. SinCola is headquartered in Cumaná, Venezuela and has offices in Chile, Puerto Rico, Peru, Mexico, Guatemala and Costa Rica. The company uses a cloud-based platform to help streamline queues and create an efficient customer experience for people that need to wait in line. An application like this comes in handy for Venezuelans in a time when resources are rationed and interactions with the government are tense. The startup continues to operate within Venezuela and in other Latin American countries.

Venezuela still has a few accelerator programs, though most programs are on pause. Wayra is a program that has helped over 45 startups in Venezuela get off the ground, 35 of which are still in business as of 2018, including Pleiq, a Magma Partners portfolio company whose founders immigrated to Chile to continue to run their business.[8] Bitpagos, now Ripio, a Bitcoin credit card provider, operates with many Venezuelan clients. Cryptocurrency usage is high and many Venezuelan developers are on the cutting edge of Blockchain projects.

As Venezuela works through political unrest and poor allocation of resources, there is no telling what the next ten years may hold, or even the next few months. Business owners are bracing themselves and locals are taking to the streets to fight back. Venezuelans will continue to innovate and create opportunities in the tech world, even through the toughest of times, but most of this innovation will likely take place outside of Venezuela.

Endnotes

1 *Business Insider.* https://www.businessinsider.com/venezuela-was-latin-americas-richest-country-heres-how-it-fell-apart-2017-7

2 *International Journalists Network.* https://ijnet.org/en/blog/venezuela-less-freedoms-more-journalism

3 *CIA.* https://www.cia.gov/library/publications/the-world-factbook/geos/ve.html

4 *Notilogia.* http://www.notilogia.com/2017/09/aumento-sueldo-minimo-venezuela.html

5 *CNBC.* https://www.cnbc.com/2017/08/30/venezuela-is-one-of-the-worlds-most-dangerous-places-to-mine-bitcoin.html

6 *World Bank.* https://data.worldbank.org/indicator/IC.REG.DURS?locations=VE

7 *Vox.* https://www.vox.com/world/2017/2/22/14688194/venezuela-crisis-study-food-shortage

8 *Reuters.* https://www.reuters.com/article/us-venezuela-politics-startups/the-venezuelan-factor-entrepreneurs-adapt-to-nation-in-crisis-idUSKBN-19R0DJ

PleIQ: Leaving Venezuela
to Build PleIQ

E dison Duran, Nastassja Palmiotto, Alejandro Perez, Ilan Duran, and Antonio De Rocha founded PleIQ after meeting at a Wayra Accelerator event in Caracas in 2014. After realizing their experiences and skills were well-complemented to build a business together, they developed PleIQ, a smart toy for early childhood that uses augmented reality to create educational experiences for children. They eventually had to leave Venezuela to find a stable place to build their business and were accepted into the 14th Generation of Start-Up Chile. PleIQ won first place at Demo Day and began to build out the business from Chile, while leaving part of the team in Venezuela.

What is it like to do business in Venezuela?

Despite being one of the wealthiest countries in the world in terms of natural resources, Venezuela also has one of the highest levels of poverty. An internet plan there reaches just 2 Mbs/second. There is almost no venture capital or funding available. The minimum wage is about US$9 a month. With triple digit inflation, you can only imagine how hard it is to innovate in any area of society, especially in technology.

We fell in love with an idea, that augmented reality (AR) could enrich the human experience, and that was the mission that always motivated us. We started Venezuela's only AR startup without any experience having built apps or used augmented reality. We applied to Wayra and were rejected, then we got in and reached break-even in four months. Within ten months, we had twelve corporate clients and we had validated the idea. Nonetheless, we eventually realized we would have to leave the country to get the resources we needed to get off the ground.

What was the inflection point for PleIQ as a sustainable business?

For us, it was crucial to be selected for Start-Up Chile in 2015 and to win first place in the Demo Day. Not only did the seed capital allow us to dedicate ourselves 100% to the business, but it also allowed us to get onto the radar of angel investors and raise our first round. That capital helped us start producing our products at scale to become the first smart toy to be exported from Chile.

What has your growth looked like since you reached Chile?

PleIQ is a smart toy for three to eight year olds, the first of its kind of be 100% produced in Chile. It includes eight physical blocks that can be used to create 48 AR experiences on your smartphone when you use the Pleiq app, which tracks children's educational progress. In August 2017, we were accepted as international members of the North

American Toy Association, which allowed us to exhibit PleIQ at the International Toy Fair in New York in February 2018. Schools in Chile, Argentina, Ecuador, and Mexico have implemented PleIQ in classrooms. We expect to reach thousands of children in 2018.

Why did you launch in Chile?

Chile is the highest-ranking Latin American country in terms of education and is a place where education is constantly on the public radar. It is also a country where children tend to spend few hours playing during childhood. That combination seemed perfect for a launch pad for an innovative, educational toy. Furthermore, Chile today is the center of innovation in Latin America. The institutional stability, the state support of entrepreneurship, the presence of venture capital, and the dynamic startup ecosystem make Chile an ideal country for startups.

Having started in one of the worst places in the world to start a business, being selected for Start-Up Chile was a lifesaver. It allowed us to prototype and validate our product, and then reach the capital we needed to scale, including CORFO, DADNEO, Magma Partners, and Chile Global Angels.

Andres Moreno, Open English: Latin America's English-Learning Powerhouse

Not all global startups were founded in a Silicon Valley garage. OpenEnglish, an online platform for teaching English with over 500,000 students in 40 countries, started in a student apartment in Caracas, Venezuela in 2007. What Andres Moreno had begun as English classes for Fortune 500 companies' Latin American offices was brought online so that it could reach a wider audience. Andres is the CEO of OpenEducation, the parent company of OpenEnglish, Next U, and OpenEnglish Jr. and has raised over US$125M in venture capital from investors in the US and Latin America.

How did you start OpenEnglish?

My dad was a diplomat, so I grew up traveling all over the world and quickly realized that speaking English could get you almost anywhere. After graduating from university, I decided to start a business bringing Ivy League graduates to teach English at the Latin American offices of Fortune 500 companies. That business would not ever have scaled because of the cost of flying people around, so one day, in our student apartment in Caracas, we decided to bring the business online. In 2007, the internet in Latin America had just gotten stable enough to build such a platform, so we started connecting Latin Americans to native English speakers who could teach them English.

How did you raise funding for a Latin American startup based in Venezuela?

In 2007, an English-teaching startup in Venezuela was far from any angel investor's mind, either in Latin America or the US. But I realized that it would be almost impossible to raise money in Latin America; I tried very hard but we never got anywhere. So I moved to Silicon Valley and slept on a friend's couch for a year, meeting with dozens of investors until eventually we were able to raise a few million. I still think it is hard to raise money in Latin America, although we have managed to raise with Latin American firms as well. The capital is here, but the culture of investing in early-stage, risky ventures, is still missing. We first had to go to the US where that culture is more understood.

What tips do you have for Latin American entrepreneurs looking to raise capital in the US?

Make sure your idea can scale across borders. Unless you are in Brazil, your idea will need to have regional impact to capture the attention of VCs in the US, because that's the only way the market will be big enough. Also make sure you have a good understanding of your unit economics, customer churn, lifetime value, etc., so you can leverage your location. Keep your overhead low; it is easy to find affordable talent and office space in Latin America so don't waste capital. It will always take longer than you think to get to where you want to be.

You can listen to our entire conversation on the *Crossing Borders* podcast on Itunes, Stitcher or wherever you get your podcasts, or on my blog:

http://www.nathanlustig.com/2018/09/11/ep-54-andres-moreno-helping-latin-america-learn-english-through-openenglish/

XII

Paraguay

The landlocked country of Paraguay flies below the radar for many entrepreneurs and travelers alike. Home to 6.7 million people, Paraguay has a GDP of $29.73B as of 2017, representing ~0.4% of the world economy. Minimum wage is 1,964,507 Guaranies per month, which comes out to roughly US$353. Paraguay is a major producer of hydroelectricity, and the Itaipú dam, the world's largest generator of renewable energy, is on the Paraná river. Paraguay had the highest economic growth in South America from 1970 – 2013, averaging 7.2% per year, albeit from a low base.[1] Paraguay has a moderate inflation rate of 5% on average and international reserves of 20% of GDP, twice the amount of the external national debt.[2]

Paraguay is the second-largest producer of both stevia and tung oil in the world, and the sixth-largest producer of soybeans and corn. While unemployment remains low at roughly 4.9%, studies estimate that 30-40% of the population is poor, and in rural areas, 41.2% of the population lacks the monthly income to cover basic necessities.[3]

For investors and entrepreneurs, there are distinct advantages to doing business in Paraguay. By 2015, there were as many cell phones in the country as there were Paraguayans, partly because of poorly run fixed-line telecommunications services. For investors, the agriculture climate is ripe for high returns.

Foreign investors have the same guarantees, rights, and obligations as Paraguayan investors. Unlike neighbors Argentina and

Brazil, Paraguay allows free flow of capital both into and out of the country. The only difference between local and foreign investment is that foreign investments are subject to 5% additional tax and a 15% tax on international remittances to nonresidents. You must be a Paraguay resident to manage a Paraguayan company or serve on a board of directors. Entrepreneurs can comply with this restriction by finding a local partner.

There are also drawbacks to those wanting to do business in Paraguay. According to the *World Bank Doing Business Report*, Paraguay ranks 143 for Starting a Business, 153 for Paying Taxes, and 116 for Trading Across Borders (all out of 190).[4] Corruption and lack of transparency hinder the possibility of becoming more competitive on a global scale. Workers' rights, child labor, and women's rights issues are problems as well.

On the entrepreneurial side, Paraguay is growing. According to Angel.co, there are only 29 companies in Paraguay and our portfolio company Founderlist doesn't show many more either...the ecosystem is just really getting started. Co-working spaces such as Welco and Loffice help unite the entrepreneurial community and Koga Labs helps social entrepreneurs. Startups like Argentina's PagoRural operate in Paraguay's agtech sector. The Landfill Harmonic, a program to teach disadvantaged Paraguayan kids how to play musical instruments, is one of the coolest social projects I've seen during my time in Latin America. Google their appearance on 60 Minutes or check YouTube for some inspiration.

Roughly 70% of the population is under 35 years old, creating strong entrepreneurial potential. Jóvenes Empresarios del Paraguay (Young Entrepreneurs of Paraguay), which helps entrepreneurs between the ages of 18 and 40, has 120 partners and remains dedicated to the sustainable development of Paraguay through strengthening young entrepreneurs, fostering business opportunities, and providing necessary services. Fundación Paraguaya, a sustainable

NGO, spearheads micro-finance and entrepreneurship in Paraguay and offers entrepreneurial guidance for startups.

Local startups are seeing success. Guaranglish is a language-learning app that helps Paraguayans learn English and foreigners learn Guarani, a local indigenous language. The Paraguayans who created the app wanted to ensure the local language would be understood by future generations. Another company, UnoWifi, leverages free Wifi hotspots to give demographic information about customers, allowing companies to run targeted marketing campaigns. The startup operates in Paraguay and Uruguay and is now looking for international expansion.

There are some practical startups helping to bring Paraguay into the digital world. For instance, Movilpy is an online directory of all businesses related to automobiles, motorcycles and the motor world in Paraguay. Juhu lists all events around the country for movies, arts, and more. Paraguay En Tu Mano serves as the "Yelp" across the country, where businesses can register, and users can find restaurants and events nearby. TAXit! is an app that helps Paraguayans manage taxes.

Paraguay has one of the least-developed ecosystems in Latin America and it's likely one of the harder places to do business when compared to Chile, Colombia or Uruguay. It's ripe with opportunities, but entrepreneurs should remain aware of the high amount of bribery and corruption they may run across. Those in the Agtech fields should consider Paraguay for its high ROI opportunities but should also consider working with a local partner in the area. Since the population is so young, expect to see more startup movement and a growing ecosystem in Paraguay in the coming years.

Endnotes

1   *Wikipedia.* https://en.wikipedia.org/wiki/Paraguay#Economy

2   Ibid

3   IBid

4   *World Bank.* http://www.doingbusiness.org/data/exploreeconomies/paraguay

Paulo Duarte: Paraguay Superfoods Company Broterra

P aulo Duarte is a Paraguayan entrepreneur who is the founder of Broterra, a superfood company that supplies many multinational companies in Paraguay with sesame and chia seeds. Broterra grew from six points-of-sale to 25,000 during their first year after creating a strategic partnership with a dairy company. Paulo has now decided to create Paraguay's first sustainable superfood cereal bar that he hopes to export to the United States and sell in his home country to create a value-added export economy in Paraguay.

Why develop the superfood market in Paraguay?

My family owns land in one of the poorest areas of Paraguay, and we realized that there was a need to help farmers reach a larger market for their products. Broterra provides farmers with higher prices for their goods and a market for their products. We started testing this opportunity on our own by planting chia seeds on our land in 2013 when they were still an unknown product in the US and in Paraguay and we started exporting to the US in 2014. The business of superfoods is growing very quickly around the world. We saw chia, sesame, and amaranth seeds as an opportunity to build a brand that adds value to the simple raw material that we export. Paraguay's economy is made of 95% raw materials for export, and we need to head toward adding more value to our products.

What is the entrepreneurial ecosystem like in Paraguay?

Paraguay is a stable country that is one of the largest electricity exporters in the world. Until recently, we didn't have much of an entrepreneurial ecosystem to speak of. However, we have a young labor force, and the government is beginning to invest in turning Asunción into a startup hub. There is still a lot of bureaucracy for startups to deal with in Paraguay, so it is hard to be an entrepreneur here. Our ecosystem lags behind the region, but it is growing quickly. We have the Agora Accelerator starting to make an impact on the tech ecosystem, but we have a long way to go. The real advantage of Paraguay is that we have very low corporate taxes, which is very attractive for starting a business. As we are seeing more success stories in Paraguay, young entrepreneurs are becoming inspired and motivated to build businesses here.

Where is the Paraguayan startup ecosystem headed?

As one of our finance ministers recently said, Paraguay is condemned to be a successful country. I think Paraguay could become the next Colombia, because we are starting to share our products on the global market and we are being recognized for those products. Our products are starting to have dominance in our local market, when just a few years ago the only things available in supermarkets were imported products from the US or Europe. I think next we will see Paraguayan products competing in the US and European markets and being sold at Whole Foods or Target. Over the next few years, Paraguay will continue opening itself to the world and I think our entrepreneurial ecosystem will flourish.

You can listen to our entire conversation on the *Crossing Borders* podcast on Itunes, Stitcher or wherever you get your podcasts, or on my blog:

https://www.nathanlustig.com/2018/07/02/ep-47-paulo-duarte-broterra-a-paraguayan-superfoods-company/

XIII

Costa Rica

C osta Rica, literally "Rich Coast" in Spanish, is a fitting name for a country with diverse geography ranging from tropical rainforests to vast oceanscapes. Five million people call Costa Rica home, and the official language is Spanish. Costa Rica's GDP is US$74.9 billion with 72% attributed to exports like coffee, sugar, and fruit.[1] The average wage for Costa Ricans is about CRC654,059 (Costa Rican Colón) or US$1,150 per month.[2]

Costa Rica is a prime location for entrepreneurs because of its proximity to the United States and its many free trade agreements. Its largest foreign investments come from the United States, which led to a 2016 trade surplus of US$1.6 billion between Costa Rica and the US.[3]

In the 2010s, large tech companies like Amazon invested in the Costa Rican market.[4] Ticos, as Costa Ricans are known locally, have one of the highest literacy rates in the region at 97.8%.[5] The country has made education a top priority, and English is common among the young population.

Economically, the inflation rate remains low (0.8%), and the relative economic stability is a major plus for investors.[6] Despite Costa Rica's impressive renewable energy consumption of 98.1% of total energy generated, Costa Rica could use upgrades to both its water and transportation systems.[7] And according to the World Bank, it takes an average of 852 days to settle a claim, which leads some to say Costa Rica may require justice system reform.[8] Compared to the Latin America and Caribbean average of 749 days, it's slightly longer, but is extremely long compared to 370 in the US and 480 in Chile.

As opportunities are increasing, accelerators and coworking spaces are sprouting up to encourage entrepreneurs to get into business. For example, venture capital firm Carao Ventures invests in innovative startups and provides resources for entrepreneurs, helping them build their businesses. As partners of key networks, like EY Central America and Xcala, Carao Ventures has reviewed over 2,000 applications with some successful investments. Auge began in 2015 with a mission to incubate ideas sustainably with financial resources provided by companies like Coopetarrazu. It works with university students and entrepreneurs to help develop and grow successful ideas through collaboration, community, and partnerships in Costa Rica.

Located in Costa Rica's Capital of San Jose, Creasala is a coworking space and cafe designed to connect business professionals, students, and entrepreneurs in a creative environment. Slidebean, a Start-Up Chile graduate that helps teams create engaging and interactive presentations, is based in San Jose. It was backed by Carao Ventures, Magma Partners, Firstrock Capital and others after graduating Start-Up Chile. Gopato, another Carao Ventures company, operates through Facebook Messenger, taking orders from customers and delivering products on-demand. Gopato works with restaurants, stores, pharmacies and more to deliver consumers products via online ordering. Founders José Navarro and Leonel Peralta came up with the courier service in 2015, and by 2017, they have received US$550,000 in funding to connect messengers with consumers.[9]

It's relatively simple to set up an online business for sports betting or high stakes poker in Costa Rica. And it is completely legal, which has attracted tech and business talent. Currently, there are approximately 200 online gambling businesses in the country and that number continues to rise as the expat gambling community grows.[10] In addition to the eco-friendly movement, Costa Rica is going through a major surge in tech, attracting startups and international corporations. Companies like Amazon and Microsoft have set down roots in the country and more are likely to open offices in the future. With its stable economy, proximity to the US, wealth of diverse resources, and vibrant culture, Costa Rica is Central America's prime place to do business.

Endnotes

1   *Heritage.* https://www.heritage.org/index/country/costarica

2   *Trading Economics.* https://tradingeconomics.com/costa-rica/minimum-wages

3   *Export.gov.* https://www.export.gov/article?id=Costa-Rica-market-overview

04   *Seattle Times.* https://www.seattletimes.com/business/amazon/amazon-invests-in-costa-rica-as-it-carves-itself-a-profitable-niche-in-the-world-economy/

5   *CIA.* https://www.cia.gov/library/publications/the-world-factbook/fields/print_2103.html

6   https://www.heritage.org/index/country/costarica

7   *World Economic Forum.* https://www.weforum.org/agenda/2017/04/costa-rica-ran-entirely-on-renewable-energy-for-more-than-250-days-last-year/

8   *World Bank.* http://www.doingbusiness.org/data/exploreeconomies/costa-rica

9   *FINSMEs.* http://www.finsmes.com/2017/01/gopato-raises-550k-in-first-funding.html

10   *GBO International Services.* https://www.gbo-intl.com/costa-rica-gambling-license/

Jose "Caya" Cayasso: Making Presentation Design Easy from Costa Rica and New York City

Jose "Caya" Cayasso is a Costa Rican entrepreneur who is co-founder and CEO of Slidebean, a software-as-a-service (SaaS) company that helps people stop wrestling with presentation design. Slidebean's product, presentations that design themselves, is used by thousands of people around the world, from students to business executives. Caya traveled from Costa Rica to New York City to found his first startup, which gave him the tools and network he needed to build Slidebean. Slidebean has 20 employees in Costa Rica and two in New York and has raised funding from Start-Up Chile, 500 Startups, Carao Ventures, Firstrock Capital, and Magma Partners.

How did you go from Costa Rica to opening a tech business in NYC?

I visited New York for the first time with my first company I founded. We got accepted into an accelerator in New York City, which was an amazing experience. Coming from Costa Rica, I felt my time in New York was really a crash course on what was happening in tech and startups, and how different it was from what we had in Costa Rica. I fell in love with it. When that company didn't work out, I returned to Costa Rica and met up with my co-founders to start again. We realized the frustration of spending hours on PowerPoint presentations, or even worse, having to sit through a terrible presentation, and we set out to create a better way to present that information.

What did you learn in your first business that helped you build Slidebean?

The lesson I always talk about first is: I know exactly what it is like to run out of money. I went through the terrible process of going out of business, where I was still in love with my business, but there just wasn't enough funding to keep me and the business alive. So now I am really focused on having revenue. With Slidebean, we aimed for profitability a lot faster. That made a big difference for us in the beginning.

What made you decide that you could make it work in the US?

When we moved into NYC with Slidebean, it was not our first time there, so we already had contacts. We weren't as aimless as the first time, when it almost felt like we were tourists. By the second time, we really had it down. I can understand why Latin American founders might be hesitant about moving to NYC or San Francisco where your living costs increase by 3-4x; that is obviously very scary, but it also could make a big difference for the company. For an early stage business, it might not make sense to increase your costs that much just to be there, but you should definitely be putting your foot in the door and be portraying the right image to users by having a presence in the US.

What advice would you give to investors in the US about looking at companies in Latin America?

Consider how well the back office team is connected to the headquarters. They need to feel like the same team. Ideally, one of the co-founders should be in the Latin American office permanently. Everyone across both offices should know each other. This should not look like outsourcing. It all works as long as both teams work really closely together. I think that has been one of our best strengths, because we build up a great culture in Costa Rica. If you have a committed team that is friendly with each other, they really enjoy going to work together. That's one of our biggest achievements. We aren't afraid of separating the two offices because that culture lives across the two.

You can listen to our entire conversation on the *Crossing Borders* podcast on Itunes, Stitcher or wherever you get your podcasts, or on my blog:

http://www.nathanlustig.com/2017/06/13/ep-6-jose-caya-cayasso-ceo-slidebean/

XIV

Bolivia

B olivia, named after Simón Bolívar, the Venezuelan leader who played a major role in Bolivia's independence from Spain, is wedged between Chile, Peru, Paraguay, Argentina and Brazil. Bolivia is an amazing country of contrasts with unmatched deposits of silver, tin, zinc, natural gas, and enough lithium to power all of our modern devices for centuries. With those advantages, Bolivia should be a wealthy country. But it is one of the poorest countries in the Western Hemisphere, only slightly better off than Haiti.

Since its "discovery" by the Spanish in the 1500s, Bolivia has historically been on the short end of the stick in deals and wars with Spain, Britain, the United States, Chile, Brazil, Paraguay, and Argentina, all in partnership with its small upper class that has historically exploited its natural resources and labor.

Bolivia is known for natural beauty, and underdevelopment compared to its neighbors. From the world's largest salt flat in the southwest, Salar de Uyuni, where visitors can find pink flamingos in the 11,000 km2 landscape, to rainforest, El Camino de La Muerte and other natural wonders, Bolivia is an incredibly diverse country.

Bolivia's capital, La Paz, is the highest capital city in the world, checking in at ~11,500 feet, (3,500 meters) while the airport is the fifth highest in the world, at 13,323 feet (4033M).[1] As of July 2017, Bolivia's population is a bit over 11M, of which 51% are under age 25.[2] Bolivia is landlocked, and 19% of its 2016 exports went to neighboring Brazil and 11% went to Argentina.[3]

Bolivia is much less developed than other Latin American countries, with the exception of certain areas in Santa Cruz, the wealthiest city in Bolivia, and small parts of La Paz. The education system, infrastructure, and government system all need work. However, these areas have seen massive advances over the past 15 years, leading to Bolivia's 5.3% PPP GDP growth to $78.66 billion, but only $34B in nominal GDP.[4,5] This puts Bolivia on par with Wyoming's GDP but with 20x more people. The average wage is ~2,000 BOB/month, roughly $289 US dollars.[6] With the rise in GDP, Bolivia saw growth in the construction and telecommunications industries. The World Bank's 2017 Doing Business report ranked Bolivia 149th out of 190 countries, making it one of the hardest places to do business in the world.

Bolivia is rich in resources, but the left-wing government has rejected foreign aid in favor of internal development, which has capped its growth. Current President Evo Morales is a controversial figure, as he has clearly made improvements to the lives of the poorest Bolivians, but he has been criticized for hampering growth. President Morales says he is working to create more open policies to help expand the economy and create a more competitive landscape, but it remains to be seen whether he will do it.

Although the economy is fairly small and Bolivia is one of the poorest countries in the region, GDP is on the rise. So are some Bolivian entrepreneurs. Startups involving real estate and enterprise are popping up. UltraCasas is a platform where interested parties can search for real estate and filter by price and neighborhood. According to COO Camilo Eid, UltraCasas was the first Bolivian startup to receive foreign funding. The online platform provides a directory for Latin American businesses, offering more than 25 million businesses the chance to advertise in seven languages. Users can receive significant discounts on listed businesses, from restaurants to hotels.

Innova Bolivia connects startups with venture capitalists. The platform supports innovative ideas and encourages entrepreneurs to take their entrepreneurial ventures to the next level. Though a new concept for many, coworking spaces like Makecowork are also beginning to pop up in big cities. Currently, the most interesting opportunities in Bolivia are more traditional businesses that happen to use technology. It's not likely that entrepreneurs will use Bolivia as a base to target clients in the region for awhile, but more local businesses or export businesses are on the rise.

Bolivians are hard-working and many are just looking for an opportunity to do well. Bolivia still lags behind countries like Chile, Argentina, Peru, and others in Latin America, but there are certainly opportunities for entrepreneurs who would like to take a higher degree of risk. It's also an amazing country for tourism to places like La Paz, Lake Titicaca, Uyuni, Potosi, Sucre, and more. I've really enjoy visiting Bolivia and the people are some of the most friendly in Latin America, so I'm hoping Bolivia gets over the hump and continue to grow.

Endnotes

1 *World Atlas.* https://www.worldatlas.com/articles/the-20-highest-airports-in-the-world.html

2 *CIA.* https://www.cia.gov/library/publications/the-world-factbook/geos/bl.html

3 Ibid

4 https://www.cia.gov/library/publications/the-world-factbook/geos/bl.html

5 *Trading Economics.* https://tradingeconomics.com/bolivia/minimum-wages

6 *World Bank.* http://www.doingbusiness.org/data/exploreeconomies/bolivia

Carlos Jordan: UltraCasas, the Zillow of Bolivia

C arlos Jordan is a Bolivian entrepreneur and the founder of UltraGrupo, a startup that manages two portals, UltraCasas and UltraCreditos, to provide apartments and mortgages for the Bolivian market. Born in Bolivia and educated in the US, Carlos realized there was a need for an apartment classifieds portal in Bolivia while he was working for a mining company in Chile and living in Bolivia during his time off.

Having always wanted to be an entrepreneur, Carlos got over the fear of failure to build UltraCasas and eventually raise the biggest venture capital round in Bolivian history. He went on to develop UltraCreditos, a mortgage and loan platform that helps Bolivians get access to credit to purchase homes, cars, and other investments. Carlos is a key player in the emerging Bolivian startup ecosystem as he looks to create a success story that will jumpstart the local tech industry.

What is it like to do business in Bolivia?

Bolivia has had outstanding growth from after the 2008 financial crisis through 2018, but it is still a small market. There is still a lot to develop in the market and there are not many success stories yet, but we aim to be one of them. Our population is extremely young, with a lot of people under 25, and there is a high level of tech talent. We use a lot of software from abroad, but we are building very little of our own tech for Bolivia. But we have a very high internet penetration rate, higher than our neighbors, where 8 million of 11 million people are connected. This combination - young people, tech talent, entrepreneurial spirit - could create something very interesting in the next few years.

The other thing you need to know about doing business in Bolivia is that we are a very geographically-diverse country. We range from the hot Amazon rainforest to the freezing Andean plateau. We are an emerging market that still depends heavily on oil and mining. You should visit several parts of the country before investing to get a good understanding of our diversity and needs.

What does Bolivia's startup ecosystem need to take off?

We need a good incubator or accelerator. Ideally, we need some entrepreneur with a lot of knowledge to take charge and create this resource for the ecosystem. We have the talent and the entrepreneurial spirit here, but we need help to organize and channel it. Bolivia also needs more success stories. Young Bolivians need to see homegrown tech solutions competing with international businesses or even scaling globally, so we can show the world what Bolivia is capable of.

How did you raise a round of investment from Bolivia?

When we first realized we needed funding to help UltraCasas grow, we contacted some investors in Bolivia. At the time, they had no idea how to invest because they didn't understand our business. It's hard to invest in something that you don't understand. Until we have some success stories, we won't be able to get the private sector in Bolivia to invest. We had to go abroad and meet people through the Seedstars program to be able to raise investment. We eventually raised almost US$500K from several VCs in Europe, which was the biggest round ever for Bolivia. Going abroad helped our business a lot, since we got to network with a lot of mentors and investors; it would have been almost impossible to raise that capital in Bolivia.

You can listen to our entire conversation on the *Crossing Borders* podcast on Itunes, Stitcher or wherever you get your podcasts, or on my blog:

https://www.nathanlustig.com/2018/10/09/carlos-jordan-starting-ultracasas-the-zillow-of-bolivia-ep-58/

XV

Panama

H ome to the famous 48-mile canal, Panama is a central location for import and export, serving as a connector to ports and cities worldwide. Panama has free trade agreements with many countries, including the United States. Its population has surpassed 4 million and continues to grow along with the average wage, which is currently US$1,238 per month.[1,2]

Panama produces an impressive 65% of its energy from renewable resources, second only to Costa Rica in the region.[3] The financial sector plays an important role in Panama's GDP. Panama's economy has prospered and the government has invested heavily in infrastructure, leading to installations of Metro lines and significant city renovations. Foreign investment rose to US$5.2 billion in 2016, and in 2017 foreign investment surged again after Panama cut ties with Taiwan and recognized China in June 2017.[4] Chinese money quickly flooded into Panama, creating many business opportunities.

Panama is a prime country for foreign investment and considered a tax haven by many governments because it does not tax residents' income generated outside of Panama.[5] For income generated inside the country, all of the normal business deductions are available, and income tax rates are low.

The Balboa, the local currency, is dollarized, meaning it remains at a fixed rate of 1:1 with the dollar. You can also spend USD as legal tender in the country. Given the dollarization of the currency, Panama has had low inflation, a key attraction for investors. Panama relies heavily on foreign investment, so the government makes the investment process relatively simple. There are almost no distinctions between domestic and foreign investments and many expats from North America and Europe call Panama City home.

Though Panama does not have a shortage of investment opportunities, poverty and income inequality persist. In fact, it was the runner up for worst income distribution in Latin America. Disparities aside, sizable investments are leading to noticeable growth in the business sector, especially with startups. For example, Atlas Banc, is a Panama-based bank that will serve as a technology-centric clearing and settlement bank to support financial institutions and private bank clients in Latin America and the world.

The innovation hub of Panama is called The City of Knowledge. This impressive 120-hectare space located near the canal's Miraflores locks is where local firms, entrepreneurs, academic institutions and international organizations meet. With a coworking space, convention hall, plaza, and sports complex, there's no shortage of spaces for tech savvy people to meet up, network, and share ideas.

Kalu Yala takes its startup incubator to another level with its unique business model geared towards young entrepreneurs. The incubator, located in a town with the same name, centers around sustainable living. Similar to Yelp, Degusta is another Panamanian startup attracting attention by connecting consumers with Panamanian restaurants and offering the opportunity for users to provide feedback and add to a collective guide to the food scene.

In the housing market, GoGetIt is a real estate platform and guide to Panama's diverse neighborhoods. Users can see neighborhood reviews based on safety, walkability, and traffic. Additionally, the platform allows real estate agents to post properties for sale or rent.

Another startup on the radar is MercaTrade, a platform for companies interested in doing business in Latin America. The site provides information about free trade agreements and important upcoming projects in Latin America. My Office is a sustainable coworking space with sweeping views of Panama City and biodegradable office equipment.

While Spanish is the official language in Panama, English is also very popular because of a large English-speaking expat community and the fact that the US has been heavily involved with the Panama Canal from 1904 through 1999. A lower cost of living, high-speed Internet, modern banking and telecommunications systems makes Panama an extremely attractive place to do business.

Endnotes

1 *World Bank.* https://data.worldbank.org/indicator/SP.POP.TOTL?locations=PA

2 *Trading Economics.* https://tradingeconomics.com/panama/wages

3 *The Business Year.* https://www.thebusinessyear.com/panama-2017/renewed-improved/review

4 *Santander Trade.* https://en.portal.santandertrade.com/establish-overseas/panama/investing

5 *Investopedia.* https://www.investopedia.com/ask/answers/093015/why-panama-considered-tax-haven.asp

Kyle Wiggins & Jack Fischl: From Peace Corps to Entrepreneurs

J ack Fischl and Kyle Wiggins are the co-founders of Keteka, a tourism marketplace that provides off-the-beaten-path experiences across Latin America by connecting local guides with international tourists online. Although Jack and Kyle studied across the Charles River from each other in Boston, they didn't meet until they both became Peace Corps volunteers in Panama, where they were inspired to found Keteka after seeing how their communities struggled to market unique tourism opportunities. Kyle and Jack realized there was a need to bridge the gap between these rural communities, their skilled local tour guides, and a tourism market that operates through online transactions. Keteka started as a Wordpress website built in an internet cafe in Panama and has now grown to include over 1300 tours across 13 countries in Latin America.

How did you start Keteka when you were in Panama?

Our communities were located around fourteen hours apart by bus, but they had one thing in common: both communities wanted to take advantage of the income that can be made through tourism. We realized the main challenge for these communities was marketing the unique opportunities they offered; they had no internet or even electricity, so everything depended on word-of-mouth. At that point we decided to just build a website to help them promote their experiences.

We took turns going to the nearest internet cafes to our communities, about two hours away, to build this simple Wordpress site that included just three communities at the start. Then we started getting requests from all the other volunteers in Panama, asking us if we could add their communities to the site, because they had similar services to offer. Soon we were getting requests from Peace Corps volunteers all over Latin America, and even from Senegal, to include their communities! We realized there was a huge network available in the Peace Corps, with 7000-9000 volunteers deployed all over the world at any given time, that could all provide a unique perspective on living abroad in their country. We were then able to raise around US$15K in crowdfunding to research this idea more in Panama and Latin America before really starting to grow Keteka.

How does Keteka support tour guides in Latin America?

We realized that local communities like the ones we worked with in Panama often had no choice but to partner with large corporations if they wanted to get the word out about their tour options. Usually, this meant a clunky system with several middlemen taking a cut before the tour guide actually got paid. Tour guides usually get only about 10% of what tourists pay to participate. That doesn't give guides an incentive to provide an amazing experience. We wanted to disrupt that payment structure so that it would favor the local community, meaning that guides on Keteka receive 85% of the booking price; the rest is our commission and the transaction cost. We want tour guides to be paid fairly for their work so that they are incentivized to exceed expectations on every tour.

What lessons did you learn in the Peace Corps that helped Keteka take off?

One of the things we realized in the Peace Corps was that to many people in the developing world, time is more valuable than money. Transportation times were incredibly long and unpredictable for people to leave the communities where we were staying. It was hard to get a traditional job in the city, for example, because even crossing the Canal could take anywhere from 45 minutes to four hours, depending on the day. Trying to bring US systems and lifestyles to the jungle just wouldn't work and we had to come up with something new. We also realized that people are not reasonable; not everyone follows the same logic or solves a problem in the same way. We learned to step back and try to figure out other people's reasons for doing things, rather than assuming that our logic was the same. You have to get to know people before you can help them. But at their core, people are people, wherever they are.

You can listen to our entire conversation on the *Crossing Borders* podcast on Itunes, Stitcher or wherever you get your podcasts, or on my blog:

https://www.nathanlustig.com/2018/08/21/ep-51-kyle-wiggins-jack-fischl-taking-tourists-off-the-beaten-path-with-keteka/

XVI

Puerto Rico

B ecause Puerto Rico is a US territory, Puerto Ricans are US citizens who can live anywhere in the US, but don't have full rights in Congressional and Presidential elections when they are living in Puerto Rico.

Pre-Hurricane Maria, you probably knew Puerto Rico from Despacito, the most played video in the history of YouTube, its beautiful beaches and by its crippling debt that has stunted its growth. Entrepreneurs were working against the economic crisis' backdrop to rebuild the economy even before Maria, but now are also helping in the rebuilding effort.

Home to 3.4 million residents and surprisingly some of the largest and highest grossing retail shops in the world because of tourism, Puerto Ricans do not let the island's debt or hurricane recovery define them.[1] Many entrepreneurs hope that Puerto Rico takes these disasters as an opportunity to rethink issues and start from scratch using policies which will ideally lead to policy changes to help stimulate the economy. One of these projects that Puerto Rico is exploring is leveraging Tesla's Powerwall and solar energy technology to redo the electricity grid.[2]

Sebastian Vidal, one of Start-Up Chile's Executive Directors, saw potential to help Puerto Rico become a bridge for Latin American entrepreneurs to come to the US and for the US to access Latin America, so he helped create the accelerator program Parallel 18, to encourage growth within Puerto Rico and internationally. The accelerator supports entrepreneurs within Puerto Rico, and startups from over 48 countries have applied just to take part in the initiative. As Sebastian Vidal wrote in an article titled *Why We Need to Continue to Help Puerto Rican Entrepreneurs* in 2017:

> "Young entrepreneurs like MIT grads Eric Crespo and Brian Collazo, co-founders of delivery service Lunchera; and Alana Matos co-founder of Ed-Tech company Caila, who just finished her Master's at Harvard were returning. Innovation was also sprouting from teams living on the island, solving local business challenges with global reach, and showing strong initial results." [3]

> "Companies like Abartys Health, disrupting the insurance industry by a streamlined communications platform; GasolinaMovil, a pay at the pump mobile app that is taking over the Puerto Rican market; Burea, a loyalty platform that substitutes paper coupons with a mobile app; are growing exponentially." Brainhi, a Parallel 18 alumni company, was the first Puerto Rican company selected for YCombinator.

There are many advantages to doing business in Puerto Rico. Starting a business in Puerto Rico only takes 5.5 days compared to the Latin America average of 31.6.[4] Another major benefit to opening a business in Puerto Rico are low business taxes. With Act 20, business owners are only required to pay 4% taxes on the profit made from exporting goods out of Puerto Rico, which can include software.[5] With incentives like this, some U.S.-based companies are operating out of Puerto Rico. The average monthly wage in San Juan is ~US$2500.[6]

Coworking spaces are starting up in Puerto Rico to foster new ideas, however, due to the hurricane, many of them have closed temporarily. One of the more popular spaces, Piloto 151, offers a virtual office in addition to its two brick and mortar locations. The idea is to provide a communal space to network as well as an online community to connect with outside of the office.

Puerto Rico has other tax breaks for US citizens to move their businesses to the island. Many Wall Street hedge fund managers, best typified by Peter Schiff, have moved operations to Wall Street as a tax avoidance scheme.[7] It remains to be seen whether moving these types of businesses will actually help local Puerto Ricans and contribute to the economy, or will exacerbate the difference between the rich and the poor. I tend to think it will be the latter and would explore policies that give big rewards for actually contributing to the economy, rather than hoping it trickles down.

Despite the introduction of tax incentives and accelerators, Puerto Rico has policies in place that cripple growth. Some, like the The Jones Act, which forces all deliveries bound for Puerto Rico to first go to Miami and then be on a US-flagged ship, rather than receiving shipments directly from neighboring countries, are imposed from Washington, DC.[8] These higher costs are passed directly to consumers through increased prices. Others, like its debt, unfunded liabilities and under educated population, are issues that Puerto Rico has to fix on the home front.

With back-to-back hurricanes and many without water or power for an extended period of time, much of Puerto Rico is still operating in crisis mode as of 2018. Programs are targeting small to medium-sized businesses and providing loans up to USD$150,000 to help people rebuild.[9] The local government is providing incentives for affected companies to help rebuild business and the Department Economic Development and Commerce has provided emergency lines of credit for effected businesses. As Puerto Rico works through these difficult times, future policy changes may help restart growth and get Puerto Rico back on its feet.

Endnotes

1   *Business in Puerto Rico.* https://www.businessinpuertorico.com/en/news/1

2   *Reuters.* https://www.reuters.com/article/us-usa-puerto-rico-tesla/tesla-to-send-more-battery-installers-to-puerto-rico-to-restore-power-idUSKBN1C-B2GY

3   *Sebastian Vidal.* https://medium.com/@Sebavidal/how-technology-entre-preneurs-can-help-puerto-rico-44a4d1152f74

4   *World Bank.* http://www.doingbusiness.org/data/exploreeconomies/puer-to-rico

5   https://medium.com/@Sebavidal/this-is-why-your-startup-should-learn-about-taxes-in-puerto-rico-95352878a0c1

6   *Bureau of Labor Statistics.* https://www.bls.gov/regions/new-york-new-jersey/news-release/countyemploymentandwages_puertorico.htm

7   https://www.youtube.com/watch?v=by1OgqQQANg

8   *Business Insider.* https://www.businessinsider.com/jones-act-puerto-rico-trump-hurricane-maria-marine-merchant-2017-9

9   https://www.businessinpuertorico.com/en/news/1

Sebastian Vidal: Building Parallel 18 in Puerto Rico

S ebastian Vidal is the Executive Director of Parallel 18, an equity-free startup accelerator based in Puerto Rico. Since 2011, Sebastian has worked with over 1000 startups between his time at Start-Up Chile and Parallel 18. Originally from Chile, Sebastian worked with Start-Up Chile in its early days and helped streamline the process by which the Chilean government paid entrepreneurs through the Start-Up Chile program. He later took over as Managing Director. In 2015, he left Chile to develop an equity-free incubator from the ground-up in Puerto Rico, where he has spent the past two years creating Parallel 18.

How did you go from Chile to Puerto Rico?

I used to work for, and then led Start-Up Chile, which is an entrepreneurship initiative launched by the government of Chile to jumpstart the local innovation ecosystem by bringing in foreign entrepreneurs. The program has reached global acclaim and has nurtured more than 2500 startups since it was founded. It has also served to prove that it is possible for a government to work very efficiently and in a non-bureaucratic way that helps startups.

At the end of 2013, the Start-Up Chile team began to consult with other governments to teach them how to design new entrepreneurial policies. I visited Peru, Brazil, Jamaica, Malaysia, South Korea, and Puerto Rico. Then I was approached in 2014 to develop a Start-Up Chile-type program in Puerto Rico from scratch. At the time, I had a great job at Start-Up Chile and no one could understand why I would want to leave. But I wanted to get out of my comfort zone and take the risk. And on the day I decided I would go to Puerto Rico, the government there declared they were in default.

What are the lessons you have learned after mentoring 1000 startups?

I can see patterns in why some companies were successful. The first is focus. Sometimes you come across entrepreneurs who are developing multiple new products at once and trying to reach new markets, but they only have US$30-50K in the bank. That is a very quick way to run out of money. You need to focus on your current clients and on your solution; ignore the competitions and the trophies.

The second thing is that, although there are tons of books on working smart rather than working hard, the startups that have really gone on to raise money are the people who are working their asses off. These people are constantly in the zone, constantly connected. It is a risk, because you can spend two years in the zone and still fail. But the people who are constantly learning and trying to provide better results for their clients are always the ones that are going to win.

What have you learned from Parallel 18?

I have learned a lot about the importance of demo days in Latin America as compared to the US. I think all demo days in Latin America should include an educational component. We often have important investors at our demo days, but sometimes they are very uninformed about investing in the Latin American market. So for them it can be a bit of a learning experience. But we try to start introducing our entrepreneurs to investors long before demo day, because few investors actually invest in the first meeting. It is really important to build a relationship with investors over time so that when demo day comes, they are ready to invest.

You can listen to our entire conversation on the *Crossing Borders* podcast on Itunes, Stitcher or wherever you get your podcasts, or on my blog:

http://www.nathanlustig.com/2017/07/27/ep-14-sebastian-vidal-building-powerful-startup-accelerator-puerto-rico/

Lauren Cascio: Innovating in the Insurance Industry from Puerto Rico

L auren Cascio is the co-founder and COO of Abartys Health, a health insurance tech company that has created a system that allows seamless data flow and communication between insurers, doctors and patients in Latin America and the United States. Since she founded Abartys Health in 2016, Lauren has been selected by Walmart as one of Puerto Rico's most promising business leaders, has made the Caribbean's 40 under 40 list, and was a finalist for the Forbes 30 under 30. Lauren is also proud to have delivered the winning pitch for Abartys Health at SXSW's ReleaseIT competition in 2017 and Parallel 18 Accelerator's Investor Choice at the 2017 Demo Day and recently closing a round of funding from investors.

How did you get inspired to found Abartys Health?

In college, I studied health trends and became fascinated with the insurance market. Then when I went through my divorce, when I was already living in Puerto Rico, I decided to teach myself to program PHP because I realized I would not be able to care for my children with the work I was doing in corporate wellness. About six months in, it clicked that I wanted to combine my interest in healthcare with my newfound passion for technology. Through mutual connections, I met Dolmarie, my co-founder, who had been working in the insurance industry for over 20 years. We started building our product based on problems we were solving for our first two corporate clients, which turned out to be inefficiently-billed claims. Abartys is using technology to upgrade these antiquated systems to save money for insurers and provide more transparency for patients.

What are the benefits of founding a startup in Puerto Rico?

First of all, Puerto Rico has great tax incentives for people that manufacture, hire, and export from the island, so a lot of companies are setting up there. The government is really working to support entrepreneurship through programs like the Parallel 18 accelerator, and there is already a lot of great talent there. Of course, the quality of life and culture in Puerto Rico are also a big factor. For Abartys, Puerto Rico is an ideal location because it is geographically close to the United States, but it is still connected to the Latino culture. We operate in the US, Puerto Rico, and Latin America, so it is important for us to be at the intersection of those regions.

What is the difference between the sales process in the US and Latin America?

We currently have nine clients that cover one million providers across the US and Latin America. For us, the most important thing is understanding which issue is most critical to our client. We follow a model called "land and expand" where we provide the module that supports their most central issue, then offer more benefits later. No matter what, each client is a struggle to close, since the insurance industry moves slowly. But in the US, our sales cycle is around nine months and most people just want to see the numbers and the return before they make a decision. In Latin America, we might have to make ten trips and take the executives out to dinner or coffee several times before even setting foot in the office. Those sales cycles can take up to 18 months.

You can listen to our entire conversation on the *Crossing Borders* podcast on Itunes, Stitcher or wherever you get your podcasts, or on my blog:

https://www.nathanlustig.com/2018/06/12/ep-44-lauren-cascio-how-abartys-health-is-upgrading-the-insurance-industry/

XVII

Central America & The Caribbean

This section deviates from the previous format of one country per chapter because these countries in Central America and the Caribbean have ecosystems that are just getting started or have a very small market. My goal is to give you an even more brief primer on this region.

Although each country is very different, the smaller countries in Central America still face many of the same structural and cultural barriers that continue to hold them back. According to the Wall Street Journal, the "Northern Triangle" of Central America – which includes Honduras, Guatemala, and El Salvador – is one of the world's most dangerous regions.[1] Heavy drug trafficking and powerful organized-crime networks have overwhelmed the region's governmental institutions, creating a vicious circle of poverty and violence. These problems were exacerbated after 9/11 when increased US vigilance in the Gulf of Mexico forced more drug trafficking overland, through Central America.

Thanks to the internet and the widespread adoption of mobile devices, the first doors are opening for a new age of development in Central America in the form of entrepreneurs and innovators trying to capitalize on opportunities in countries like Nicaragua, Honduras, Guatemala, and El Salvador. Here's a brief overview of the current business environment in some of the smaller countries in Central America.

Nicaragua

Nicaragua is the largest country by area in Central America but has a population of only six million people, compared to Guatemala's 15 million. The average monthly salary in Nicaragua is approximately US$420/month, a fairly average figure for Central America, but much lower than Chile's minimum wage of US$500/month.[2]

Despite Nicaragua's relatively low GDP, US$14.3 billion and US$2,228.80 per capita, its startup scene is beginning to show signs of initial growth from a very low base.[3] Companies like Vega Coffee are breaking into the US market by selling coffee directly from producers to consumers, lowering prices and allowing farmers to keep revenue by cutting out the middleman.

If you're interested in spending some time in the Nicaragua, noteworthy coworking spaces include La Fábrica Coworking and Co-labora. Coworking options are also cropping up outside of the capital Managua and coliving spaces, such as Encuentros in Granada and NomadLife in San Juan del Sur, are successfully attracting digital nomads with Nicaragua's low costs of living and its proximity to beaches and cultural heritage sites.

Honduras

Honduras, a country of nine million, can be a challenging place to work because of its small economy, low GDP of US$21.4 billion, or US$ 2,570.80 per capita, and an average salary at 7,400 lempiras, approximately US$342/month.[4,5] Nonetheless, some of the first tech startups are starting to get off the ground. Apps like VoaComer are working in the food delivery industry. Movitext, a massive SMS texting app targeted to the Mexican and Central American market, has an impressive list of clients who use their services, including Google, Facebook, Waze, Airbnb, Microsoft, as well as many banks, universities, and retailers. Chekku, an intuitive tool that uses mobile technology and GPS to optimize resources for businesses, is another Honduran startup to keep on your radar.

Coworking spaces are also popping up in capital Tegucigalpa and even in San Pedro Sula, previously one of the most dangerous cities in the world. Entrepreneurs, freelancers, and digital nomads can check out Urban Office, Workbox, and Connect Cowork TGU, to get a foot on the ground.

Guatemala

With over 17 million people, 62% of whom identify as indigenous, mountainous Guatemala is the most populous on the Central American isthmus.[6] Guatemala's GDP reached US$72 billion in 2017, with a US$4,212.10 GDP per capita.[7] Despite being the wealthiest city in the Guatemala, the average monthly salary in Guatemala City is approximately US$600.[8] Outside of Guatemala City, new cities such as Antigua are proving to be startup hubs for Central America, with coworking and coliving spaces – such as Serendipity Lab, ImpactHub, and Chamba Coworking, attracting professionals to Guatemala.

Due to the development challenges presented by Guatemala's geography, its most innovative startups focus on providing services to the most vulnerable populations. Kingo Solar Energy provides prepaid solar energy to homes that otherwise would be lit by kerosene or candles. Iguama is making US products available to Guatemalans through a safe mail-order application that delivers straight to consumers' doorsteps. Founders like Luis von Ahn, the founder of Duolingo, and Platzi's Christian van der Henst, are originally from Guatemala but have built global businesses from the US and Latin America respectively.

Belize

This small tropical country (population of 360k) nestled under Mexico's Yucatan Peninsula has long been a top tourist destination but lags behind the rest of the region in entrepreneurship.[9] With a GDP of US$1.76B, and monthly salaries low at ~US$800 per month, the cost of living is relatively higher in Belize than in neighboring countries. Belize's official language is English, making it easier for those from the United States to work there.

Alliance Business Centers was the first and as of this writing the only coworking space in Belize City. Local startups such as Boarding Path, the Google Maps for inside airports, and Gone Green Superfoods, a manufacturer and importer of the most nutrient-dense superfoods available, target foreign market and are slowly gaining traction worldwide. Belize fame as a tourism destination many allow export products to become popular in foreign markets. Compared to neighboring Costa Rica and Panama, Belize's ecosystem is much smaller and there are fewer tech startups. It could be an interesting option for remote workers, as it's safer than neighbors like El Salvador and Honduras, but less expensive than Costa Rica and Panama.

El Salvador

El Salvador is the wealthiest of the countries in this section, however, it's a latecomer to the Central American startup scene. Most of the coworking spaces are based in the capital, San Salvador, where Internet connections are stronger and there is more access to amenities that businesses require. Deskritorio Coworking and Yawal, for example, are at the forefront of co-working/co-living spaces in El Salvador.

The top startups in El Salvador are heavily based on improving the tourism sector of the economy, however, companies like Insidey, which helps make teamwork more efficient, are starting to innovate in other sectors. Yupi and Pagadito are Salvadoran versions of Uber and PayPal, respectively. El Salvador's GDP of US$27.7 billion, US$4,486.40 GDP per capita, and average monthly salary of US$371.71 are helping it catch up with the rest of Central America.[10,11]

According to Andy Lieberman, Director of New Programs at Miller Center for Social Entrepreneurship, there are plenty of opportunities for Central America to leapfrog other regions[12]. Entrepreneurs can leverage mobile data and cloud-based tools that provide better services at lower costs without the large upfront investment that used to be necessary for a technology-based enterprise.

Lieberman also believes there is plenty of room for the region to embrace approaches already proven elsewhere in the world and apply them to the local context. While there are many challenges of doing business in Central America, and it still has a long way to go before it can be a top option for setting up a company in Latin America, there are opportunities for those who are willing to take the risk today.

The Caribbean

Cuba, the Dominican Republic, and Haiti are small countries that have varying degrees of development and openness, but all three are filled with entrepreneurial people.

Cuba

This small island nation of 11 million people has the most tightly controlled Internet in the world, so it is an unlikely candidate to join the wave of tech innovation in Latin America.[13]

With a GDP of US$87.13 billion and average monthly salary of 687 pesos (US$25), Cuba is not the ideal place for a startup venture.[14] Nonetheless, Cubans are among the most highly-educated people worldwide and often succeed in overcoming enormous hurdles to become entrepreneurs.

Two startups, YoTeLlevo and El Paquete Semanal, provide web-based services that get around the extreme lack of internet access on the island.[15] El Paquete delivers hard drives with popular web content – news, TV shows, movies, etc. – to customers around Cuba, and is even hired by local companies to help with digital marketing in a country without WiFi.

As of 2017, there are no coworking spaces on the island, but Cubans can purchase Internet by the hour at one of a few cafes or find another source through connections. One entrepreneur from a Magma Partners portfolio companies has a development team based in Cuba, and other startups are looking at hiring Cuban developers. At this stage, a it seems like building a remote work or startup ecosystem won't happen until the government liberalizes the economy and increases access to the internet.

Dominican Republic

With a population of 10 million, the Dominican Republic has grown to become a middle-income country, with average salaries rising to US$363/month and a GDP of US$71.58 billion.[16,17]

Though the startup scene is relatively new, the Dominican Republic hosts multiple tech companies, including Ravn and Jompeame. Ravn is a highly secretive messaging app that can be hidden within other fully functioning apps so that only the users know its location. Jompeame is a fundraising platform for extreme poverty causes – the first of its kind in Latin America.

Another noteworthy organization is the Luma Project, which has built a campus to provide free education to entrepreneurs in the Dominican Republic to help empower more innovation on this Caribbean island nation.

The Dominican Republic produces a well-trained developers, leading companies like Instacarro, a Brazilian car marketplace, to open development offices.

Haiti

Most of Haiti's population of 10 million people subsist on a US$4.50 per day minimum wage. With a GDP of US$8.023 billion, Haiti is one of the least developed and lowest income countries in Latin America.[18,19]

The local languages are French and Creole, making it harder to operate if you're not a speaker. One company, ManmanPemba, offers a weekly newsletter of events across Haiti, as well as a Yelp-like search function to find any local restaurant, bar, or business. More than 250,000 Haitians have immigrated to Chile since 2010 to try to get out of poverty and pursue a better life.

Other notable startups include Lajan Cash, Venmo for Haiti, and Ramase Lajan, a program that creates jobs for Haitians through recycling. Haitians are trying to move away from being synonymous with disaster relief and towards innovation and entrepreneurship to build businesses that meet local basic needs.

Endnotes

1 *Wall Street Journal.* https://www.wsj.com/articles/how-to-revive-central-america-1499029385

2 *Check In Price.* http://checkinprice.com/average-and-minimum-salary-in-managua-nicaragua

3 *Global Finance Magazine.* https://www.gfmag.com/global-data/country-data/nicaragua-gdp-country-report

4 https://www.gfmag.com/global-data/country-data/honduras-gdp-country-report

5 *Central America Data.* https://www.centralamericadata.com/en/article/home/Honduras_Minimum_Wage_Increases_Between_55_and_8

6 *CIA.* https://www.cia.gov/library/publications/the-world-factbook/geos/print_gt.html

7 https://www.gfmag.com/global-data/country-data/guatemala-gdp-country-report

8 http://checkinprice.com/average-and-minimum-salary-in-guatemala/

9 https://www.cia.gov/library/publications/the-world-factbook/geos/bh.html

10 https://www.gfmag.com/global-data/country-data/el-salvador-gdp-country-report

11 *Numbeo.* https://www.numbeo.com/cost-of-living/country_result.jsp?country=El+Salvado

12 *Miller Center.* https://medium.com/@millersocent/social-entrepreneurship-in-central-america-733e371970ec

13 *Index Mundi.* https://www.indexmundi.com/cuba/

14 *Miami Herald.* https://www.miamiherald.com/news/nation-world/world/americas/cuba/article89133407.html

15 *BBC.* https://www.bbc.com/news/technology-33816655

16 https://www.cia.gov/library/publications/the-world-factbook/geos/dr.html

17 https://www.numbeo.com/cost-of-living/country_result.jsp?country=Dominican+Republic

18 https://www.cia.gov/library/publications/the-world-factbook/geos/ha.html

19 *New York Times.* https://www.nytimes.com/2014/05/06/world/americas/haiti-minimum-wage-increases.html

Kevin Valdez: From Guatemala to GroupRaise

Kevin Valdes moved from rural Guatemala to Houston, Texas when he was just 12 years old. He didn't speak any English at all when he moved to the US, but quickly learned in school so he could help his parents start a family business and later attend university. At university, he met Devin Baptiste, who eventually became his co-founder at GroupRaise. Kevin is passionate about helping Latin American students reach their potential by providing them with the opportunities he received when he moved to the US with his family.

Did you always know you would be an entrepreneur?

I grew up in a family of entrepreneurs. When my mom arrived in the US, she decided to start creating a business based on what my grandfather was doing in New Jersey. With my aunt, she started delivering packages to families in Guatemala; they started with just three to four packages, then grew to having warehouses. At age 15, I was helping them deal with all the legal documents since they didn't speak English. Doing that, I realized I was not interested in following the same path as my college classmates, and I think Devin felt the same. Devin and I met in class and quickly became friends, spending time outside of class talking about our entrepreneurial aspirations. I think I was destined to be running a business, since I have been working in my parents' business from the start.

How does your connection to Guatemala affect your career?

I originally considered my immigration status to be a disadvantage. I now see it as an advantage, as I have a different perspective on a lot of things than my counterparts from the US. When I was in school, I would always think that there were so many other great students like me in Guatemala who never had the chance that I had. If I had not been given the opportunity to come to the US, we would not be speaking today. One time, Vicente Fox, former President of Mexico, came to speak at my university and told us that Latino students in the US had a responsibility to make more opportunities for those that were studying in Latin America. That really resonated with me, since the only thing that separates me from them is the opportunity I got from my parents. I keep working on my business to create more opportunities in Latin America and uncover the untapped potential of the region.

What did you learn from your parents about running a business?

My dad's advice to me was always that time is precious and we should always seize the opportunity to make the most our time. He had the vision to take our family to the US and he instilled that same vision in us. I also learned how important it is to be fully customer-focused, because I watched my mom go far out of her way to help customers, even answering phone calls late at night. We have used that model at GroupRaise from the start and it pays off. It doesn't matter if you're a mom-and-pop shop or a giant international chain, you have to pay attention to your customers.

You can listen to our entire conversation on the *Crossing Borders* podcast on Itunes, Stitcher or wherever you get your podcasts, or on my blog:

http://www.nathanlustig.com/2018/05/08/ep-39-kevin-valdez-from-guatemala-to-groupraise/

XVIII

Conclusion: Latin America's First Press

A s I sit in Bogota, Colombia in October 2018, many of the things that entrepreneurs, investors and government have been hoping for have finally started to happen. Looking back, I think we will see 2018, and September 2018 specifically, as an inflection point for tech in Latin America.

In September, Grin, an electric scooter company based in Mexico City, raised Latin America's biggest seed round, at $28M and quickly raised another round of $45M. Yellow, Brazil's electric scooter company, raised $63M in Latin America's largest ever Series A. Rappi, a Colombian last-mile delivery company, closed a $200M venture capital round, making it the second Latin American startup with a $1B valuation this year. OmniBnk, an invoice-backed lending platform, secured $200M to lend to SMEs in Latin America, the largest fintech lending deal in the region. Nubank received $180M from Chinese giant Tencent and Ualá got a $34M series B from notable Wall Street investors. Last, but not least, Cornershop, a Chilean/Mexican last-mile delivery business, was acquired by Walmart for $225M.

Looking back at 2010, or even 2016, any one of these milestones would have been enough to generate excitement for an entire year. But they all happened during an 8 week period in August, September and

October. Latin American startups received more venture capital during this time, $850M, than in all of 2016!

Cornershop's acquisition not only generated waves in the ecosystem, but also in Chilean and Mexican public policy, marking a cross over from tech into the mainstream. Cornershop's cofounders where also the cofounders of Groupon Latin America which exited in 2010. The team, investors and founders have gone on to create many more businesses, to become like a Latin American version of the PayPal Mafia. Movile, MercadoLibre, Rocket Internet and Groupon each have trained a number of future entrepreneurs who went on to build startups across the region, starting the virtuous cycle that Latin America needed to get the startup ecosystem really moving. They're showing people that you can start a startup, raise funds from top venture capitalists from around the world and generate a profitable exit in Latin America.

September 2018 really has been a before and after. In the days after Cornershop's acquisition and OmniBnk's $200M deal, more than five family offices who had previously decided not to invest in Magma contacted me because they were rethinking getting more involved in technology, either as an investor or as part of their family businesses. While companies like Rappi, Grin, Yellow and others still need to create profitable business models and still have the possibility of failing, I believe 2018 will be an inflection point for the region. Latin America's opportunities have been getting more exciting every year, and I see no reason why it shouldn't continue be be more interesting and profitable with each passing year.

Over the past five years that we've been investing with Magma Partners, we've seen several trends consolidating that will play a significant role in the development of the ecosystem. China is investing heavily in Latin America; as President Trump's trade war intensifies, Chinese FDI into the US has dropped by 92% to $1.8B, while Chinese FDI to Latin America has surged to $15.3B in the first half of 2018. At the same time, Fintech in Latin America has become widely accepted as the solution to financial inclusion in the region. Mexico's new Fntech law and the funding of Latin America's first 2018 unicorn, Nubank, exemplify how this trend is starting to play out. There are already 85+ foreign Fintech startups and 271 social impact-based Fintech startups across Latin America. Remote workers from all over the world are using Latin America, but especially Colombia and Mexico as bases to service global clients. As remote work becomes mainstream, expect Latin American countries to flourish, becoming a more attractive location than Eastern European and Indian because Latin American is on the same time zone as much of the US.

If I had to pick one country to watch, it would be Colombia. Fifteen years ago, Medellin was too dangerous to visit. Now, it's murder rate is down more than 90% Colombia has received the fourth-most global investor commitments in Latin America, after Brazil, Mexico, and Argentina. Medellin, and Colombia as a whole, is seen as a miracle of development. This story is still evolving, but I predict the example of Colombia's transformation will drive investment to Colombia and the rest of the region, bringing jobs and capital to stabilize Latin America. If I had to pick the next countries for technology investment, it would be Mexico, followed by Brazil.

As GroupRaise's Devin Baptiste puts it, the recent deals are a part of Latin America's first press of the startup ecosystem. How so? When you make olive oil, the first press has the highest quality and highest quantity of olive oil. I think those who are involved in the ecosystem are now part of the first press, which will generate the highest quality and highest quantity of startups that will have an impact in the region and ideally the world.

I hope this book, along with all of the interviews with these top founders and investors from across the region, will give you an overview of what's going on in Latin America. If you're interested in learning more, there are many resources that will help you dig deeper. To stay up to date with Latin American startup news, subscribe to LatAm List (http://www.latamlist.com) or my blog, http://www.nathanlustig.

com. You can also reach out to founders and entrepreneurs mentioned in the book or listen to the more than 70 podcasts that we've produced to showcase entrepreneurs and investors doing business across borders.

If you have questions about anything you've read in this book, please feel free to reach out **info@magmapartners.com,** @nathanlustig or @magmapartners on Twitter and the same on Instagram and LinkedIn. We'd be happy to try to help answer any questions or help you vet any opportunities you see.

Acknowledgements

There are hundreds of people who have made Magma Partners and this book possible. I can't possibly thank them all individually, but want to highlight some. If I miss you, I'm sorry, it wasn't on purpose!

Thank you to my partner Francisco Saenz, for taking a leap of faith on Magma Partners after three meetings in 2013. He's continued to be the best complimentary partner I could have asked for over the past five years as we've built Magma from Chile to the rest of the region. Thanks to Diego Philippi for thinking of me when you heard Francisco might be interested.

This whole Latin American adventure started with my old business partner Jesse Davis, who saw the original Forbes article that ended up taking us to Chile. Without his push, I wouldn't have ended up in Chile in the first place. I'd like to thank Brenna Loury and Diego Philippi for picking us for the pilot round in 2010 and for Nicolas Shea, Jean Boudeguer and the rest of the Start-Up Chile team for making our 6 months during the program as amazing as it was.

Nicolas Orellana introduced me to what it was really like doing business in Chile, Argentina, Colombia and Brazil and gave me the freedom to really explore in my role as an employee. He still is the only "boss" I've ever had in my adult life. Thanks Nico and the rest of the Welcu team, especially Camila Carreño, who put up with my bad Spanish and helped me learn.

None of this would have been possible without my friends I made during Start-Up Chile, both inside and outside of the program. Tiago Matos, Vijay Kailas, Raj U, David Lloyd, Amir Salihefendic, Jorge Diaz, Enrique Fernandez, Gonzalo Saieg, Pedro Navarro, Stephen Stynes and the rest of the crew who made my first years in Chile amazing.

I owe a debt of gratitude to the extended Magma team, past and present. Magma and this book wouldn't be what it is today without all of your help. Thanks Sophia Wood, Alejandra Dugarte, JT Li, Angel Andraca, Pedro Pablo del Campo, Eugenio, Pedro, Rita, Monica,

Francisco, Diego, Pierre Wolff, Neil Coleman, Codie Sanchez, Jie Hao, Nora and Katie. Sebastian Vidal for introducing me to Puerto Rico, and to Horacio Melo and Catalina Boetsch for being amazing friends.

I'll forever be grateful for all of the investors who backed Magma from a very early stage. I'm sure it felt crazy to back a gringo chilenizado to invest in startups in Latin America. We literally couldn't have done it without your money, but most of all, your support and eagerness to learn about technology and startups.

Thanks to everyone who has supported us and a special thanks to Angel and Sophia for producing the podcast that later turned into these chapters in the book and Nora and Katie for your help creating some of the original content for the blog that turned into chapters for this book. Special thanks to Jie Hao for opening the doors to China and showing me what the future could look like and taking me to amazing restaurants on each of our trips.

Thank you to all of the more than 65 entrepreneurs who have been willing to make time to talk with me on the Crossing Borders Podcast. It's been a privilege to get to know you all and share your stories with the English speaking market. I'm also smarter by talking with all of you and look forward to recording each and every episode. I can't wait to learn more from all of you in the future and be able to follow your successes.

Magma would be nothing if not for the entrepreneurs we've been privileged to be able to support. I've learned so much about business, operations, technology and human nature from all of you since we got started in 2014. Special thanks to Adrian Fisher, Cecilia Pierola, Diego Caicedo, Maria Paz Gillet, Devin Baptiste, Jack Fischl, Pedro Varas and the rest of the amazing entrepreneurs we've been able to support.

Last but not least, thanks to my parents, brother and aunt. They've been willing to come visit Latin America, open my mail and help with anything and everything over the past 8 years in Latin America. They've even been willing to edit multiple drafts of this book. Thanks for all of your support, even when I'm thousands of miles away.